T0265534

# INGENIOUS

## ALSO BY RICHARD MUNSON

*Tesla*

*Tech to Table*

*From Edison to Enron*

*The Cardinals of Capitol Hill*

*Cousteau*

*The Power Makers*

# INGENIOUS

A Biography of
**BENJAMIN FRANKLIN,**
Scientist

## RICHARD MUNSON

**W. W. NORTON & COMPANY**
*Independent Publishers Since 1923*

For information about permission to reproduce selections from this book,
write to Permissions, W. W. Norton & Company, Inc., 500 Fifth Avenue,
New York, NY 10110

For information about special discounts for bulk purchases, please contact
W. W. Norton Special Sales at specialsales@wwnorton.com or 800-233-4830

Manufacturing by Lake Book Manufacturing
Book design by Daniel Lagin
Production manager: Lauren Abbate

ISBN 978-0-393-88223-0

W. W. Norton & Company, Inc.
500 Fifth Avenue, New York, N.Y. 10110
www.wwnorton.com

W. W. Norton & Company Ltd.
15 Carlisle Street, London W1D 3BS

1 2 3 4 5 6 7 8 9 0

*To Kathryn*

# CONTENTS

# INGENIOUS

# 1

## THE KITE

Benjamin Franklin, forty-six years old in June 1752, strode into a field just north of the burgeoning village of Philadelphia. He had told no one other than his twenty-two-year-old son about his plan to demonstrate the connection between lightning and electricity, both of which were then considered mysterious and terrifying. The Franklins carried only a ball of twine, a metal key, and a kite.

Benjamin wasn't the first to observe that both forces emit light, move swiftly in crooked directions, and discharge a sulfuric smell. He did, however, devise the first replicable experiment that proved their connection. About two years before, he had written detailed plans for placing an iron pole, about forty feet long, atop a tall building or church steeple. Reprinted in European journals, his proposal theorized that a brass-pointed tip would draw electrical discharges from clouds and send them via wire into glass jars that stored the energy. Although Franklin felt the bodily risks from a lightning strike were small, he recommended experimenters shield themselves within a sentry box like that of a guard's booth.

At the request of the French king, Thomas-François Dalibard, on

May 10, 1752, conducted Franklin's experiment by raising such a pole above a church bell tower in Marly-la-Ville, about twenty-five miles north of Paris. Adding to Franklin's precautions, Dalibard and his assistants avoided electrocution by standing on insulated pads placed atop four empty wine bottles—they were, after all, in France. He described their findings three days later at the French Académie des sciences, declaring, "M. Franklin's idea has ceased to be conjecture; here it has become a reality."[1] Within about a month, other scientists in France, England, and Germany all performed the sentry-box experiment as Franklin had designed it.

Because of slow communications between Europe and the American colonies—ships took about six weeks (though weather conditions could stretch that to two or three months) to sail the almost four thousand miles across the Atlantic—Franklin hadn't learned of these successful demonstrations before he decided to experiment in a "different and more easy manner."[2] A kite tipped with a foot-long wire solved the problem that Philadelphia then did not possess buildings tall enough to support an iron rod rising into the clouds; a common kite, he theorized, "could have a readier and better access to the regions of thunder than by any spire whatever."[3]

The notion of flying a wire-tipped kite in an afternoon thunderstorm had to seem a little crazy in an era when lightning regularly ignited buildings. Franklin, moreover, feared "the ridicule which too commonly attends unsuccessful attempts in science." Still, he ventured into a field in the rain simply out of curiosity about the nature of electric charges.[4]

He avoided the common paper kite, making his of silk since that material "is fitter to bear the wet and wind of a thunder gust without tearing." He crafted "a small cross of two light strips of cedar, the arms so long as to reach to the four corners of a large thin silk handkerchief when extended." After adding a tail and loop, he fixed a foot-long pointed wire to the top of the upright stick. For the string from the kite to the ground, he chose hemp twine that when wet would "conduct the electric fire freely." He added some protection from shocks by inserting an insulated ribbon between the end of the twine and a sealing-wax handle that he held. Between the twine and ribbon, Benjamin fastened a metal house key that he felt would collect charges captured from the clouds.[5]

As the sky darkened ominously, Franklin and his son stood just inside a shed's door and raised their kite . . . with no effect. Benjamin began "to despair of his contrivance," yet as the clouds blackened further, despite the absence of lightning, the string's filaments began to stand erect. As the line became wet from the emerging drizzle, Benjamin noted that electric sparks "stream(ed) out plentifully from the key at the approach of a person's finger."[6] Franklin's experiment worked.

Although schoolchildren learn a little about this effective test, historians tend to dismiss Franklin's science, focusing instead on his diplomacy and writings. Benjamin Franklin (1706–1790) is mostly heralded for being the only patriot to sign the four key documents that created the United States, including the Declaration and Constitution. He negotiated the financial and military support from France that allowed the united colonies to win independence, and he settled the peace terms with Britain. Moreover, his witty insights and self-help advice—such as "Early to bed . . ."—still permeate popular culture.[7]

Yet with all due respect to Franklin's standing as a founding father of our country, we wouldn't be discussing his political prowess were it not for his fame as a leading scientist, which opened doors for him in the worlds of diplomacy and nation-building. Science, rather than being a sideline, is the through line that integrates Franklin's diverse interests.

Benjamin's work extended well beyond a simple-sounding kite experiment to include leading-edge research on electricity, heat, ocean currents, weather patterns, and chemical bonds. Building on the work of Francis Bacon, he also outlined a clear and straightforward process for careful observation, induction, measurement-based testing, and fact-focused conclusions. This empirical procedure, which would be called the *scientific method*, democratized the obtaining of knowledge, making natural philosophy, as science was then called, available to more than an educated and well-heeled elite.

Science even drove Franklin's patriotism. His American Philosophical Society was one of the earliest efforts to enable the autonomous American colonies to work together, and he regularly promoted New World researchers, boasting that their intellectual prowess matched that within the Old World's staid, and often arrogant, universities. His commitment to reason, moreover, helped frame the founders' approach to laws and politics.

Although Franklin was among the eighteenth century's most famous scientists, too many historians have written off his explorations as a hobby rather than an underlying passion, treating them as an aside or relegating them to a single chapter.[8] One of the most cited biographies asserts that "human life, civic duties, and morality were all more important to him than philosophical amusements."[9] An encyclopedia maintains that "Franklin never thought science was as important as public service,"[10] and as recently as 2002, a distinguished historian elides Franklin's accomplishments, writing that his "scientific discoveries would count for little beside public service."[11] In fact, observation and experimentation not only pervade Franklin's life, but he preferred talking science with his "philosophic friends" to discussing politics with "all the grandees of the earth."[12]

A few scholars feature Franklin's practical inventions, such as pointed rods and efficient stoves that divert lightning and smoke from homes, yet they tend to portray him as a mere tinkerer. One popular profile claims Benjamin showed "little appreciation for abstract theories" and was anything but "a profound conceptualizer."[13] A rare countervailing argument came from Bernard Cohen, who asserted in the 1940s that Benjamin "made a fundamental and vital contribution to the general structure of electrical theory,"[14] and he hinted that "the scientific-empirical temper of (Benjamin's) thought could be discerned in his social and political programs."[15] Yet even Cohen downplayed Benjamin's examinations of refrigeration, the movement of ocean currents, the behavior of ants, how our blood circulates, and so much more.

Also routinely ignored are Franklin's demographic studies, which influenced Adam Smith and Thomas Malthus, and even Charles Darwin on his way toward a theory of natural selection. Few biographers, moreover, view his science-based associations as democracy-building or his policy pamphlets as political science.

Experimenting with a child's toy suggests to some that Franklin was more playful than philosophical. It is offered as evidence that his findings should have been obvious, that he was a genial codger and not an insightful contributor to our knowledge about the world. Yet before Franklin no one had designed repeatable experiments revealing the nature of electricity. Almost two centuries after Benjamin flew his kite, the poet Robert Frost paid tribute to his ingenuity by asking, "How many times it thundered before Franklin took the hint!"[16]

Benjamin, admittedly, is a hard man to know. No doubt he left behind an extensive paper trail, penning a best-selling memoir and *Poor Richard's Almanack*, along with a multitude of articles that he wrote for his *Pennsylvania Gazette*. Yet these documents often display a detachment—from objectivity to downright ventriloquism. Benjamin regularly adopted aliases or spoke in the voice of some mouthpiece he conjured. In fact, he was an inventor who reinvented himself several times over, moving from a teenage runaway and struggling tradesman to a well-to-do publisher, clever diplomat, and admired scientist.

When Franklin's kite experiment is portrayed in popular culture, the enduring images often are fanciful, mischaracterize his contributions to science, and provoke misconceptions that surround Benjamin today. Perhaps the best-known representation came from Currier and Ives more than a century after the event in a hand-colored lithograph that depicts an old man comforting his frightened young son and holding a kite string in an open field as jagged flashes cross the sky. Yet as noted before, Franklin was vibrant; his son was a mature twenty-two-year-old; these careful scientists sheltered in a shed to avoid electric bolts; and no lightning ever appeared that afternoon, simply clouds holding electrostatic energy.

A Benjamin West painting of 1816 advances a more grandiose view of this moment in science: a purple-robed Franklin, surrounded by cherubs, reaches skyward to receive sparkling fire from the gods. Such renditions create crude caricatures that undermine our understanding of this complex individual. They also present competing, but inaccurate, legends—a foolish fanatic practically begging to be electrocuted versus a godlike creature capturing power from the heavens. Rather than illuminate Franklin's thought processes or the science itself, the images offer a simplistic spectrum of scientist portrayals, from daydreamer to demigod, complete with scraggly hair.

Our modern narratives also don't give Franklin his due. A 2022 Ken Burns documentary focused on his diplomacy and ownership of slaves, virtually ignoring his science.[17] A Broadway musical from 1964 embellished tales of his Paris romances, prompting a journalist to label him "our founding flirt."[18] The crass commercialization of his image in advertisements for investment funds and foods threatens to render him an eccentric and comic character who elicits neither controversy nor adulation.[19]

Benjamin deserves to be rescued from such trivializing images. I assert that we do not appreciate Franklin as well as we believe or as richly as he deserves. We need to recognize how experimentation and reason pervaded his entire life, as well as acknowledge that his scientific discoveries surpassed pragmatic inventions.

What if scientists—rather than historians or artists—crafted his biography? Noting his insights into energy, molecules, climate, and refrigeration, Joseph Priestley, who isolated oxygen in 1774, declared Franklin's discoveries to be "the greatest, perhaps, that [have] been made in the whole compass of philosophy since the time of Sir Isaac

Newton."[20] English physicist J. J. Thomson, the man credited with detecting the electron in 1897, said that what Franklin "rendered to the science of electricity...can hardly be overestimated."[21] Robert Millikan, who won the Nobel Prize for Physics in 1923, labeled Franklin's research "probably the most fundamental thing ever done in the field of electricity."[22]

Yet Benjamin was more than a respected experimenter. He became a science celebrity, in part because he strategically networked with others who could spread his ideas. His early success as a newspaperman also ensured his theories and tests were communicated clearly and engagingly.

Assessed through the lens of science, we find a more complete portrait of what John Adams called "one of the most curious characters in history."[23] That expression of fascination alone, particularly from a Franklin critic, prompts us to examine anew this man. Yet in an indirect way, Adams also accentuated Benjamin's core and consistent attribute: curiosity.

The ingenious Franklin faced the world with wonderment and systematic study—offering rich perspectives on the Enlightenment and the American experiment. His commitments to reason, experimentation, and tolerance also reveal his relevance to our modern era, when science, facts, and democracy face rising challenges.

# 2

## INGENIOUS ANCESTORS

"Ingenious" conveyed a rich meaning in Benjamin's era, suggesting intellect but also imagination, diligence, and playfulness. Franklin used that term seventeen times in his memoir, *The Autobiography of Benjamin Franklin*, to describe the manual and mental talents of his family of craftsmen, blacksmiths, and candlemakers. Despite hailing from a modest rural English village with limited schooling, these ingenious ancestors were considered people of learning and a proud part of an emerging middle class.

Family trees do not necessarily reveal the personality of a single member, but Benjamin enjoyed exploring his heritage and began his autobiography with these words: "I have ever had a pleasure in obtaining any little anecdotes of my ancestors."[1] Offering a glimpse into his own self-image, he paid particular attention to his family's independence, inventiveness, and love for learning. He highlighted the family name (Francklyne or Franklin) as having originated in the late Middle Ages to describe a growing class of freeholders who owned property but were not aristocrats.

Benjamin's earliest known ancestor was his great-great-grandfather, Thomas Franklin, born about 1540 in the village of Ecton within the county of Northamptonshire, amidst the southern part of the English Midlands. Thomas displayed an independent streak, particularly regarding religion. When Queen Mary, known as "Bloody" by her Protestant opponents, tried to reimpose Catholicism at mid-century, Thomas hid a banned English Bible beneath his kitchen stool; when safe, he turned the furniture over onto his knees and read the Holy Book, which could quickly be concealed if royal guards approached.

Thomas's son, Benjamin's great-grandfather Henry Franklin (born in 1573), extended the rebellious tradition and spent a year in jail for writing poetry that "touched the character of some great men."[2] He also displayed an interest in public affairs and, with some irony, was elected parish constable. Henry's eldest son—Benjamin's grandfather—was another Thomas (born in 1598); the gregarious tinkerer worked in Ecton as a blacksmith, read extensively, built a clock, and lived to the age of 83, more than twice the life expectancy of his era.

As was tradition, Thomas's oldest son inherited the family's thirty-acre farm, and a forge. That Thomas Franklin (born in 1637) was Benjamin's uncle and a man of many talents; in addition to being a blacksmith, lawyer, and solicitor, he became "a gunsmith, a surgeon, a scrivener, and wrote as pretty a hand as ever I saw. He was a historian and had some skill in astronomy and chemistry."[3] If that sounds like the multifaceted Benjamin to you, you're not alone. When Thomas died in 1702, four years to the day before Benjamin's birth, one relative noted: "Had he died on the same day, one might have supposed a transmigration."[4] Benjamin was proud to add that his uncle Thomas was "much employed in public business. He set on foot a subscription for erecting chimes in their steeple and completed it. . . . He found out an easy method of saving their village meadows from being drowned. . . . His advice and counsel were sought for on all occasions, by all sorts of people."[5]

Benjamin's father Josiah, the youngest of Thomas Franklin's four sons, was born in 1656 in Ecton, a sleepy hillside village above the River Nene. At the age of fourteen, he moved to nearby Banbury, a thriving market town on the River Cherwell, where he apprenticed to become a silk and cloth dyer. While arduous and odorous, that craft required a technical understanding of how fabrics interact with colors held by various alkalis and acids.

Josiah aligned, but not fanatically so, with the Puritans who rejected the Anglican Church's rituals and ornaments, which they considered too affiliated with Catholicism. After Oliver Cromwell's Puritan rule ended around 1660, Charles II took the British throne and demanded that dissenters accept his new Book of Common Prayer, as well as a traditional hierarchy of ordained bishops, priests, and deacons. Authorities banned dissidents from organizing their more democratic gatherings and barred Puritans from obtaining public office. That's when Josiah left for Massachusetts "to enjoy the exercise of (his) religion with freedom." Economics, however, probably played a bigger role in Josiah's decision as he faced the pressures of a rapidly expanding family and the end of his apprenticeship in a town that could not support another dyer.

Josiah set sail in August 1683 at the age of twenty-five, accompanied by his wife, Anne, and three children: Elizabeth, Samuel, and Hannah. The rough nine-week trip cost him the equivalent of six months' earnings, and his initial prospects in Boston appeared bleak because the town already hosted several dyers of fabrics. Demand for colorful cloth, moreover, was limited since modestly attired Puritans dominated the population, and the colony in 1651 imposed sumptuary, and rather undemocratic, laws that forbade the wearing of bone lace, silk hoods, or scarves by persons whose estates did not exceed 200 pounds.[6]

An upside of the new American settlement was that trades initially required no long apprenticeships, so Josiah quickly shifted to a new profession—making soaps and candles. The job of tallow chandler required long, hot, and smelly hours boiling cattle carcasses, lime, and potash into lye for soap and jelly for candles, but the demand for those products expanded along with Boston's population.

The Franklins rented a small, clapboard house on Milk Street, across from the Old South Meeting House. After two years Josiah became a junior member of a congregational church, and he rose slowly through the Puritan ranks over another twelve years to finally become a tithingman who monitored "nightwalkers, tipplers, Sabbath breakers . . . or whatever else tending toward debauchery, irreligion, profaneness, and atheism."[7] After six more years, Josiah graduated to being a constable, one of eleven Puritan elders supervising the tithing-men, a position that allowed him to mix business with religion; specifi-cally, his expanding connections gave him the profitable concession for selling candles to these night-watchmen.

As Josiah's business grew, he moved to a slightly larger building on the corner of Hanover and Union Streets, in the center of town and about a ten-minute walk to Long Wharf. The family lived in the back, behind the workroom. Above the front door hung a big blue ball, a sign of Josiah's trade as a candlemaker and soap-boiler.

Despite the family's progress, they faced hardships. In 1688, five years after arriving in Massachusetts, Anne gave birth to their sixth child, a son who perished as a newborn. A year later, she delivered another boy and died from childbirth; that son succumbed a week later. Such devastating tragedies were not unusual during those times; about 20 percent of Boston children died within their first week of life. A grieving husband, needing help with not only his five surviving chil-dren but also shop management, Josiah quickly remarried. Less than five months after burying Anne, he wed Abiah Folger, who would give birth to ten other children, including Benjamin. The reconstituted fam-ily faced its own heartaches; Abiah's sixth child, Ebenezer, died at six-teen months when he "drowned in a tub of suds," probably having fallen into Josiah's boiling soap vat.

Benjamin's mother, according to his autobiography, had "an excellent constitution; she suckled all her ten children,"[8] and he told a friend that she was "full of wisdom." When he spent too much for a tiny whistle, for instance, Abiah offered this practical advice:

"Every time you really want a thing, say to yourself first of all—how much is the whistle worth?"[9] Josiah and Abiah remained married for fifty-six years, prompting Benjamin in 1744 to describe his father as "a pious and prudent man" and his mother "a discreet and virtuous woman."[10]

Benjamin added that his father had "an excellent constitution of body, was of middle stature, but well set, and very strong." Josiah, he wrote, "could draw prettily, was skilled a little in music, and had a clear-pleasing voice, so that when he played psalm tunes on his violin and sung withal . . . it was extremely agreeable to hear."[11] Benjamin also praised his father's "solid judgment" in public affairs: "I remember well his being frequently visited by leading people, who consulted him for his opinion in affairs of the town or of the church."[12] Perhaps most telling, he further described Josiah as having "a mechanical genius" and being "very handy in the use of other tradesmen's tools."[13]

Benjamin appreciated his father's resourcefulness. He described their family living between two rivers, only one of which supported herring, so to snare more of his favorite fish, Josiah collected and carried masses of eggs to the other waterway, where they "hatched, and therefore herring spawned there."[14] And so, as much as learning mechanical dexterity at his father's knee, you could say Benjamin dined on his father's ingenuity.

———————

APPRECIATING BENJAMIN FRANKLIN REQUIRES SOME UNDER-standing of the place of his youth. Boston at the turn of the eighteenth century was beginning to thrive, to shed its Puritan restrictions, and to become a vibrant commercial center that hosted more than a thousand ships transporting goods—especially fish, lumber, and food—throughout the colonies and Europe. Its population of seven thousand would double within two decades, despite deadly outbreaks of smallpox in 1702 and 1721. And while Boston's streets remained unpaved and crowded with animals, the town enjoyed a building spree, including the Old State House in 1713, Old North Church in 1723, and Faneuil Hall in 1742.

The Massachusetts capital also emerged as an intellectual center. It long had hosted the first higher-education institution in the English colonies, yet Harvard College during this period began to shift its focus from divinity to science. The school hired its first secular president in 1708, assembled a substantial collection of technical books and equipment, placed a telescope atop Massachusetts Hall, and appointed in 1728 the colonies' first full-time professor of natural philosophy. Boston also hosted three newspapers and several book publishers, and its intelligentsia, later to become known as "Boston Brahmins," cultivated a culture of literature and learning.

Boston and other North American towns may have lacked Europe's respected libraries and learned societies, but they were poised for growth, and they offered fresh landscapes, flora, and fauna to explore. More important, Massachusetts was not tied to Old World traditions. With its vibrant intellectual and cultural scene, Boston in the early eighteenth century was an opportune place and time for the curious and ingenious.

Cotton Mather epitomized the evolution from Puritan rigidity to scientific experimentation. New England's religious eminence obtained a reputation for intolerance from his denunciations of women "afflicted" by witchcraft and his involvement in the Salem trials of 1692–1693 (some thirteen years before Benjamin's birth). Yet this stickler for moral earnestness believed that the natural world revealed God's glories and was worthy of study, and he advocated for integrating old religion with new science, for linking Puritanism with rationalism. "Philosophy [science] is no enemy," he declared, "but a mighty and wonderous incentive to religion."[15] Mather possessed a three-thousand-volume library and wrote extensively on botany, particularly plant hybridization, astronomy, and medicine. The cleric in 1723 also received the rare honor of being elected a non-English fellow of the Royal Society of London (a distinction Benjamin would obtain thirty-three years later).

This era became known as the Enlightenment,[16] and "Dare to know!" became its motto.[17] Benjamin came of age as scholars and tradesmen began to celebrate reason over superstition, trusted their senses as sources of knowledge, questioned traditional authority, and believed in the power of education. They advanced rationality and truth-seeking, rejected piety and purism, and asserted that observations would be more accurate, and valuable, if not stifled by dogma. Rather than ostracize those with different views, they increasingly appreciated the uncertainties associated with both nature and politics and welcomed feedback from other fact-seekers.

Immanuel Kant further described this time of discovery, this age of reason, as "humankind's emergence from . . . dogmas and formulas," as well as from religious and political authority.[18] Historian Ritchie Robertson said the epoch produced an "uneven but decisive transformation of people's understanding of the world and of their basic assumptions."[19]

This intellectual movement was built on scientific developments from previous decades. Francis Bacon, who died in 1626, advanced empiricism, in which knowledge is considered to result mainly from sensory experience and the process of observing and experimenting. René Descartes, who died in 1650, invented analytic geometry and gave us the best-known statement in philosophy: "I think, therefore I am." And Isaac Newton formulated the laws of motion, advanced "proof by experiments," and wrote in 1687 the widely referenced *Mathematical Principles of Natural Philosophy.*[20]

Enlightenment values spread rapidly in the eighteenth century to a widening range of acclaimed observers and experimenters, including the chemist Antoine-Laurent Lavoisier, the philosopher Voltaire, the economist Adam Smith, and the botanist Stephen Hales. They substituted inductive reasoning (whereby judgments are based on observation) for deductive reasoning (whereby inferences are based on widely accepted premises).

European natural philosophers tended to be gentlemen of means who could afford the equipment and time to explore their interests. Often linked to established universities or elite clubs, most looked down on Americans, asserting that unsophisticated colonists could not become true scientists.

Yet across the Atlantic, diverse researchers increasingly embraced scientific rationality, religious toleration, and experimental political organizations. Several became professional researchers—such as astronomer David Rittenhouse, metallurgist Jared Eliot, and chemist Benjamin Rush—but key roles were played by the numerous amateurs who collected diverse plants, discovered mammoth bones, recorded the movement of stars, and mapped America's geography. They set a tone for viewing the world differently, their age-of-discovery ideas permeated popular discussions and papers, and their recognized insights fostered pride among Americans.

Benjamin Franklin was influenced by and advanced those calls for experimentation. Born in Boston in 1706 to a soap- and candle-making father, he would become an American paragon of this era of Enlightenment.

Benjamin was Josiah's fifteenth child and youngest son, born when his father was forty-eight and his mother thirty-eight. He arrived on Sunday, January 17, 1706,[21] and was taken within a few hours to be baptized at Old South Church, as was the custom because many newborns died early.[22, 23]

The snippets we know of Benjamin's early life come from his own recollections as an old man. His first recorded memory is of thirteen Franklins sitting around a cramped dinner table at their Boston home. He later told a friend that "he lacked for nothing in his childhood" and enjoyed youthful games, such as blowing soap bubbles from a tobacco pipe and feeding pet pigeons living in a box nailed to the side of his house.

Benjamin joined in discussions with neighbors and family friends whom Josiah invited for dinners to debate "some ingenious or useful topic for discourse which might tend to improve the minds of his children."[24] He and his siblings regularly viewed four large maps in the parlor and were quizzed on the names of mountains, oceans, and rivers. They also enjoyed access to their father's modest library, remarkable for the home of an uneducated tradesman.

Benjamin could not recall a time when he didn't read, claiming to be "addicted to all kinds of reading."[25] He noted that "all the little money that came into my hands was ever laid out in books."[26] Although Franklin carefully read the proverbs that embraced diligence and frugality—attributes that would become a core of his future writings—this precocious child, not yet a teenager, sought out sophisticated biographies, particularly Plutarch's *Lives of the Noble Greeks and Romans* ("which," he observed, "I read abundantly"). That Greek philosopher conveyed to Franklin the potential for progress, not by God's grace but from humans' search for knowledge and struggle against obstacles.

Franklin also devoured Daniel Defoe's *An Essay upon Projects*, which proposed pensions for seamen, fire insurance associations, and other community enhancements—several of which Benjamin would later develop in Philadelphia. Franklin learned from that author the power of satire, with one cheeky essay suggesting that institutions for the developmentally disabled should be paid for by a tax on arrogant authors who, by no effort of their own, claimed to have obtained more intelligence at birth.

Benjamin received an informal education from his Uncle Benjamin, who arrived from London in October 1715 in bad shape, having recently lost his wife and daughter and failed at his dyed-silk business. Despite such setbacks, Franklin deemed his uncle "ingenious," his highest praise, for publishing two quarto-sized volumes of his own poetry and devising a unique shorthand. As a pious gentleman, Uncle Benjamin also took down "sermons of the best preachers" and assembled into multiple volumes the "principal pamphlets relating to public affairs."[27] Yet he failed to find a job in Boston and after four unemployed years was thrown out of the cramped house by his brother Josiah.

Both Benjamin's father and uncle hoped he would become a minister, perhaps studying divinity at Harvard College. Yet young Franklin proved to be irreverent and impious, finding, for example, the "long graces by his father before and after meals very tedious."[28]

Benjamin's formal education was limited. Josiah placed his other boys directly into apprenticeships with different tradesmen, but he recognized his young son's intelligence and sent the eight-year-old to the Boston Latin School, where he shined, jumping a grade ahead in his first year. But school proved to be unaffordable for a soap maker. As a less expensive alternative two blocks from home, Josiah contracted with George Brownell, a tutor known for his "mild, encouraging methods," to teach Benjamin calligraphy and spelling (at which he excelled) as well as arithmetic (which he failed, a surprising fact in view of his later prowess with calculations).

The costs were still too high, so at the age of ten, with only two years of school-based instruction, Benjamin reluctantly joined his father as a tallow chandler and soap boiler, assigned to cut wicks for candles, attend the shop, and run errands. Because Franklin "disliked the trade,"[29] Josiah slowly sought to find his son more engaging employment and systematically introduced him to the city's bricklayers, joiners, blacksmiths, cobblers, coppers, and wheelwrights. In hindsight, Benjamin expressed "pleasure . . . to see good workmen handle their tools," appreciation for the middling class, and confidence in his own ability to "construct little machines for my [scientific] experiments while the intention of making the experiment was fresh and warm in my mind."[30]

Benjamin grew into a six-foot-tall teenager, with broad shoulders and a lean build from boxing as well as swimming in the Charles River. His rather large head featured thin, light-brown hair, a wide mouth, and a pointed upper lip. Friends commented on his alert eyes and kind smile.

He appeared early to be a clever experimenter. His love of swimming, for instance, led to one of his first inventions—flippers. Benjamin believed his speed in the water was limited by the size of his hands and feet, so he devised two oval palettes with holes for his thumbs and "fitted to the soles of my feet a kind of sandals." These paddles and ten-inch-long flippers enhanced his pace, but they also irritated his extremities and exhausted his shoulder and leg muscles.

Young Franklin seemed obsessed with "what if?" possibilities. When he came across a kite tethered to the shore of a mile-wide pond, he wondered if it could pull him across to the other side. "Holding the stick in my hands," he waded into the pool and "was drawn along the surface of the water in a very agreeable manner." The kite, he boasted, "carried me quite over without the least fatigue and with the greatest pleasure imaginable."[31]

Young Benjamin saw himself "a leader among boys,"[32] albeit an immature one who regularly steered them into scrapes. In one youthful episode, he and his friends decided to build a wharf close by a salt marsh on which they could stand and fish for minnows. Unfortunately, the stones Franklin identified for that structure were intended for a new house being constructed near the marsh. When the homebuilders left for the evening, Benjamin "assembled a number of my playfellows, and working with them diligently like so many emmets [ants], sometimes two or three to a stone, we brought them all away and built our little wharf." The next morning, laborers located the missing stones and identified the thieves. Franklin later quipped, "Several of us were corrected by our fathers, and, though I pleaded the usefulness of the work, mine convinced me that nothing was useful which was not honest."[33]

Benjamin, continuing to complain about his tasks at the tallow shop, expressed a desire to "break away and get to sea." His father strongly objected since Josiah Jr., his second oldest son, had set sail two years before Benjamin's birth and reportedly died off the coast of China. Josiah initially tried to convince his nephew Samuel, "who was bred to the business" of making cutlery and grinding blades, to take in Benjamin as an apprentice, but Samuel demanded a high fee. Josiah's next option, noting Benjamin's fondness for books, was for him to join his twenty-one-year-old brother, James, in the printing profession.[34] The younger Franklin later noted in his memoir: "My father was impatient to have me bound to my brother [and block my hankering for the sea]. I stood out some time, but at last was persuaded and signed the indentures when I was yet but twelve years old."[35] Although brothers, James and Benjamin barely knew each other. James was nine years older and had been living in England.

The apprenticeship contract required Benjamin to serve for nine years, two longer than the norm, and to face numerous restrictions: "Taverns, inns, or alehouses he shall not haunt. At cards, dice, stables, or any other unlawful game he shall not play. Matrimony he shall not contract." In return, Benjamin was to obtain "meat, drink, apparel, washing & lodging, and a complete new suit of clothes."[36] The strict arrangement portended conflicts between master and apprentice, with James demanding his brother do his bidding, as would other trainees, while the willful Benjamin expected "more indulgence" from a family member.

Benjamin displayed "great proficiency in the [printing] business"[37] and grew to find it a noble profession. In his last will and testament, he described himself proudly as "I, Benjamin Franklin of Philadelphia, printer."[38]

The work demanded intelligence and creativity. An apprentice, for example, stretched paper so it would remain flat and not buckle, dried those pieces overnight to avoid paper shock, and prepared them the following day to hold an image from lead type.

Benjamin appreciated how the job allowed "access to better books." He borrowed copies from friends at other printshops, "careful to return (them) soon and clean," and he often sat in his room "reading the greatest part of the night."[39] Books expanded Franklin's imagination and insights. From John Bunyan's travel saga, he met indi-viduals overcoming adversity and was introduced to "the first (writer) that I know of who mixed narration and dialogue, a method of writing very engaging to the reader."[40] From John Locke's treatises, he learned how observation and reason—not divine revelations from God—led to knowledge.

The apprenticeship also afforded Benjamin the opportunity to write. Printers regularly crafted articles and advertisements for their clients, and they offered edits to increase the clarity and impact of words. At the request of James, who had seen London folksingers mar-ket their lyrics, Benjamin composed short poems, but his own father criticized them for falling "far short in elegance of expression." After being exposed to better literature, Benjamin admitted he "saw the jus-tice of his [father's] remarks" and turned from poetry to prose, "deter-mined to endeavor at improvement."[41]

And so, Benjamin was shifting from printer to writer by the age of thirteen. He found inspiration in an old volume of the *Spectator*, a short-lived English daily known for the quality and good-humored detach-ment of its writing. The publication aspired to be civilized and urbane as well as to offer a voice of reason. Benjamin found the journal's style "excellent and wished, if possible, to imitate" it. The resolute teenager crafted short notes on the sentiment of each sentence within a *Spectator* article. He laid those hints aside for several days and then reconstructed the piece, compared his version to the original, and "discovered some of my faults and corrected them." He also expanded his stock of words, searching for synonyms that would have "the same import but of differ-ent length, to suit the measure, or of different sound for the rhyme." He admitted being "extremely ambitious" to become "a tolerable English writer," and he devoted his evenings, early mornings, and Sundays to such exercises.[42]

An opportunity to test his writing skills came after his brother James began publishing the *New England Courant* in August 1721.

Boston already hosted two newspapers, both of which enjoyed connections with the Puritan and political establishments. Owned by a single businessman and beholden to no religious or political dogma, the *Courant* marked the birth of an independent press—and launched the tradition of cheeky journalism. James and his talented cadre of writers took aim at Boston's elite, singling out the Mathers: Increase, who had been a leading Puritan clergyman and president of Harvard College for twenty years, and his son Cotton, another preacher. The *Courant* staff faulted the ministers for offering only mild opposition to the Salem witch trials, which had occurred some thirty years earlier, and they regularly mocked clergymen as hypocrites for having left England to avoid religious persecution only to marginalize Quakers, Anglicans, and people of other faiths in New England. James claimed his editorial missions were to provide "nothing but what is innocently diverting" and to offer "a full and methodical account of foreign and domestic affairs, as well as something charming or amusing."[43] The *Courant* also provided basic logs on the ships entering and leaving the port as well as sensationalistic stories about horrid murders and risqué acts.

Benjamin's official assignment at his brother's business was to "carry the papers through the streets to the customers," but he was drawn to men "who amused themselves by writing little pieces for this paper," usually under clever pseudonyms.[44] Since his brother rejected pieces he wrote for the *Courant*, the fifteen-year-old "contrived to disguise my hand, and wrote an anonymous paper,"[45] which he slipped under the editor's door.

Benjamin devised his first mouthpiece to be an opinionated, widowed, and middle-aged woman he named Silence Dogood, with the first name a contrast to her verbosity and the last name playing off Cotton Mather's *Essays to Do Good*. Franklin introduced her as "a mortal enemy to arbitrary government and unlimited power. I am naturally very jealous for the rights and liberties of my country; and the least appearance of an encroachment on those invaluable privileges is apt to make my blood boil exceedingly."[46]

Through Silence Dogood, a comic character with serious intent, the saucy Benjamin anonymously commented on current events and challenged religious leaders having political authority. A not-so-humble "humble servant,"[47] she questioned "whether a common-wealth suffers more by hypocritical pretenders to religion, or by the openly profane?" She concluded the more dangerous were the hypo-crites, who sought to "betray the best men in his country into an opin-ion of his goodness."[48]

The teenager tested contemporary journalistic limits in his four-teen letters, spaced every fortnight between April and October 1722. One piece verged on the ribald: "Women are the prime causes of a great many male enormities."[49] Dogood even praised prostitutes as agents of compassion who attend to "the health and satisfaction of those who have been fatigued with business or study."[50]

The Dogood letters gained attention and acclaim in their time. In good part because of them, the *Courant* was praised as "the most enter-taining, news-filled, and controversial paper of its day."[51] From a histor-ical perspective, they launched the uniquely American style of satirical humor later advanced by such masters as Mark Twain and Will Rogers. Yet when the authorship of these crafty essays became known, James felt deceived, and he beat Benjamin physically, an action the younger brother "took extremely amiss."[52]

Believing he needed to stoke debate to sell even more newspapers, James printed an antivaccine piece by a Boston physician, ignoring the advice of Harvard's Thomas Robie, perhaps the colony's top doctor, as well as James's personal physician who had immunized many Bos-tonians against smallpox. James took the stance largely to challenge Cotton Mather, who had read about Turkish inoculations in medical literature and had heard from one of his enslaved workers about effec-tive immunizations in parts of Africa. Noting that smallpox killed nine hundred Bostonians in 1721 and struck more than half the city's population, Mather responded to the *Courant*'s editorializing by condemning the "notorious, scandalous paper called the *Courant*, full freighted with nonsense, unmanliness, raillery."[53]

Trying again in 1722 to stir up controversy and circulation, the *Courant* condemned the colony's political leaders for being slow to combat pirates. Without a trial, those officials charged James with "high affront," sent him to jail for three weeks, and prohibited him from publishing. James countered by pretending to release Benjamin from his indenture and printing the paper under the younger brother's name. The sixteen-year-old, as a result, found himself in charge of a newspaper whose imprint temporarily read "printed and sold by Benjamin Franklin."

When James returned from custody, he tried to rein in his brother, who rather enjoyed his brief independence. While admitting he might have been "too saucy and provoking" and that James was "otherwise not an ill-natured man," Benjamin resented "the blows his passion too often urged him to bestow upon me."[54] James restricted Benjamin from leaving his employ by convincing Boston's other printers not to hire his brother. So the young Franklin decided to run away, correctly reasoning that James would neither reveal nor be able to enforce the secret apprenticeship agreement he had signed when imprisoned.

Benjamin arranged for a friend, John Collins, to convince a sloop captain bound for New York that the young printer needed to quickly skip town since he "had got a naughty girl with child."[55] He sold some of his prized books for passage and snuck aboard the *Speedwell* on the evening of September 25, 1723. Over the next three days, the one-masted sailboat covered almost four hundred miles and arrived in New York City, where Benjamin claimed he was "without the least recommendation to, or knowledge of, any person in the place, and with very little money in my pocket."[56]

But Franklin did know of William Bradford, New York's only publisher critical of the "oppressors and bigots" who had harassed Benjamin's brother. Bradford had no job openings, but he suggested Franklin sail another hundred miles south to Philadelphia, where his own son, Andrew, had just lost his principal printer's aide. That trip proved arduous, with a fierce squall tearing the boat's sails, a subsequent calm forcing a full day's rowing, a drunken Dutchman falling overboard, and Benjamin catching a fever during the frigid October nights. Upon his arrival at the Market Street wharf, Franklin possessed just a single Dutch dollar and a shilling in copper pennies. When he crossed the street to a bakery and begged for whatever three pennies would provide, he was surprised to receive "three giant puffy rolls," two of which he gave to a woman and her child from his boat.

Philadelphia was a Quaker outpost of two thousand residents scattered across a flat plain between the Delaware and Schuylkill Rivers. Despite a visionary grid design, the main streets were dirt roads blighted by numerous vacant lots. One historian described Philadelphia as a destitute village with "wooden shacks and narrow alleys, wells and water pumps too close to privies, poverty by the waterfront."[57] Yet within this squalor appeared signs of construction and seeds of opportunity, particularly for a runaway looking to make his mark.

Walking up Market Street, which ended after just three blocks, Franklin passed the Read home, outside of which his future wife coincidentally stood by the door. Benjamin later guessed he presented "a most awkward, ridiculous appearance." He stumbled along with a group of clean-dressed people into the Quaker meetinghouse, where the Friends sat down and proceeded, as was their custom, to say nothing. The drowsy Franklin, who had not rested the previous night, fell fast asleep, dreaming of a better future.

# 3

✂

# SEARCHING FOR OPPORTUNITY

A refreshed Franklin headed off to meet Andrew Bradford, the printer he had heard of in New York. Since Bradford could offer no immediate work, Benjamin "made himself as tidy as he could" and paid a visit to the town's other printer, Samuel Keimer, whom Franklin found to be poorly qualified for his business and his equipment worn out and outdated. Although Keimer presented himself as something of a scholar, Franklin found him "very ignorant of the world," acting with "enthusiastic agitations," and possessing "a good deal of the knave in his composition." Yet Keimer offered employment, and the destitute seventeen-year-old accepted.[1]

The teenager seemed to be drawn to schemers, another one being Sir William Keith, the royal lieutenant governor of Pennsylvania. Gallant and well dressed, the British official flattered Benjamin for his writing style and volunteered to help him establish his own business and obtain printing contracts from the provincial government. A political man, Keith quietly hoped to gain a talented ally, while Franklin misjudged the lieutenant governor to be "the best man in the world."[2]

In April 1724, Keith sent Benjamin off to Boston with a glowing letter meant to convince Franklin's father to underwrite the printing venture. The ever-practical Josiah, however, responded with cordiality but bluntness, writing that his son was "too young to be trusted with the management of a business so important."[3] Keith subsequently vowed to finance Benjamin himself and to send the young printer to London to select the appropriate equipment, estimated to cost around one hundred pounds sterling, as well as to make acquaintances in the printing, bookselling, and stationery businesses. The lieutenant governor pledged to prepare letters of credit to cover Franklin's inventory and passage aboard the fittingly named *London Hope*, which annually sailed from Philadelphia to London.

In the months before the ship's departure, the lieutenant governor frequently invited the young printer to his house for dinner, which Franklin viewed as a great honor. Yet despite Keith's assurances that his letters were aboard the ship, when the vessel arrived in London on Christmas Eve, 1724, the captain opened the mail bags and found nothing from the lieutenant governor. A distraught Benjamin sought out a Keith acquaintance who laughed at the idea of the politician offering credit since, as he said, the governor had "no credit to give." Franklin reluctantly realized he had been taken in, this time by someone "too liberal of promises which he never meant to keep."[4]

Benjamin suffered another miscalculated relationship with James Ralph, a fellow Philadelphia tradesman and lover of books. Ralph, although married and raising a child, joined Franklin on the *London Hope*, claiming he would obtain goods in London to sell on commission in the colonies. Franklin and Ralph initially were "inseparable companions . . . [who] took lodgings together in Little Britain," one of the oldest sections of London.

Soon, Franklin realized that Ralph had no intention of returning to his family, and that the struggling merchant was quite happy spending Franklin's money on their joint dinners, evenings at the theater, "other places of amusement," and foolish "intrigues with low women."[5] Yet ultimately, Benjamin's own flirting destroyed the relationship. When Ralph finally found a job teaching in a village school outside of London, he asked Franklin to look after his mistress, a young milliner identified only as Mrs. T. Benjamin checked in on her, lent her a little money, and proceeded to seduce her, or, as he put it, "attempted familiarities."[6] A very displeased Ralph refused to speak to Franklin or repay his debts, which totaled a substantial twenty-seven pounds.

London—a city of 600,000 compared to Philadelphia's 7,000— would prove formative for the rather unfocused nineteen-year-old Franklin. England's vibrant capital was enjoying a building boom, with fashionable suburbs spreading north and rickety tenements rising throughout. In the early eighteenth century, London featured numerous public projects, with the founding of Westminster and Guys Hospitals, the first professional police force, and a commission established to pave and clean downtown streets. The metropolis also embraced public dialogue, as evidence by the growth of coffeehouses, scientific journals, and daily newspapers, all of which further introduced young Franklin to ideas advanced by Isaac Newton, Edward Gibbon, and other early Enlightenment leaders.

Benjamin possessed demonstrable skills with presses and fonts, and he quickly landed a job at Palmer's, a well-regarded printing house in Bartholomew Close. He worked there for a year, after which he took a higher-paying job at John Watts's, an even larger printshop that employed nearly fifty tradesmen. Franklin distinguished himself for his speed and ability to carry two sets of heavy type up and down stairs while other workmen struggled to transport only one.

Benjamin spent most of his spare time reading. Showing an appreciation for science, he repeatedly studied Theophilus DeSaulnier's *A Course in Experimental Philosophy*, which illustrated how testing equipment worked. Embarrassed by his failing grade in mathematics, he "took Cocker's book on arithmetic and went through the whole by myself with great ease. I also read Seller's and Shermy's books on navigation and became acquainted with the little geometry they contain."[7] Such readings expanded Franklin's expertise and prepared him to conduct his own experiments.

At work, he tested the chemistry associated with printing, offering another early sign of scientific ingenuity. He became particularly adept at creating iron-based inks, a delicate process that involved mixing oak galls, copper sulphate, ferrous sulphate, and gum Arabic. Carbon inks, depending upon the press and the temperature, demanded varying textures of soot, while disparate papers held distinct viscosities that required different ink formulas.

While clearly skilled, Benjamin could be haughty with his print-shop colleagues, and he was not initially popular at John Watts's, particularly after he stubbornly refused to pay "a new Bienvenu, or sum for drink," the terms used for pitching in to cover the team's alcohol, which averaged each day about a quart per person, serving as a safe alternative to the city's tainted water. Franklin's coworkers, he wrote, responded by "mixing my sorts, transposing my pages, breaking my matter." Ignored and ostracized, the newbie claimed to be an "excommunicate" until he finally took a realistic view of his prospects and covered his share of the group's beer and fortified wine.

Benjamin, however, increasingly loved "company, chat, a laugh, a glass, and even a song,"[8] and the charming conversationalist demonstrated a talent for networking at the coffeehouses and pubs popular with writers and scientists. He engaged and charmed William Lyons—a surgeon and the author of *The Infallibility of Human Judgment*—who brought him to Horns, an alehouse in Cheapside, to introduce him to Dr. Bernard Mandeville, author of the *Fable of the Bees*, a political satire on private vices. Later, Lyons went with Benjamin to Batson's Coffeehouse, where Dr. Henry Pemberton promised to introduce him to Sir Isaac Newton, an encounter for which Franklin was "extremely desirous." Alas, that meeting never happened, but Benjamin did talk at length about experiments with Sir Hans Sloane, a member of the Royal

Society whose extensive collections became the basis for the British Museum; that senior scientist gravitated to Franklin's "curiosities" from the New World, particularly "a purse made of the asbestos, which purifies by fire."[9]

Franklin's networking skills were notable in a city with wide economic and social disparities. Powerful aristocrats made up about 2 percent of the population and had little interaction with Franklin's group of skilled but low-paid artisans, let alone the 60 percent that depended upon charity during periods of unemployment, illness, or old age.[10] Yet as difficult as it was to bridge English classes, the gregarious Benjamin increasingly engaged with both the "middling sort" of professionals and the few wealthy gentlemen interested in natural philosophy.

Stimulating as his London conversations were, Franklin longed for his Philadelphia home. From a financial perspective, his trip was a bust. He had saved almost no money and even lacked the funds for a return voyage, in large part because of his and Ralph's extravagant expenditures. Desperate for cash, Benjamin considered offering swimming lessons to the sons of aristocrats. "If I were to remain in England and open a swimming school," he later wrote about his life-defining decision, "I might get a good deal of money. And it struck me so strongly, that had the overture been sooner made me, probably I should not so soon have returned to America."[11]

The eighteen months in London nonetheless marked a turning point for the maturing Franklin. In his own words, "I had by no means improved my fortune, but I had picked up some very ingenious acquaintances, whose conversation was of great advantage to me; and I had read considerably."[12] The alehouse discussions expanded his interest in the natural world and the ideas of Enlightenment thinkers. His successful experiments with the chemistry of printing revealed to him his own ingenuity. His befriended writers and researchers formed an initial network of scientists who later would publicize his research and advance his celebrity.

In England, an evolving Franklin also overcame his habit of befriending knaves, and he began to connect with more reliable colleagues, particularly Thomas Denham, a successful Quaker merchant. Seeing potential in Franklin, Denham offered to advance the ten pounds sterling needed to pay for his trip home, as well as an annual salary of fifty pounds if he would help open a general store in Philadelphia. Benjamin felt the role of shopkeeper to be more distinguished than tradesman, but more important, Denham, according to Franklin, "counseled me as a father, having sincere regard for me."[13] The pair set sail on the *Berkshire* in July 1726 to return to Philadelphia.

Benjamin used the eleven-week voyage to launch two endeavors that would occupy the rest of his life. First, he planned to improve his character—systematically. Embarrassed by his profligate spending, cavorts with prostitutes, and seduction of Ralph's mistress, Benjamin crafted self-improvement rules. "Let me," he declared, "make some resolutions and some scheme of action that, henceforth, I may live in all respects like a rational creature." His four-part "plan of conduct" called for being "extremely frugal," to "speak truth" and "aim at sincerity in every word," to work industriously, and to "speak ill of no man."[14] Franklin's behavior, not unexpectedly, would stray from these aspirations and he subsequently would outline more substantive goals, yet with Denham's encouragement, the twenty-year-old acknowledged he must enter a new phase, growing from a teenager who "never fixed a regular design as to life" into a man who "regulates his future conduct."[15]

Benjamin's other shipboard undertaking was to observe nature—carefully. Building on his London conversations and readings, he displayed a growing curiosity and commitment to scrutiny. As an example of his newfound appreciation for observation, Franklin described in detail a flying fish as having "about the bigness of a small mackerel, a sharp head, a small mouth, and a tail forked somewhat like a dolphin, but the lowest branch much larger and longer than the other and tinged with yellow."[16]

Showing his growing interest in calculations and experiments, Franklin also tracked the ship's location by the timing of a lunar eclipse and the appearance of grampuses and larks. He studied tiny "vegetable animals" found living on a branch of sargassum, a brown alga floating in the sea. How telling that he became fascinated by a bit of seaweed. As the small creatures grew, Franklin suggested they resembled miniature crabs, "about as big as the head of a tenpenny nail," that "were visibly animated, opening their shells every moment and thrusting out a set of unformed claws." He kept "the weed in salt water, renewing it every day till we came onshore, by this experiment to see whether any more crabs will be produced or not in this manner."[17] Recalling Francis Wollaston's writings he had read in London, Franklin wondered if he was witnessing the spontaneous emergence of one organism—a tiny shellfish—from another kind of creature—sargassum. His guess proved to be incorrect, but his inquisitiveness grew.

His last day at sea featured clear skies and gentle breezes, prompting a buoyant Benjamin to declare, "The immediate prospect of liberty, after so long and irksome confinement, ravishes us."[18] Ravished by liberty, a self-proclaimed new and improved Franklin returned to Philadelphia, where his career as a shopkeeper awaited.

# 4

~>-≈-<~

# BUILDING A
# BUSINESS EMPIRE

Thrilled as Benjamin was to be back in Philadelphia, the city did not offer him brotherly love. Thomas Denham opened a general store on Water Street, where Franklin declared himself an "expert in selling," but within four months, Benjamin developed pleurisy. The sharp chest pains caused a great deal of suffering and "nearly carried me off."[1] Worse was Denham contracting distemper and dying. Benjamin not only lost the man he "respected and loved" but also his employer, as Denham's executors closed the Water Street shop.

Yet Philadelphia, although still a bit of a frontier town, welcomed new immigrants opening businesses and building houses. As the capital of Pennsylvania—a proprietorship founded by the Quaker William Penn, and one of what would become thirteen British colonies—the city also attracted politicians and professionals. To succeed there, Benjamin understood he needed to expand his network of allies and friends.

So, in the autumn of 1727, not long after his return, the convivial Benjamin formed a social organization called the Leather Apron Club, and commonly known as the Junto. Unique for that time, members were to be young workingmen, his own "ingenious acquaintances" of professionals and artisans wanting to improve their prospects; inaugural members included a glassmaker, copier of deeds, surveyor, printer, shoemaker, joiner, and merchant's clerk. Franklin drafted precise rules for how the group would consider morals, politics, and science; discussions, for instance, were "to be conducted in the sincere spirit of inquiry after truth, without fondness for dispute or desire of victory."[2] Whatever their skills, participants had to pledge their love for mankind in general and truth for truth's sake, and they needed to cherish reading, poetry, mechanics, mathematics, and sensible conversation. They met weekly on Friday evenings, first at the Indian Head Tavern on Market Street and then in a room at a house they pooled their money to rent. One Sunday afternoon each month, except during the winter, members assembled outdoors for calisthenics, reflecting Franklin's commitment to exercise and health.

The Junto became a "club for mutual improvement," enabling its members to help other up-and-coming tradesmen and to hone their oratory.[3] Never far from his attentions, Benjamin regularly steered the Junto's discussions toward science. He posed numerous questions for discussion, including: "Is sound an entity or a body?" "How may the phenomena of vapors be explained?" "Why does the flame of a candle tend upwards in a spire?"

Despite the pleasures of networking, Franklin had little money and few employment prospects, so he returned to Samuel Keimer's printing house. Although the proprietor initially treated him "with great civility," Franklin got wind that the short-tempered, shortsighted printer planned to dismiss him after he tutored four young workers. Perhaps because of his very industriousness—Franklin was among the first persons in the colonies to manufacture type and brew his own ink—tensions with the owner rose. Hearing a loud noise one day, Benjamin poked his head out the workshop window to see Keimer screaming from the street that Benjamin should "mind my business, adding some reproachful words that nettled me the more for their publicity, all the neighbors who were looking out on the same occasion being witnesses how I was treated."[4] The quarrel continued indoors, prompting Franklin to quit the shop.

That evening Benjamin arranged to meet with another workman to discuss their options. Hugh Meredith arrived with his father, a well-off farmer and a recently elected member of the Pennsylvania General Assembly. Together, the trio devised an inventory for a new printshop and secretly sent their order to London.

Unaware of those plans, Keimer begged Franklin to help him with a new contract to print New Jersey's paper currency, an exacting job that required substantial sophistication and science. The assignment revealed Benjamin's ability to experiment with new approaches; for example, to prevent counterfeiting, a major concern for the colony, Franklin devised elaborate engraving designs, and he even developed invisible ink. He settled on distinctive watermarks obtained by pressing tree leaves into soft plaster or wet papier-mâché and using those molds to make lead printing blocks.[5] He also tested adding various amounts of mica to make the currency more durable.

Benjamin did a professional job of it, while engaging the province's legislators and influential officials. It was Franklin rather than Keimer whom they invited to their homes for dinner and introduced to their friends. Franklin bragged that "these friends were afterwards of great use to me."[6]

After Benjamin successfully finished the New Jersey contract and the printing equipment arrived from London, he and Meredith settled their affairs with Keimer and in early 1728 opened their own shop near the town market. His partnership with Meredith did not last, though. Hugh—whom Franklin once called "honest, sensible"—returned to drink and began to play "low games at alehouses." Even Meredith eventually realized he was "not fit for" the trade and moved to North Carolina, where cheap land allowed him to manage a small farm. With financial support from two other friends, Franklin paid off the partnership's debts and advertised under his own name an enterprise publishing flyers and pamphlets. At the young age of twenty-two, Benjamin Franklin had become a Philadelphia printer.

While his shop faced competition from both Keimer and Bradford, Benjamin gained business from his growing group of acquaintances, including lucrative jobs from the Society of Friends or Quakers.[7] Mindful of the power of appearances, he worked past eleven in the evening, dressed plainly, and avoided "places of idle diversion."[8] Rather than hire an assistant and be seen as extravagant, he carted his own supplies through the public streets.[9] One leading Philadelphia resident, or so Franklin recounts, found his industry to be "superior to anything I ever saw of the kind."[10]

Benjamin proved to be a skilled printer of high-quality products. Bradford, in contrast, may have held the valuable contract to print documents for the Pennsylvania government, but his work appeared "coarse and blundering." Franklin took it upon himself to reprint one such document "elegantly and correctly," and sent copies to every legislator.[11] The House thereafter chose Franklin as its official printer.

Benjamin was about to expand his operations by issuing his own newspaper when Keimer one-upped him, debuting a weekly he promised to be "a most useful paper of intelligence [that would include] the most complete body of history and philosophy ever yet published since the creation." To undercut this upstart competition, Franklin abandoned his independent plan and formed an alliance with Bradford. As he had done in Boston with letters from Silence Dogood, Benjamin wrote under the byline "Busy-Body," enlivening Bradford's periodical with entertaining barbs and gossip. Readers were delighted. Franklin admitted such tales were "nobody's business," but "out of zeal for the public good" he was taking "nobody's business wholly into my own hands."[12] To this mix, he added ridicule, calling his competitor "a sour philosopher" and his newspaper a "book of crudities."[13]

Keimer's response was to brand Franklin "every Ape's epitome."

Yet the unwieldy name Keimer adopted for his publication was an easy target: *The Universal Instructor in All Arts and Sciences, and Pennsylvania Gazette.* After only nine months, Keimer's incompetence caught up with him. He took on substantial debt, tumbled briefly into prison, and—after selling his paper to Benjamin in October 1729 "for a trifle"[14]—fled to Barbados.

Despite winning the publishing skirmish, Franklin admitted that "to publish a good newspaper is not so easy an undertaking as many people imagine it to be." In 1731, he released a frank defense of the press, entitled *Apology for Printers*, in which he asserted "that when men differ in opinion, both sides ought equally to have the advantage of being heard by the public; and that when truth and error have fair play, the former is always an overmatch for the latter." He crafted this call for journalistic freedom after including an advertisement for a ship sailing to Barbados, whose copy read: "No sea-hens (aka prostitutes) nor black gowns (aka ministers) will be admitted on any terms." Clergymen howled, arguing that Franklin had attacked morality and religion. They demanded a retraction, to which the twenty-five-year-old responded: "If all printers were determined to not print anything until they were sure it would offend nobody, there would be very little printed."[15,16]

WHILE FRANKLIN'S PUBLISHING BUSINESS ADVANCED, HIS PERSONAL life appeared far less organized, in large part because he failed to follow his own self-improvement dictates crafted on the boat returning from London. With surprising candor, Benjamin wrote that his "hard-to-be-governed passion of youth had hurried me frequently into intrigues with low women that fell in my way, which were attended with some expense and great inconvenience." Perhaps the greatest "inconvenience" came when the lusty printer fathered a son.[17]

Speculation abounds regarding William Franklin. We don't even know his birth date, although William himself said he was 82 in 1813, suggesting he arrived sometime in 1730 or 1731. We also don't know the identity of William's mother. One theory is that she was a well-to-do woman able to hide the pregnancy because her husband traveled, perhaps as a sea captain. During a nasty political campaign for the Pennsylvania Assembly in 1764, Franklin's opponents charged that the boy was the son of a prostitute named Barbara, whom Benjamin supposedly had abandoned.

Franklin, now a father, realized he needed to marry and increasingly turned his attentions to Deborah Read, the woman who happened to be standing outside her house as Benjamin in 1723 first walked up Market Street from the Philadelphia wharfs. Franklin in subsequent months admitted to having "a great respect and affection for her," yet he virtually ignored Deborah while gallivanting in London.[18] When her father died, she felt the need to marry but gave up on the wandering Franklin, linking instead with John Rogers, an amiable but unprofitable potter whom, she learned later, had ditched a wife in England. When Rogers's Philadelphia-based business failed, he stole a slave and sneaked off to the West Indies, leaving behind substantial bills; Benjamin later referred to Rogers as "a worthless fellow."[19]

Utilizing his new method for making difficult personal decisions—one he suggested was built on Isaac Newton's vision for balances and what we might call a ledger mentality—Benjamin divided a sheet of paper into two columns, one labeled "Pro" and the other "Con." The actual ledger, which was not saved, might have noted Deborah lacked a dowry, was "seldom cheerful," and possessed a fierce temper. On the "Pro" side, she was industrious and frugal, owned a piece of property, and agreed to help raise the "bastard child." She certainly was not Benjamin's equal in inquisitiveness or intelligence; although inaccurately described by some historians as illiterate, her letters often included grammatical and spelling errors, and she showed no interest in travel or philosophical conversation. Upon his return to Philadelphia, Franklin wrote dispassionately about "where the balance lies," and the couple "revived their mutual affection." Since Deborah could not prove the rumors that John Rogers had died in a fight in the Caribbean, she could not legally remarry; bigamy in 1730 was a crime that called for life imprisonment. And there was the fear of getting stuck with Rogers's substantial debts. The pair simply moved in together on the first of September. Benjamin referred to Deborah as "my plain country Joan." [20]

The common-law wife quickly merged marriage and commerce. She expanded the printshop's sundry offerings to include groceries, ointments, and cloth; managed the store's bookkeeping; folded and stitched pamphlets; and gathered linen rags for the papermakers.[21] Capable of being assertive, Deborah maintained order, an attribute Franklin admitted did not come easily for him.

HAVING SHED SOME RESPONSIBILITIES OF RUNNING THE BUSINESS to Deborah, Franklin sought to expand his civic engagement, entrepreneurial activities, and science reading. He proposed to improve the Philadelphia community and his own standing within it by having Junto members pool their books into a common library. Yet since their collections were disappointingly small, Benjamin in 1731 launched a subscription library, his "first project of a public nature," in which club participants asked reading devotees to pay forty shillings up front and ten shillings a year to purchase and circulate a broad array of books. They reached their initial goal of fifty subscribers within a few weeks and then doubled it.

A few years later, Franklin focused on Philadelphia's night watch, whose patrols often were relegated to drunken ragamuffins. Benjamin complained that policing was supported inadequately by a six-shilling tax imposed on all buildings, whether owned by "a poor widow housekeeper" or "the wealthiest merchant," and he convinced legislators, after much lobbying, to impose taxes on each property's value and hire trained constables. Franklin also formed a company of thirty firefighting volunteers—who maintained their own leather water buckets, ladders, and hooks. He reported that this bucket brigade "never lost more than one or two houses at a time, and the flames have often been extinguished before the house in which they began has been half consumed." Near the end of his life, he noted proudly that the "Union Fire Company still subsists and flourishes."[22]

Franklin's community-enhancing projects were generally met with positive reviews. In 1731, he was elected to be a member of the elite St. George's Lodge of the Freemasons, which included Philadelphia's most successful businessmen and respectable landlords.

Benjamin further expanded his business ventures in late December 1732 with the publication of *Poor Richard's Almanack*. Numerous printers, including six in Philadelphia, profited by selling annual predictions of the weather, tides, dawns and sunsets, and eclipses. Yet the imminently nimble Benjamin brought the almanac to a new level, adding entertaining stories and clever sayings that still are prevalent in American popular culture.

Under the pseudonym Poor Richard Saunders, Franklin mocked the pretentious and celebrated the amusements of everyday life. While trying to avoid "all libeling and personal abuse," he made the publication both entertaining and useful, offering advice, recipes, witticisms, and proverbs. Annual sales climbed to ten thousand copies, outpacing even the Bible, and reaped "considerable profit" for the publisher.

Franklin viewed the almanac as more than a moneymaker; it was to be a "vehicle for conveying instruction among the common people" who rarely read books. He filled the spaces around the calendars with pithy proverbs advancing his worldview that industry and frugality lead to wealth and virtue. To encourage people to better themselves, for example, he wrote: *It is hard for an empty sack to stand upright.* To spur readers to develop options, Poor Richard suggested: *Necessity never made a good bargain.* Among that almanac's best-known maxims are *"Haste makes waste"* and *"Early to bed and early to rise makes a man healthy, wealthy, and wise."*[23]

Franklin admitted Poor Richard's sayings were not always original but "contained the wisdom of many ages and nations."[24] His genius was to make them pithy. For instance, he edited the old English dictum *Fresh fish and new-come guests smell, but that they are three days old* into the more memorable *Fish and visitors stink in three days.*

Franklin's advice-giving almanac was just one of his business triumphs. He also published popular books, including America's first novels; edited a wide-circulation newspaper; held jobs with the Pennsylvania Assembly and postal service; built a network of printing partnerships and franchises throughout the colonies; helped construct a paper mill in Williamsburg, Virginia; and invested in Philadelphia and seaside properties. By 1734, the increasingly respected businessman became grandmaster of the Freemason lodge.

Yet Franklin was no Midas. His literary weekly failed, as did his *Die Philadelphische Zeitung*, an attempt to service Pennsylvania's large German-speaking population. After six weeks of aggressive marketing, that journal attracted only fifty subscribers.

Franklin realized he needed to further discipline his behavior if he were to advance his prospects. He had broken a contract with his brother, romanced his best friend's mistress, and squandered substantial time in London's pubs and brothels. Even after crafting a set of self-improvement dictates on his 1726 voyage back to Philadelphia, he fathered a son out of wedlock. While some would label such acts as sinful or immoral, it's worth noting that Franklin initially preferred "errata," a rather mild term used typically to describe printing errors that can be easily corrected.

Conventional religion did not satisfy his quest for maturity and personal reformation. He found church services "uninteresting and unedifying" and rejected the clergy's efforts "to make us good Presbyterians [rather] than good citizens."[25]

The closest Benjamin came to metaphysics was a flirtation with being "a thorough Deist,"[26] a believer in an emerging theology that insisted truth came from human action rather than God's grace. Complementing Benjamin's growing interest in science, Deism embraced close observation of nature and argued reason revealed life's wonders. Rather than contemplate his soul, grace, or salvation, Benjamin felt this rationalistic theology might help guide his personal behavior.

Still, the twenty-seven-year-old wanted something more "bold and audacious" to help him succeed as a businessman and natural philosopher. He proposed "moral perfection." Building on his four rules for conduct, Franklin in 1733 selected a dozen virtues to strive for, adding a thirteenth, "humility," after a Quaker friend "kindly" informed him of his "pride" and "overbearing and rather insolent" attitude. The list and his tenets included:

- Temperance (eat not to dullness; drink not to elevation).
- Silence (speak not but what may benefit others or yourself; avoid trifling conversation).
- Order (let all your things have their places; let each part of your business have its time).
- Resolution (resolve to perform what you ought; perform without fail what you resolve).
- Frugality (make no expense but to do good to others or yourself).
- Industry (lose no time; be always employed in something useful; cut off all unnecessary actions).
- Sincerity (use no hurtful deceit; think innocently and justly, and, if you speak, speak accordingly).
- Justice (wrong none by doing injuries or omitting the benefits that are your duty).
- Moderation (avoid extremes; forbear resenting injuries so much as you think they deserve).
- Cleanliness (tolerate no uncleanliness in body, clothes, or habitation).

- Tranquility (be not disturbed at trifles, or at accidents common or unavoidable).
- Chastity (rarely use energy but for health or offspring, never to dullness, weakness, or the injury of your own or another's peace or reputation); and
- Humility (imitate Jesus and Socrates).[27]

Franklin proposed tackling these virtues in sequence, focusing on one each week. He tracked his progress with a little book of thirteen pages, each devoted to a single principle.

Benjamin marked infractions with a black mark, and it was not long before he "was surprised to find myself so much fuller of faults than I had imagined." "Habit," he concluded, "took the advantage of inattention; inclination was sometimes too strong for reason." To be "completely virtuous" and avoid "slipping," he declared that "contrary habits must be broken, and good ones acquired and established."[28] Now he saw the evidence before him, admittedly self-reported but no less flattering.

"Order," Franklin admitted, "gave me the most trouble." Not only was he easily distracted at work, but he also failed to devise a system for organizing papers and things. He claimed his "exceedingly good memory" allowed him to avoid the "inconvenience attending want of method," yet he admitted his struggle with this virtue became more difficult with age. Benjamin rationalized this shortcoming, suggesting that "a benevolent man should allow a few faults in himself" to "keep his friends in countenance."[29]

Also difficult was humility. "In reality there is perhaps no one of our natural passions so hard to subdue as pride," he admitted. "For even if I could conceive that I had completely overcome it, I should probably be proud of my humility." Again, the image-conscious Benjamin hedged, arguing that he might not have acquired "the *reality* of this virtue, but I had a good deal with regard to the *appearance* of it."[30]

More easily mastered was industry. Having embraced family traits as well as toiled in shops from an early age, Franklin believed hard work to be "a means of obtaining wealth and distinction."[31]

Admittedly, what we know about Benjamin's effort at moral perfection comes from his recollections as a seventy-nine-year-old trying to explain his transition away from being a disjointed and unfocused youth. Obviously self-serving, it offers his tale of maturing into a careful adult who organizes his ways and controls his behavior.

Franklin preached what he practiced. While adjusting his own conduct, he offered his guidelines to others, believing that "one man of tolerable abilities may work great changes, and accomplish great affairs among mankind, if he first forms a good plan."[32] Moral perfection, in effect, became a democratic exercise. As noted by historian Ralph Lerner, Franklin, perhaps our first pop psychologist, argued that "ordinary folk, using the proper method, can acquire the necessary habits. No longer is perfection to be seen as the preserve of rare individuals of high character and high motivation."[33]

Franklin's zealous discipline led him beyond a checklist of virtues. He taught himself, in varying degrees of fluency, to read Latin, French, Spanish, and Italian, in large part so he could review scientific journals in their original language. He endeavored to become a polished public speaker. While a charming and engaging teller of tales in small groups, he admitted being a poor orator to a crowd, claiming to be "never eloquent, subject to much hesitation in my choice of words, hardly correct in language."[34] He also strove to become a more effective—and apparently humbler—debater. In the Junto's early days, he had argued assertively for his scientific or ethical opinions, laying rhetorical traps for his opponents, until realizing that his colleagues disliked such arrogance and doubled down on their own positions. Benjamin slowly turned to "modest diffidence," avoiding words like "certainly" or "undoubtedly," and, instead, using "I conceive" or "I apprehend." The increasingly disciplined—and pragmatic—Franklin added, "The modest way in which I proposed my opinions procured them a readier reception and less contraction."[35]

In 1736, Benjamin's more diplomatic approach secured him a position as clerk to the General Assembly, where he recorded legislative proceedings. Although a low-profile position, it allowed him to expand his interactions among prominent officials and to secure "the business of printing the votes, laws, paper money, and other occasional jobs for the public that, on the whole, were very profitable."[36] Historian Jill Lepore calculated that just the printing of paper currency made Franklin more money than the combined profits of his *Pennsylvania Gazette* and the popular *Almanack*.[37]

Not all was going well, however. In 1736, six years after moving in together, Benjamin and Deborah's four-year-old son, Francis, died from smallpox. They had not vaccinated Franky because he had been too sick with dysentery, yet Benjamin's bitter sense of guilt comes through in the single paragraph of his memoirs devoted to this tragedy, in which he warned other parents "who omit [inoculation] on the supposition that they should never forgive themselves if a child died under it."[38] It took seven more years for Deborah and Benjamin to try again for a family, and Sarah ("Sally") was born in 1743.

FRANKLIN, WITH HIS NEW POLITICAL CONNECTIONS AND OWNERSHIP of the renamed *Pennsylvania Gazette*, decided to take on Bradford's *American Weekly Mercury*. That journal, derided as sloppy and dull, nonetheless turned a profit, largely because the older printer enjoyed access to politicians, who secured his appointment as Pennsylvania's postmaster, which gave him control over the distribution of broadsheets.

Benjamin launched this new journalistic war by using higher-quality type and paper, as well as publishing "spirited remarks" that became "much talked of." Audiences especially liked the *Gazette*'s crime tales, including reports on a couple charged with murdering the man's daughter from a previous marriage."[39] Sex advice sold too, such as an anonymous letter, presumably crafted by Franklin, asking whether a husband, who had learned of a neighbor seducing his wife, could use such information to seek sex with that neighbor's wife.

Franklin also outmaneuvered Bradford politically. His growing network of allies alerted Col. Alexander Spotswood, the British head of the colonies' postal service, to Bradford's sloppy accounting, and convinced him to name Franklin in 1737 the postmaster of Philadelphia. The position offered a small salary but, more important, it allowed Benjamin faster access to news and wider distribution of his newspaper. As a result, circulation and advertisements doubled, affording Franklin "a considerable income" and making the *Pennsylvania Gazette* the most widely read paper in the American colonies. A triumphant Benjamin boasted that his "old competitor's newspaper declined proportionately."[40]

WHAT GREW ALONG WITH FRANKLIN'S BUSINESS AND GOVERNMENT responsibilities was his interest in science and mathematics. As Assembly clerk, for example, he found the rambling discourses by monotonous politicians to be "often so unentertaining that I was induced to amuse myself with making magic squares."[41] Demonstrating a newfound mastery of arithmetic, he arranged numbers so their sums in each row, each column, and across both main diagonals would be the same. Crafting such a square of nine numbers may not be too difficult, but Franklin completed complex cubes of sixty-four integers. He admitted some considered squares to be a trivial waste of time, but he became fascinated by the magic of numbers, and he boasted that he "had acquired such a knack at it that I could fill the cells of any magic square, of reasonable size, with a series of numbers as fast as I could write them."[42]

Franklin's every activity, in fact, seemed an opportunity to practice his inquisitiveness. When a popular itinerant preacher spoke on Philadelphia's courthouse steps, Benjamin, rather than contemplate the sermon, sought "to learn how far [the minister's] voice could be heard" and to calculate the crowd's size. As Franklin counted his steps to the back of the throng along Market Street, the sermonizer's words finally became obscured by the noise from the wharfs several blocks away. Franklin then used that distance from the revivalist to form the radius of a semicircle, and, assuming each listener occupied two square feet, he "computed that [the full-throated preacher] might well be heard by more than thirty thousand."[43]

With his growing financial resources, Franklin assembled a cadre of skilled craftsmen to join him in scientific research at a larger home in "a more quiet part of the town." This four-story, ten-room brick house stood in the middle of a courtyard off Market Street; its separation from the printshop symbolized his move from tradesman to "the better sort of people." To convey respectability and demonstrate his growing wealth, he even paid Robert Feke, a popular Boston-based artist, to paint his portrait wearing a dark green velvet coat, ruffled shirt, and curled wig.[44]

Franklin's opportunity to totally "disengage from private business" occurred in 1748 when David Hall, his foreman, whom Franklin called "obliging, discreet, industrious, and honest," bought out Franklin's share of the Philadelphia printing house, paying Benjamin over eighteen years some eighteen thousand pounds (equal to approximately $3.8 million in 2024).[45]

Benjamin savored his newfound freedom, writing, "I am in a fair way of having no other tasks than such as I shall like to give myself, and of enjoying what I look upon as great happiness, leisure to read, study, make experiments, and converse at large with such ingenious and worthy men as are pleased to honor me with their friendship or acquaintance, on such points as may produce something for the common benefit of mankind, uninterrupted by the little cares and fatigues of business."[46]

Franklin was forty-two years old, which happened to be the half-way point of his long life. Just twenty-two years after returning to Philadelphia virtually penniless, he had become a respected gentleman, with annual income probably five times that of a lawyer and equal to the governor's, but still far less than that of Pennsylvania's proprietors and other large landowners.[47] Financially successful and more disciplined, he finally could focus his attentions energetically on science, turning it from a pastime to a vocation.

# 5

# ELECTRICITY AND HEAT

As Enlightenment thinking evolved in the early eighteenth century, electricity became the greatest mystery in natural science, and Benjamin found himself on the cutting edge of discovery. No doubt the phenomenon's properties had been observed, if not understood, for millennia. In 600 B.C., Thales of Miletus rubbed amber—fossilized tree resin—across animal fur to generate flickers and attract light objects. Ancient Egyptians marveled at electric fishes that shocked their prey. Isaac Newton in 1713 speculated that "an electric spirit" permeated matter,[1] and several decades later Émilie, Marquise du Châtelet, described this "fire" in her dissertation as "the breadth of life that god has spread throughout his handiwork."[2]

The era's scientists initially considered electricity to be the result of human action—the rubbing itself—rather than a natural force. They knew nothing about its relationship with magnetism, nor the role of electrons. They didn't understand how to generate this energy, store it, or harness it to run machines and lights. They couldn't fathom how it would slash human drudgery and revolutionize industry and commerce.

Electricity long remained mostly a source of entertainment. In one popular demonstration, showmen suspended a young man from the ceiling with insulated cords; when they rubbed amber and slightly electrified the adolescent's feet, small sparks shot from his fingers, and he delivered shocking kisses to any daring lady. Another crowd pleaser featured an electric charge igniting a cup of alcohol. Abbé Jean-Antoine Nollet in 1746 staged a grand electrical performance to delight King Louis XV and the French court; he gathered about two hundred monks in a large circle, had them hold an iron wire, and when the clerics at both ends of the line touched the terminals of a rudimentary battery, thus completing a circuit, the entire devout crowd jumped simultaneously.

Benjamin's passion for electricity was sparked in 1740 when Isaac Greenwood, who had been dismissed from his Harvard professorship for excessive drinking, lectured in Philadelphia on "various experiments concerning electrical attraction and repulsion."[3] Franklin's interest grew when he witnessed Dr. Archibald Spencer, an Edinburgh-educated physician and itinerant showman, present electrical displays in 1744.[4] Benjamin called Spencer's exhibition "imperfectly performed, as (the doctor) was not very expert; but being on a subject quite new to me, they equally surprised and pleased me."[5]

The Greenwood and Spencer lectures inspired Franklin to read everything he could find about this seemingly magical form of power. More than a decade before his kite experiment, Benjamin started with De Magnete by the Englishman William Gilbert, who in 1600 examined lodestones, naturally occurring magnets, and coined the word electricus (from the Greek word for amber). He paid particular attention to Otto von Guericke, who in 1660 invented a device that produced static electricity, and he carefully tracked the contemporary efforts of numerous natural philosophers investigating this enigmatic wonder. French chemist Charles Du Fay, for instance, electrified rocks, wood, and animals, and he sent a small charge more than two-and-a-quarter miles!

Yet no one had explained electricity's features, how to generate large quantities of it, or how to regulate its power. Perhaps the most substantive advancement occurred in 1745 when Ewald Georg von Kleist in Germany and Pieter van Musschenbroek at Leyden, in South Holland, independently devised the first known means to store electricity and provide portable power. We know that device as the Leyden jar, essentially a flask wrapped in foil and filled with water, into which was inserted a metal bar electrified by a rotating generator.

Franklin referred to that bottle as "miraculous" and tried regularly to improve it. He discovered that the jar's glass, rather than its metal or water, as others suspected, held the electric charge. He subsequently outlined modifications that made what he called an "electrical battery, consisting of eleven panes of large sash-glass, armed with thin leaden plates pasted on each side, placed vertically and supported at two inches' distance on silk cords, with thick hooks of leaden wire, one from each side, standing upright, distant from each other, and convenient communications of wire and chain from the giving side of one pane to the receiving side of the other; that so the whole might be charged together and with the same labor as one single pane."[6]

Franklin sought to expand his research and create a sophisticated laboratory. Taking advantage of his new and larger home on Market Street, he collected additional equipment as well as "little machines I had roughly made for myself."[7] Although the date is a bit uncertain, Peter Collinson—a London-based cloth merchant and accomplished botanist—donated notes on electrical experiments conducted in England, Holland, and Germany.[8] Thomas Penn, Pennsylvania's proprietor, who would become Franklin's political foe, also forwarded a few sophisticated tools, including a rotating electrostatic generator.

With a mix of joyful play and serious research, Franklin spun glass tubes, powered up rudimentary batteries, and tested how far he could throw sparks. "I never was before engaged in any study that so totally engrossed my attention and my time," he claimed.[9]

Still several years before he flew a kite in a storm, Benjamin carefully designed basic research experiments that contradicted conventional wisdom and revealed electricity's fundamental nature. He showed, for instance, that rubbing does not create electricity but causes it to flow. Put another way, he discovered that electricity was "not *created* by the friction but *collected* only," thereby disproving the prevailing belief that it was a new form of matter resulting from an experimenter's intervention.[10]

Franklin and his inquisitive team—particularly Ebenezer Kinnersley, a Baptist minister and English professor; Thomas Hopkinson, a lawyer; and Philip Syng, a silversmith—further demonstrated electricity to be a single "fluid" with positive and negative qualities. That "electric fire," they observed, remains in a neutral state until forced into an imbalance by frictional forces. Previous natural philosophers, particularly Charles Du Fay and L'Abbé Jean-Antoine Nollet, had theorized that electricity was composed of two fluids, and that materials could either emit (be "effluent") or collect (be "affluent") charges. By focusing instead on charging and discharging, Benjamin explained how electricity moves from one body to another since, as he put it, "common matter is as a kind of sponge" that soaks up this fluid.[11] Robert Millikan, identified earlier as the 1923 winner of the Nobel Prize for Physics, called Franklin's single-fluid thesis the progenitor of the modern electron theory.[12]

The Philadelphia team also discovered that total electrical charges maintain equality and regularly seek balance. From this observation, Benjamin proposed a law known as "conservation of charge," which predicted accurately the outcome of numerous electrical experiments. The law asserts that the overall charge in an isolated system never alters, and that positive and negative states of electrification seek neutrality, which is the cause of electrical shocks.[13] "The equality is never destroyed," Franklin wrote, "the fire only circulating."[14] In future years, this concept provided a basis for the development of electricity as a source of power, and it helped nuclear physicists predict the composition of a reaction's final product. Franklin's conservation law alone was enough to cement his fame as a scientific pioneer.

Despite having no formal education in theoretical physics or higher mathematics, Benjamin identified several of electricity's other basic characteristics. Beginning around 1745, some seven years before lofting his silk kite, Franklin described the differences between conductors and insulators, demonstrating that electricity moves through metal (a conductor) but not wood (an insulator). He showed that like charges repel each other while unlike charges do the opposite. (Admittedly, an explanation for this mutual repulsion of similarly charged bodies had to wait almost fifteen years on others, particularly Franz Aepinus, a German-based physicist.) Benjamin outlined the role of capacitors and batteries that store electrical charges, and he even created a language for this new science, introducing more than two dozen electrical terms, including "condenser," "armature," as well as "plus" and "minus" charges.

Franklin reveled in testing electricity's attributes, writing that for months in 1747 he had "little leisure for anything else." He and his colleagues frequently repeated their experiments for "friends and acquaintances, who, from the novelty of the thing, come continually in crowds to see them."[15]

Benjamin's notes reveal a refreshing inquisitiveness and are filled with expressions of happy discovery: "It is amazing to observe"; the "experiment more than surprises us"; and the results "appear more surprising."[16] Reflecting on the unforeseen thrills associated with his tests, Franklin wrote: "Though we miss what we expected to find, yet something valuable turns out, something surprising and instructing, though unthought of."[17]

Franklin and his colleagues found joy in their experiments, such as when they tried multiple ways to break the charge around an electrified object. Historian Joyce Chaplin described how the exuberant Philadelphians "breathed on the air around the [electrified, three-inch, iron] shot, sifted sand over it, waved woodsmoke toward it, plunged it in darkness, and lighted it with a candle.[18]

Benjamin's laboratory notes also displayed humbleness, not one of his usual attributes. He warned a colleague, for instance, that his science writings might "bring you nothing new, which may well be, considering the number of ingenious men in Europe continually engaged in the same researches."[19] Franklin even admitted what he didn't know, including, "I am very little acquainted with the nature of magnetism,"[20] and "I am much in the dark about light."[21]

Not all his experiments worked. To determine electricity's possible health benefits, Benjamin sent a small charge into a man's lame hand, which he could not lift off his knee. By the next morning, he could raise it four or five inches, and even more the following day, enough to feebly take off his hat. Yet the improvements stopped after a while, and the patient, disliking painful shocks, avoided further treatments.

Franklin argued that an effective scientist must maintain an open mind, a willingness to question his own theories and tolerate challenges from others. "I must own that I have some doubts about (my own hypotheses)," he admitted, "yet, as I have at present nothing better to offer in their stead, I do not cross them out; for even a bad solution read, and its faults discovered, has often given rise to a good one in the mind of an ingenious reader."[22] Benjamin conceded one personal benefit from embracing corrections and new insights—that they "make a vain man humble."[23]

Dangers associated with electrical experiments added to that humility. On Christmas Day 1750, Franklin inadvertently took a substantial charge from two large glass jars, and he later wrote: "My senses being instantly gone. I neither saw the [flash] nor heard the [crack], nor did I feel the stroke on my head, though I afterwards found it raised a round swelling where the fire entered as big as half a pistol bullet."[24] That experience prompted the following wry reflection: "If anyone should doubt whether the electricity matter passes through the substance of bodies, or only over and along their surfaces, a shock from an electrified large glass jar, taken through his own body, will probably convince him."[25]

Franklin regularly gave credit to his clever and crafty colleagues, and most of his experiment descriptions referred to "we" or "us." The team, meanwhile, credited their leader. Consider Ebenezer Kinnersley, a key collaborator who became master of the English School at the Academy of Philadelphia and lectured throughout the colonies on the science of electricity. When William Smith, who would become a political enemy of Benjamin's, asserted that Kinnersley was the "chief inventor . . . of the electrical apparatus, as well as author of a considerable part of those discoveries in electricity published by Mr. Franklin," Kinnersley responded that Franklin had the "undoubted right" to all the honors he received. He added that no one should "deprecate the merit of the ingenious and worthy Mr. Franklin in the many curious and justly celebrated discoveries he has made in electricity."[26]

Another key player was Peter Collinson, to whom Benjamin reported his team's theories and assessments. The first note in March 1747 simply stated that "we have observed some particular phenomenon that we look upon to be new."[27] Although based in London, the merchant and botanist played an important role in American science, turning his counting house, as historian Brooke Hindle phrased it, into a clearinghouse.[28] While Collinson managed one of England's finest gardens and became a botanist of some note, his greatest contribution was as a networker, circulating theories and findings among natural philosophers in Europe and the colonies.

When Collinson arranged for Franklin's notes to be read at meetings of the Royal Society of London, Benjamin worried some of his theories would be "stifled" or "laughed at by the connoisseurs."[29] William Watson, a rather pompous English scientist, did suppress some of Franklin's letters and tried to discount others by suggesting Benjamin's experiments "coincide with and support those which I some time since communicated to the Society."[30] Yet interest in Franklin's unique findings grew, and in 1751 (still a year before the kite experiment), his British supporters assembled many of his notes into a pamphlet entitled *Experiments and Observations on Electricity, Made at Philadelphia in America,* which gained popular attention throughout Europe, particularly in France. With ten separate editions, it was one of the most widely read treatises and certainly the most noted scientific book by an American of the eighteenth century. (Ironically, New World publishers felt Franklin's letters and essays would not sell and did not publish the work until 1941.)

With the pamphlet, Benjamin became something of a continental celebrity. "All Europe is in agitation on verifying electrical experiments," Collinson wrote to him. "All commends the thought of the inventor."[31]

AFTER WORKING FOR SEVERAL YEARS ON EXPERIMENTS WITHIN HIS laboratory, Franklin began going outdoors to observe clouds, which he suspected accumulated electrical charges. When such "electrified clouds pass over," he wrote, "high trees, lofty towers, spires, masts of ships...draw the electrical fire and the whole cloud discharges." That observation prompted one of Franklin's early proverbs, a wise one to follow: "Dangerous therefore it is to take shelter under a tree during a thunder gust."[32]

Most religious people of the early and mid-eighteenth century feared lightning as a terrifying demonstration of God's wrath or the devil's punishment; Cotton Mather referred to lightning as "the arrows of god."[33] The faithful rang church bells during storms to invoke the almighty's protection and ward off discharges, a practice not good for the long-term health of bellringers. One study found that lightning in the mid-eighteenth century struck more than 386 churches in Germany and electrocuted 103 sextons. Other adherents stored gunpowder within churches, believing holy structures offered a divine shield. In a village in northern Italy in 1769, lightning struck a religious building holding hundreds of tons of explosives, killing more than three thousand people and destroying much of that city.

In addition to confronting the superstitious, Franklin challenged natural philosophers who commonly viewed lightning as the earth's combustible liquids being vaporized and burned, much like what happens in a mine explosion. He did, however, build on the efforts of a few other scientists such as Englishmen Francis Hauksbee, who in 1705 linked lightning and electricity by suggesting that bolts were static electricity discharges, and the Frenchman Abbé Nollet who listed similarities between the two phenomena. Yet Franklin was the first to devise trials to prove the connection between lightning and electricity. With perhaps the clearest expression of his hard-charging inquisitiveness, Benjamin declared, "Let the experiment be made."[34]

Franklin imagined that clouds often contain negative charges near their bases and positive ones above; as a cloud drifts, it can push its negative charges into trees or buildings and then into the ground. Alternatively, electrical charges can travel from cloud to cloud or rise from the earth into the sky.[35] He felt that when differences in charge exceed what the air can withstand, ascending and descending discharges seek a balance through a lightning bolt. Yet Franklin admitted to being "at a loss" about how clouds "become charged with electricity; no hypothesis I have yet formed perfectly satisfying me."[36]

As Benjamin observed new evidence, he willingly altered his theories. For instance, he changed his view of lightning's path being from the shortest possible route to the one of "least resistance."[37] He moved from believing that lightning melted metals by "cold fusion" to understanding it burned those materials through heat.[38]

Franklin hypothesized that pointed conductors would attract electrical charges from clouds. He could not initially explain the properties "of points, sending off or drawing on the electrical fire," but he wrote clear and detailed descriptions of their "truly wonderful" effects. Rejecting the typical placement of round balls made of wood or metal atop weather vanes, he advocated for a point from "a rod of iron, eight or ten feet in length, sharpened gradually to a point like a needle, and gilt to prevent rusting."[39] Many months before his kite experiment, he predicted, in what even he admitted "may seem whimsical," that "the electrical fire would, I think, be drawn out of a cloud silently" by such tapered tips.[40] In 1750, he proposed a lightning bolt could be neutralized by a wire strung from the point to the ground, his first suggestion for a lightning rod.[41]

As noted in the first chapter, Benjamin could not conduct his own sentry-box experiment—which called for a researcher to stand protected within a small structure and draw sparks from a raised iron pole—since he felt no structure in Philadelphia rose high enough to extend a rod into the sky. In France, M. Delor, considered a "master of experimental philosophy," repeated several of Franklin's lab-based experiments for King Louis XV, who then encouraged Thomas-François Dalibard to perform the "sentry-box" experiment outdoors.[42]

Franklin's directions explained the experiment's risk. "If the electrical stand be kept clean and dry," he wrote, "a man standing on it when such clouds are passing low, might be electrified." "Apprehensive persons," he suggested, should feel safer if they periodically brought a grounded wire, held by insulated handles, close to the iron rod, thus "drawing off any sparks without endangering himself."[43] Franklin further encouraged kite flyers to seek shelter in a shed and to keep the silk portion of the kite's string dry, and he later added that "care must be taken that the twine does not touch the frame of the door or window," which could burst into flames.[44]

Despite such warnings, flying a kite lent whimsy to a significant effort, and the use of a child's toy discounted the danger of early electrical science. On August 6, 1753, a Russian researcher, Georg Wilhelm Richmann, who flouted some of Benjamin's dictates, died by electric shock when he confronted rare ball lightning in a severe storm. So, it wasn't whimsy that Franklin was practicing—or it wasn't only whimsy—and his experiment was neither a lark nor divine revelation.

When word of Dalibard's sentry-box experiment reached Philadelphia in July 1752, Franklin announced it briefly in the *Pennsylvania Gazette*. However, Benjamin waited until mid-October before revealing his own kite-flying results in both the *Gazette* and *Poor Richard's Almanack*, and then noted simply: "It may be agreeable to the curious to be informed that the same experiment has succeeded in Philadelphia, though made in a different and more easy manner."[45]

Franklin's confounding reaction to his own experiment adds to his enigma. It is odd that for such a noteworthy experiment, he made no immediate record of the location or actual date in June 1752, and he took four months to describe his work, and then only in a few paragraphs that did not reveal his own role. Afraid of not being believed, did he hold back until others confirmed the experiment?[46] Did Benjamin-the-businessman simply wait until October to garner more attention by printing the news in both his twice-weekly newspaper and annual almanac?[47] Did Franklin-the-scientist discount the kite flying to prioritize his more theoretical work on physics? Was this "toy story," as one historian deemed the effort, nothing more than another Franklin hoax, this one on Britain's stuffy scientific establishment?[48]

Later in October, Franklin shared more details about the kite experiment in a letter to Peter Collinson and concluded: "I was pleased to hear of the success of my experiments in France, and that they began to erect points on their buildings. We had before placed them upon our Academy and State House spires."[49] That note, which Collinson read to the Royal Society, revealed two pivotal assertions: first, Franklin's priority claim that the European efforts were based on his directives, and second, to be elaborated on in more detail below, that he was the first to install lightning rods on public buildings.

Benjamin's notes read like a how-to manual. Suggesting "anyone may try," he explained his use of silk, hemp twine, pointed wire, and a metal house key.[50] He described how the charge could be stored in a Leyden jar and used later to conduct experiments, and he boasted that "the sameness of the electric matter with that of lightning is completely demonstrated."[51]

Almost fifteen years passed before the English scientist Joseph Priestley, who would become distinguished for discovering oxygen, offered a fuller explanation of Franklin's experiment and its meaning.[52] It is worth noting that Benjamin had met Priestley the year before, while living in London in 1766, and had given him books and resources needed to write a two-volume history of electrical research as well as reviewed the manuscript. While Priestley's description of Benjamin's kite experiment within his *History and Present State of Electricity* is maddeningly short, the Englishman refers to it as "astonishing" and "so capital a discovery."[53] He adds: "Let the reader judge of the exquisite pleasure [Franklin] must have felt at that moment."[54]

The successful sentry-box and kite trials changed minds, as evidenced by a French philosopher's admission: "You must remember, sir, how much we ridiculed Mr. Franklin's project for emptying clouds of their thunder, and we could scarce conceive him to be any other than an imaginary being. This now proves us to be but poor virtuosi."[55]

Even haughty English scientists paid attention, praising the clarity and simplicity of Franklin's work and writings. According to Lord Brougham, who would become the lord high chancellor, "He could make an experiment with less apparatus and conduct his experimental inquiry to a discovery with more ordinary materials than any other philosopher we ever saw. With an old key, a silk thread, some sealing wax, and a sheet of paper, he discovered the identity of lightning and electricity."[56]

Even some seventy years after the kite experiment, when Benjamin's descriptions and ideas were no longer on the cutting edge of science, the celebrated chemist Sir Humphry Davy still recommended Benjamin's notes to his students, saying Franklin's "style and manner... are almost as worthy as the doctrines it contains."[57] Davy went further, asserting that Benjamin "has written equally for the uninitiated and the philosopher, and he has rendered his details as amusing as well as perspicuous, elegant, as well as simple."[58] Part of Franklin's scientific prowess, in fact, resulted from the clarity of his writing, an attribute he honed by recrafting articles from the *Spectator* and fashioning Dogood tales for the *Courant*. By demonstrating a unique ability to clearly explain his theories and experimental results, he entertained as well as enlightened his readers.

The French king also applauded Franklin, and Britain's Royal Society in November 1753 awarded him the Sir Godfrey Copley gold medal, its highest honor, "on account of his curious experiments and observations on electricity . . . (a topic only a few years ago that) was thought to be of little importance."[59] Benjamin, lowly born and with but two years of school education, also received honorary degrees from Yale and Harvard. In 1756, he was elected to the Royal Society, where his hero, Isaac Newton, had been president for almost twenty-five years; Franklin received no negative votes, "an instance of unanimity" that the association's president said "he never before saw."[60]

And so, a self-educated tradesman from the colonies revealed secrets about nature that the Old World's intelligentsia had failed to recognize. He converted a mystery into a wonder, and he became lionized for snatching fire from the gods, with Immanuel Kant declaring Benjamin to be "the Prometheus of recent times."[61] Almost two-hundred years later, historian Carl Van Doren described Benjamin's growing notoriety: "To the public, as it gradually heard about him, he seemed a magician. To scientists, from the first, he seemed a master."[62]

FRANKLIN CAPTURED PUBLIC ATTENTION IN PART BECAUSE HE CONducted understandable experiments: who could not comprehend flying a kite? Adding to his popular appeal, he hid his brilliance behind a trickster's sense of fun. He rigged a statue of George III with a gilded crown that produced "high treason" shocks when touched, and, to the delight of visitors, he placed a slight electric charge along the metal fence surrounding his Philadelphia home. He even proposed a "party of pleasure" on the banks of the Schuylkill in which electrical charges cooked the meals and ran through the river to ignite alcoholic spirits on the opposite bank.

Such humor prompted some historians to dismiss Franklin's science. Yet jokes aside, Benjamin, as noted above, made key discoveries as well as democratized science by showing how observation and experimentation are available to the ingenious and not just the rich.[63] He embraced consistent refinements, claiming that interpretations must change with new experimental results. He encouraged others to build on his "short hints and imperfect experiments" and to obtain "more complete discoveries," and suggested even imperfect experiments "have oftentimes a good effect, in exciting the attention of the ingenious to the subject and so become the occasion of more exact disquisition and more complete discoveries."[64]

Unlike pretentious philosophers, Benjamin candidly admitted when he was wrong or lost confidence in previous opinions. "I have observed a phenomenon or two that I cannot at present account for on the principles laid down in [my previous] letters," he confessed to Collinson, "and am therefore become a little diffident of my hypothesis, and ashamed that I have expressed myself in so positive a manner."[65] Part of practicing science, he observed, is to construct "many pretty systems" that we "soon find ourselves obliged to destroy."[66]

FRANKLIN SLOWLY MADE A TRANSITION TO APPLIED SCIENCE. HE embraced the argument by Francis Bacon—the English philosopher credited in the early seventeenth century with devising what would become known as the scientific method—that advances in fundamental research could eventually lead to practical developments that help humans.

Building on his kite experiment, Franklin realized that pointed rods could do more than draw electrical charges silently from clouds. They also could divert an actual lightning strike safely by wire into the ground or water. He initially noted that blocking a bolt "before it came nigh enough to strike secures us from that most sudden and terrible mischief,"[67] but he added that pointed rods would "either prevent a stroke, or, if not prevented, would conduct it, so as that the building should suffer no damage."[68]

As with his sentry-box experiment, Franklin issued detailed instructions for installing lightning rods. The instrument, he advised, should be placed six or eight feet above the building's highest point, tapered to a sharp point, and gilded to prevent rusting. For the wire, he noted that "a small quantity of metal is found able to conduct a great quantity of this fluid," and he concluded that "the lower end of the rod should enter the earth so deep as to come at the moist part, perhaps two or three feet; and if bent when under the surface so as to go in a horizontal line six or eight feet from the wall, and then bent again downwards three or four feet, it will prevent damage to any of the stones of the foundation."[69]

In September 1752, three months after the kite experiment, Franklin installed a lightning rod on his own house. He extended a metal spear nine feet above the top of his chimney and attached a wire—"the thickness of a goosequill"—from the rod's base, through a covered glass tube in the roof, down the staircase, and into an iron spike in the ground. Franklin wanted more than his house protected from lightning; ever curious, he sought data on the frequency and severity of atmospheric electric charges. Across from his bedroom, therefore, he divided the wire with "a little bell on each end; and between the bells a little brass ball, suspended by a silk thread, to strike the bells when charged clouds passed."[70] How appropriate that Franklin's first musical instrument was played by lightning.

Franklin's lightning-rod invention saved lives and structures, allowing belfry bellringers and munition warehouses to be spared death and destruction. More fundamentally, he transformed in the popular mind a frightening force that represented divine anger into a natural phenomenon that humans could control.

Yet some remained superstitious. The Reverend Thomas Prince, pastor of Boston's Old South Church, took to his pulpit to denounce lightning rods, arguing that they circumvented heaven's fury. Even a couple of scientists expressed skepticism; one French philosopher, although motivated mostly by envy of Franklin's growing fame, argued the lighting rod "was an offense to god." Stephen Hales, an English botanist and clergyman, took a different tack, claiming that parts of the earth charged with an "electrical substance" became "more exposed to more shocking earthquakes." This Royal Society fellow continued: "Although the rods may avoid God's wrath in the air," the charges "may grow more fatal . . . in the earth."[71] Franklin, through the voice of Poor Richard, cheekily dismissed the earthquake theory and countered religious skeptics by claiming the rod's development reflected divine intervention. "It has pleased God in his goodness to mankind," he wrote, "to discover to them the means of securing their habitations and other buildings from mischief by thunder and lightning." After adding rods in June 1752 at Philadelphia's academy and State House, he continued: "Surely the thunder of heaven is no more supernatural than the rain, hail, or sunshine of heaven, against the inconvenience of which we guard by roofs and shades without scruple."[72]

Other scientists joined Franklin's defense. John Winthrop, the Boston-based mathematician and astronomer, wrote that lightning rods, "by the blessing of God, might be a means of preventing many of those mischievous and sorrowful accidents, which we have so often seen to follow upon thunderstorms." Challenging the pious, Winthrop didn't believe that "in the whole town of Boston" there was so much as "one person who is so weak, so ignorant, so foolish, or . . . so atheistical" as to believe that "it is possible, by the help of a few yards of wire, to 'get out of the mighty hand of God.'"[73]

FRANKLIN SLOWLY REALIZED THAT SOME OF HIS OBSERVATIONS, AND even terminology, associated with electricity could be applied to heat. Both forms of energy are conducted through certain materials, such as metal wire. He expressed particular interest in how heat moves and becomes absorbed. Ever observant of everyday occurrences, he remarked that "beer much sooner warms in a black mug set before the fire, than in a white one, or in a bright silver tankard."[74]

Benjamin built on work by other scientists, particularly Robert Boyle, who in the mid-seventeenth century advanced laws about gases, observed that heat resulted from the movement of particles, and wrote *Experimental History of Colours*. Franklin added another straightforward experiment, this time to show how different-colored cloths absorb thermal energy differently. He and Joseph Breintnall, a Junto colleague and scrivener, placed a variety of fabrics on snow in a sunny field and measured the rate of melting. The results may now seem obvious— darker patches absorb more energy—but in the mid-eighteenth century they provided some of the first experimental data on heat transfer.

Franklin also observed and analyzed convection, or the tendency of hotter air to rise. He reviewed the writings of European physicists, particularly Evangelista Torricelli, an Italian mathematician who showed that air had weight and, therefore, must be made of something physical. Franklin joined Daniel Bernoulli, a Swiss mathematician, to suggest that air was composed of tiny particles too small to be seen or felt. He described how those particles, when heated, became lighter, "rarified," and "(take) up more space." Conversely, he reasoned, cooler particles became dense, heavy, and sink because of gravity.

A particularly clever test addressed conduction, showing how heat moves at different speeds through distinct substances. Franklin placed wax rings around the middle of rods made from discrete metals, heated the ends of those rods, and then calculated how quickly the waxes melted. He found that iron warmed slowly but retained its heat longer than other substances.

Applying such findings, Franklin the pragmatist began to wonder how best to heat a room. Existing fireplaces tended to emit choking smoke and inefficiently burn large quantities of wood or coal. Referring to himself as someone "dealing with smoke,"[75] he read all the available literature on stoves, experimented for six years with different designs, and then in 1742—a full decade before his kite flying—proposed a cast-iron unit, to be placed within a fireplace or in the center of a room, that would efficiently and cost-effectively warm the space. Building on theories by Isaac Newton and Hermann Boerhaave, a Dutch chemist, about heat being able to "descend," Franklin deployed an iron plate to separate smoke, which went up the chimney, from heat, which fell into an inner metal chamber that released it slowly into the room through louvered vents. Benjamin convinced an ironmaker and Junto member, Robert Grace, to cast the stove's plates, a job he found profitable.

Franklin printed advertising pamphlets to promote the new stoves. The canny publicist claimed that the stove reduced drafts, which dried and shriveled skin, thus ensuring that women remained looking young and beautiful. He translated the ads into Dutch, German, French, and Italian, and he employed two of his brothers and several friends as marketing agents.

Franklin boasted that his stove, unlike typical closed units, allowed homeowners to enjoy the "pleasant" sight of fire while also being able to "boil the tea-kettle, warm the flat-irons, heat heaters, keep warm a dish of victuals by setting it on the top."[76] He further claimed it made his common room "twice as warm as it used to be with a quarter of the wood I formerly consumed there."[77]

Yet this clever design proved to be complex and challenging. Before its chimney and back channels were sufficiently heated, the stove failed to draw sufficiently, and smoke drifted into the house. Sales declined dramatically, but Franklin continued simplifying and improving the unit. David Rittenhouse, a respected astronomer, more successfully modified Benjamin's design, which mistakenly became known as the Franklin Stove or Pennsylvania Fireplace. Even more popular were the Holland Stove, which warmed large assembly halls, and the Six-Plate Stove, which featured multiple metal sides.

Benjamin refused to accept a ten-year patent on his device from the governor of Pennsylvania, claiming his goal simply was to benefit mankind. "As we enjoy great advantages from the inventions of others," he asserted, "we should be glad of an opportunity to serve others by any invention of ours; and this we should do freely and generously."[78]

Benjamin's studies of smoke led to other practical improvements. Although John Clifton proposed lamps to brighten Philadelphia's streets, Franklin perfected the globe's design. The lamps sent from London tended to smoke and obstruct the light after only a few hours, requiring cleaners to be hired each morning to wipe away the smudge and to replace spheres that had overheated and exploded. Benjamin tested a variety of alternatives, settling on a design with "four flat panes with a long funnel above to draw up the smoke and crevices [that] admitted air flow to facilitate the ascent of the smoke." The useful upgrade, he bragged, "continued bright till morning, and an accidental stroke would generally break but a single pane, easily repaired."[79]

Benjamin also investigated refrigeration and the nature of cold. On a hot summer day in Philadelphia, with the temperature nearing one hundred degrees Fahrenheit, he observed that he remained relatively cool when wearing a sweaty shirt and sitting before an open window, but he became markedly warmer upon changing into a dry top. He questioned the then-common belief that breezes alone swept away warmth, and he suggested people become cooler mostly by the evaporation of their sweat, whereby the water on our skin turns into a gas that releases heat into the air. He was building on the work of Antonie van Leeuwenhoek, the accomplished Dutch microbiologist who wrote about evaporation, but the process of sweating remained a mystery for almost a century until Czech physiologist Johannes Purkinje discovered actual sweat glands.

In the summer of 1758, Franklin traveled to Cambridge University to expand on his hypothesis and conduct experiments with chemist John Hadley. Having previously observed that different fluids vaporize at different rates, the pair focused on ether, a colorless and volatile liquid that can turn quickly into a gas. Franklin and Hadley poured ether around a thermometer bulb and blew air onto it from a bellows. "We continued this operation," wrote Franklin, "one of us wetting the ball, and another of the company blowing on it with the bellows to quicken the evaporation, the mercury sinking all the time until it came down to 7, which is 25 degrees below the freezing point." He concluded: "From this experiment one may see the possibility of freezing a man to death on a warm summer's day."[80] Fortunately, Benjamin did not test that theory on any unsuspecting soul.[81]

Heat and cold turned Franklin's attention to the weather. Poor Richard long had been guessing temperatures and precipitation a year out, but Franklin sought something more certain. Elementary meteorology can be traced back some five thousand years to the time when Indian observers wrote about cold formations and the water cycle, yet explanations and forecasts remained primitive. Contradicting conventional wisdom, Franklin suggested that weather patterns along the Atlantic seaboard often moved from the south to the north, and he offered an analogy to the air in a room when wood in a fireplace is lit: "Immediately the air in the chimney, being rarefied by the fire, rises; the air next the chimney flows in to supply its place, moving towards the chimney; and in consequence the rest of the air successively, quite back to the door." Some Atlantic coast storms, he theorized, begin with "some great heat and rarefaction of the air in or about the Gulf of Mexico; the air thence rising has its place supplied by the next more northern, cooler, and therefore denser and heavier air; that, being in motion is followed by the next more northern air, etc."[82] From this comparison between fireplaces and storms, he became the first to document storm movements in the Northern Hemisphere.

———————

BENJAMIN'S LETTERS OF THE 1740S REVEAL A WIDENING RANGE OF interests. He wrote to Cadwallader Colden, his New York–based friend, about the earth's rotation and his theory that light is a subtle elastic that becomes visible when vibrated. In a note to Jared Eliot, a Connecticut farmer and clergyman, he discussed the best soil for growing hemp, the operations of oil mills, the source of most freshwater streams, the folly of Connecticut's tax on goods imported from other colonies, the price of linseed oil, and the probable weather for the summer farming season. He regaled the Swedish botanist Peter Kalm with his theories about communications among ants, noting his experiment in which a single ant climbed out of an earthen pot of molasses and somehow informed the location of the sweet treat to a swarm that arrived within half an hour. He wrote to another friend about the relationship between the breeding of pigeons and the availability of habitation boxes. He studied the luminescence of seawater creatures; suggested that light moves in waves, well before physicists found supporting data; and, as you'll read in chapter 9, provided perhaps the first evidence of the thinness of molecules.[83]

His inventions also varied. In response to his brother's complaints about painful kidney stones, for instance, Franklin designed a catheter, made of flexible and aseptic silver, that allowed John to drain urine each day from his bladder. It was more malleable than the bulky metal tubes then in use, and Benjamin bragged that the device "will readily comply with the turns of the passage."[84]

Franklin also worked to engage more people in science. Building on his community-enhancing efforts with police and fire squads, he organized a variety of institutions to share research updates, assemble libraries, and advance technology and medicine. These North American organizations, according to Franklin, symbolized the next step in the New World's development. "The first drudgery of settling new colonies, which confines the attention of people to mere necessaries, is now pretty well over," he noted, "and there are many in every province in circumstances that set them at ease and afford leisure to cultivate the finer arts and improve the common stock of knowledge."[85]

In 1743, he launched the American Philosophical Society, a scholarly association devoted to the pursuit of "useful knowledge." Franklin felt colonists would be recognized as capable by European elites only if they could demonstrate technological and scientific strength. The organization drew participants from throughout the colonies, and Franklin helped its members share news and findings via letters and pamphlets. The naturalist John Bartram probably was the first to propose the idea, but Franklin—with his networking skills, printing press, and access to the postal system—made the American Philosophical Society a reality.

The group prompted intellectual exchanges on a variety of subjects, including "newly discovered plants, herbs, trees, roots, their virtues, uses, etc. . . . improvements in any branch of mathematics . . . methods of improving the breeds of animals . . . new improvements in planting, gardening, and clearing land . . . and all philosophical experiments that let light into the nature of things, tend to increase the power of man over matter, and multiply the conveniences or pleasures of life."[86]

One key supporter was Cadwallader Colden, then New York's surveyor general, an expert on the Iroquois and a respected researcher who correlated filthy living conditions with high rates of infection. Colden recognized the need for intercolonial cooperation, writing: "The encouragement to a mere scholar is very small in any part of North America. We are very poor in knowledge and very needy of assistance."[87]

John Bartram, a Philadelphia-based botanist who collected and shared North American plants and seeds with European scientists, was another advocate. He appeared to be "a downright plain country man," yet the esteemed taxonomist Carl Linnaeus called him "the greatest natural botanist in the world."[88] With funding from the British government, Bartram explored diverse ecosystems from Florida to New England, and published numerous papers on insects as well as minerals, the aurora borealis, snake teeth, and mollusks. He grew increasingly angry at haughty English scientists who viewed him as a "wonderful observer" but never trusted him to form botanical principles or make taxonomic classifications.

James Logan, a society member from Philadelphia, assembled the largest library in the colonies, with a particular emphasis on science books and papers. A wealthy but temperamental fur trader, he served as Philadelphia's mayor and Pennsylvania's acting governor, but he was most noted as a botanist, the first to show the function of pollen and various plant organs in the fertilization of maize and other crops. Logan wrote several scholarly papers for the association, and he became a mentor to Franklin, who considered him to be the "best judge of books in these parts."[89]

The American Philosophical Society floundered initially—Franklin blamed some of its members for being "very idle gentlemen"—yet it represented one of the first efforts to integrate the colonies to a common purpose. Members of the group proudly demonstrated the ingenuity of North American scientists.

Franklin, of course, was not the only North American to advance science. Harvard College was transitioning itself from a "ministry factory" to an institution that housed an impressive collection of scientific equipment and respected researchers. One professor, the astronomer John Winthrop, worked closely with Franklin to monitor from several locations around the globe the 1761 and 1769 transits of Venus across the sun. The resulting international efforts allowed a calculation of the sun's distance from the earth, and the resulting ninety-six-page report on transit observations gained substantial recognition for American scholarship.

Yet most colonial higher-education institutions—such as Yale in Connecticut, William and Mary in Virginia, and the College of New

Jersey (later Princeton)—tended to focus on classic texts. Franklin wanted something more "useful" for Pennsylvania that would help all "aspiring" young men understand and advance technology. His efforts for a Pennsylvania academy began in 1743 with Junto discussions and a pamphlet entitled *Proposals Relating to the Education of Youth in Pennsylvania*. He called for the school "to serve mankind, one's country, friends, and family."[90]

As usual, Benjamin described his plan in some detail. The institution, he wrote, should be "not far from a river, having a garden, orchard, meadow, and a field or two"; it should have a library "with maps of all countries, globes, some mathematical instruments, an apparatus for experiments in natural philosophy and for mechanics"; students should "diet together plainly, temperately, and frugally" and "be frequently exercised in running, leaping, wrestling, and swimming." Noting that "drawing is a kind of universal language," he encouraged its instruction so "the workman may perfect his own idea of a thing to be done before he begins to work."[91]

Franklin raised about two thousand pounds to purchase a building and hire staff, and the school, called the Academy and College of Pennsylvania, opened in January 1751. (Forty years later, it changed its name to the University of Pennsylvania.) As is typical within academic institutions, arguments flared, particularly over curriculum. The largest financial supporters hailed from the Anglican establishment and wanted a classical approach based on Latin, while Franklin favored focusing on English and science. As the classicists gained control and Benjamin's influence floundered, he moved on to his next project, raising money for a public hospital that would train physicians and medical researchers.

The Pennsylvania Hospital would, he wrote, "care for the sick, poor, and insane who were wandering the streets of Philadelphia,"[92] and he patriotically predicted it would "give to the beggar in America a degree of comfort and chance for recovery equal to that of a European prince in his palace."[93] To obtain funding, he considered alternatives, much as he did with his science experiments, and advanced a unique approach—the matching grant—to spur the generosity of both the government and individuals. "In soliciting subscriptions among the people," he wrote, "we urged the conditional promise of the law as an additional motive to give, since every man's donation would be doubled." He further argued that legislators "might have the credit of being charitable without the expense."[94]

FRANKLIN IN 1747 BEGAN TO ADVANCE A NEW, AND MORE CONTROversial, civic organizing effort in response to French privateers raiding towns along the Delaware River and Indian tribes harassing Pennsylvania's western settlers. Noting that pacifist Quakers, who dominated Pennsylvania's Assembly, blocked the colony's spending on defense, Franklin wrote a new pamphlet—entitled *Plain Truth* and signed "a tradesman of Philadelphia"—that called for a militia to protect the province, and he criticized the colony's "great and rich men, merchants, and others, who . . . take no one step themselves for the public safety."[95]

*Plain Truth* tempered Quaker opposition by proposing a voluntary association rather than the mandatory militia imposed by other colonies. A pleased Franklin admitted, "the pamphlet had a sudden and surprising effect," with about ten thousand men volunteering to form more than one hundred military units. Benjamin also organized a lottery that raised three thousand pounds for rifles, cannons, and ammunition. Not surprisingly, the province's proprietor, Thomas Penn, feared an independent fighting force he did not control, and he called the militia "a contempt to government" and "little less than treason." Penn referred to Franklin as "a dangerous man" and "a very uneasy spirit," yet he recognized Benjamin to be "a sort of tribune of the people," and admitted, "he must be treated with regard."[96]

Pennsylvania's safety and future, Franklin argued, depended upon "middling people," whom he affectionately described as "the trades-men, shopkeepers, and farmers of this province and city."[97] The growth of a middle class in the early eighteenth century marked a stark societal transformation, shattering what had been a strict distinction between "gentlemen and plebes." As historian Jonathan Lyons put it: "Many in this rising social cohort acquired considerable wealth and, with it, greater intellectual curiosity, and political sophistication about the world around them, as well as the necessary leisure time to devote to these new pursuits. Printers such as Franklin stepped in to meet this growing demand for new information, ideas, and opinions."[98]

Military threats from the French and Indians dissipated by the sum-mer of 1748 and the militias dispersed, yet Franklin and many other Pennsylvanians would remember the willingness of "middling people" to join forces and defend themselves. Although the militia could be seen as an early effort to create an independent force, Benjamin remained loyal to the English king. That year, Franklin, now well-known for his science and associations, was elected to Philadelphia's Common Coun-cil, and three years later to the province's assembly.

In 1753, Franklin won a royal appointment to be deputy postmas-ter for the colonies, a position for which he authorized London-based Collinson to spend three hundred pounds lobbying on his behalf. (Ben-jamin, beginning in 1737, had been postmaster for the city of Phila-delphia.) The new multi-colony job gave Benjamin an excuse (and a stipend) to travel up and down the coast and make new acquaintances. He paid particular attention to networking among North American sci-entists, enhancing greatly the exchange of ideas and test results. The job enabled him, for instance, to freely distribute scientific updates to colleagues, become a clearinghouse for research reports, and expand on his work as secretary of the American Philosophical Society.

At this stage of his life, Benjamin viewed the postmaster position as a means to enhance the empire by bolstering intercolonial and trans-atlantic bonds. "I should hope that with such a union," he wrote, "the people of Great Britain and the people of the colonies would learn to consider themselves, not as belonging to different communities with different interests, but to one community with one interest."[99]

To appreciate the communication challenges within colonial America, one historian explained that voyagers had to endure "lame horses, disreputable travel companions, uncertain ferry service, unmarked roads, and cramped lodgings, including one public house where (a traveler) was forced to sleep in the same room as the proprietor, his wife, and daughters."[100] Letters and newsletters initially were carried by virtually anyone going in the needed direction; parcels would be left at taverns, inns, or other popular places where a friend or coworker of the recipient might notice and deliver the package. Seeking efficiency, Franklin created far more reliable routes among key cities, purchased wagons to travel throughout the day and night, and established standardized postal rates.

---

MANY BIOGRAPHERS SPOTLIGHT FRANKLIN AS POLITICIAN, BUT HE often expressed disdain for politics. In a late June 1755 letter to Collinson, he wrote: "I like neither the governor's conduct nor the Assembly's. I should be ready to swear never to serve again as assemblyman, since both sides expect more from me than they ought and blame me sometimes for not doing what I am not able to do, as well as for not preventing what was not in my power to prevent."[101]

In contrast, Franklin regularly, and enthusiastically, explored nature, as evidenced by his afternoon ride, also in 1755, across the Maryland estate of Col. Benjamin Tasker. On horses with other gentlemen, he observed "in the vale below us a small whirlwind beginning in the road and showing itself by the dust it raised and contained." As the spinning debris approached the group, Franklin described it to be "in the form of a sugar loaf, spinning on its point, moving up the hill towards us, and enlarging as it came forward. When it passed by us, its smaller part near the ground appeared no bigger than a common barrel, but, widening upwards, it seemed at forty or fifty feet high to be twenty or thirty feet in diameter."[102]

In the key line of his writing that day, Franklin declared, "The rest of the company stood looking after (the whirlwind), but *my curiosity being stronger*, I followed it." He rode close by the twister's side, watching it kick up more and more dust. Referring to "a common opinion that a shot fired through a waterspout will break it," he used his whip frequently against the whirlwind, but to no effect. When the funnel entered the woods, it whipped up dry leaves in an "amazingly rapid" circular motion, making a great noise and bending trees. The twister finally left the woods and crossed an old tobacco field, where because of the lack of dust or leaves it began to subside.

Several years later, the Royal Society printed Franklin's observations about weather conditions that formed such large eddies—whirlwinds on land and waterspouts at sea. Benjamin theorized that they resulted from air ascending or descending in a circular motion. The air within, he wrote, receded "from the middle of the circle by a centrifugal force and leaving there a vacancy. . . . When the air descends with violence in some places, it may rise with equal violence in others, and form both kinds of whirlwinds."[103] James Cook, the British explorer who would become famous for his voyages in the Pacific Ocean and to New Zealand and Australia, commended Franklin for "the most rational account I have read of waterspouts."[104]

When Benjamin returned to the group in Maryland, he asked Tasker whether whirlwinds were common in that area. "No, not at all common," announced the colonel, "but we got this on purpose to treat Mr. Franklin."[105]

# 6

## FIGHTING THE PENNS

Franklin increasingly brought science to politics, particularly when he helped launch the study of demography. Contrasting the roles of land in England and America, he noted that Britain featured a high ratio of people to territory, which made real estate expensive. As a result, Englishmen tended to work for others, either as laborers for landed gentry or as mechanics in urban factories; since such workers were numerous, wages remained low. From these observations, Franklin surmised that English workers tended to marry late and birth relatively few children. In America, Franklin countered, land was plentiful (and, therefore, cheap) while laborers were relatively scarce (and, therefore, higher-paid). Since well-compensated workers could afford to buy their own farmland and support a family, they tended to marry early and raise more kids. In fact, Franklin calculated that Americans wedded and bore sons and daughters at twice the rate of Englishmen, and he estimated that America's population "must at least be doubled every twenty years." He went further to forecast that this trend would continue for an extended period: "so vast is the territory of North America," he wrote, "that it will require many ages to settle it fully."[1]

In 1751, while many English politicians were trying to protect British businesses by limiting manufacturing and population growth in the colonies, Franklin published his predictions in a well-read political science pamphlet entitled *Observations Concerning the Increase of Mankind*. It boldly forecast that America's population in one hundred years would surpass England's, a prediction that proved to be correct.[2] Referencing such calculations, Franklin argued for English ministers to treat the colonies as emerging jewels of the British Empire and as hubs for industrial expansion. Later, during the Revolution, he would emphasize such growth of inhabitants as evidence the United States would prevail.

Franklin's influential demographic theories, as mentioned in the first chapter, were cited by Adam Smith in 1776 in *The Wealth of Nations* and by Thomas Malthus in 1798 in *An Essay on the Principle of Population*. Conway Zirkle, a historian of science, further claimed that "Franklin is really the source of Darwin's inspiration, for he gave Malthus the clue to the theory of population we now call Malthusian, and Malthus gave Darwin the clue which led to the discovery of natural selection."[3,4]

Benjamin also used botany and zoology analogies to address statecraft. He observed that there is "no bound to the prolific nature of plants or animals but what is made by their crowding and interfering with each other's means of subsistence."[5] His political point was that America could support substantial growth amidst its vast open lands, and that England's less-prolific economy would benefit by partnering with the colonies.

Despite his support for population expansion in North America, Franklin displayed a stark nativism that protested the rapid immigration into Pennsylvania of Germans, whom he derided as "Palatine Boors." Why should his colony, he asked, "founded by the English, become a colony of aliens, who will shortly be so numerous as to Germanize us instead of our Anglifying them, and will never adopt our language or customs, any more than they can acquire our complexion."[6] He also referred to Irish indentured servants as a "lousy stinking rabble,"[7] and he argued that the emerging country should be limited to English and Indians, the "lovely White and Red," and exclude Germans and Blacks.[8] "Perhaps I am partial to the complexion of my country," Benjamin asserted, "for such kind of partiality is natural to mankind."[9] Such prejudices, as we'll see, would come back to haunt him politically.[10]

APPRECIATING FRANKLIN'S EARLY POLITICAL EFFORTS REQUIRES understanding his relations with the Penn family. The patriarch, William Penn, obtained in 1681 a royal grant of almost thirty million acres between the Delaware River and the Allegheny Mountains as settlement for a sixteen-thousand-pound debt King Charles II owed his deceased father, who had been an admiral in the Commonwealth Navy. Penn and his family, as a result, became sole proprietors and gained sovereign rule of the territory, unlike other North American colonies controlled by the king and his ministers.

William Penn, raised within a distinguished Anglican family, joined the Religious Society of Friends, or Quakers, at the age of twenty-two, while he was still living in England. Quakers believed their "inner light" came directly from God and declined to bow to other authorities; their refusal to swear an oath of loyalty to Cromwell or the monarch led to their persecution in Britain. Penn was not only expelled from Oxford University but also imprisoned several times in the Tower of London. Later, he decided to form a Quaker settlement in North America that would guarantee jury trials, just imprisonments, and fair elections. Most important, unlike Cotton Mather in Puritan-dominated Massachusetts, Penn wanted the colony to be a "holy experiment," the "seed of a nation," and an asylum for Friends and other persecuted believers, including French Protestants, Mennonites, Amish, and Lutherans from Catholic German states.

Penn proved to be a visionary in more ways than his democratic ideals. In 1682, he founded Philadelphia—which in Greek translates into "brotherly love" and which he advertised as a "green country town." He designed the city as a grid with numerous parks and broad streets to be lined by solid brick houses. Each plot, boasted Penn, had "room enough for a house, garden, and small orchard, to the great content and satisfaction of all here concerned."[11]

As Mather did with Puritanism, Penn linked Quaker beliefs to science. He embraced rationality as the best means to appreciate the natural world, and he advocated "right reasons," meaning actions grounded in "mechanical and physical or natural knowledge."[12]

Yet the visionary Penn also hoped Pennsylvania would be a money-making enterprise, and he marketed its land in several languages throughout Europe. Although settlers flocked to the rich fields and emerging villages, the colony never provided the proprietor with a profit. Considered a poor businessman, William Penn died penniless in 1718.

William's children, particularly Thomas, worked to turn the province into a commercial pursuit that would enrich the proprietors with leases, rents, and steadily rising land values. This harder-nosed generation of Penns, like feudal lords, had no interest in being beholden to the local Assembly or in offsetting provincial costs for building roads or protecting settlers from hostile Indians. The bad-tempered Thomas renounced his father's Quaker faith, joined the Church of England, lived like an aristocrat in Britain, restricted Catholics from coming to the province, and appointed governors who tried to weaken the power of elected representatives.

Squabbles between Thomas and Benjamin began over taxes. Penn wanted to avoid paying any costs associated with the province's defense; if levies were to be imposed, he demanded that his family's vast estates be excluded. Franklin, now an elected member of the assembly, mocked this "incredible meanness" as an "injustice," and he labeled the Penn-appointed governor, Robert Hunter Morris, a "hateful instrument of reducing a free people to the abject state of vassalage." The governor protested the term *vassalage*, which triggered Franklin to accelerate the war of words: "Our lord would have us defend his estate at our own expense!," he wrote to Thomas Penn. "This is not merely vassalage; it is worse than any vassalage we have heard of; it is something we have no adequate name for; it is even more slavish than slavery itself."[13] Thomas, not surprisingly, came to despise Franklin, denouncing him as "vile."[14]

Delaware Indians, meanwhile, grew increasingly angry at Thomas Penn for subverting the "Walking Purchase," an old deed that gave his family a tract of land to be measured by a man walking for a day and a half. Thomas cunningly hired practiced runners to sprint for thirty-six hours, thus claiming far more acreage than was his due. For Franklin, that deceitful act added to his antipathy toward the proprietary family, and it amplified his call for the colonies to jointly make alliances with the Indians. In 1753, Benjamin joined a rather inconclusive summit with several tribes at Carlisle, Pennsylvania. The next year, he participated in a more promising conference—organized in Albany, New York—of colonial and Indian representatives, ostensibly to advance a united defense against the growing French presence in the Ohio valley.

While most Albany-meeting participants also wanted more autonomy from Britain, they expressed little interest in rebelling against the mother country, particularly since they needed Britain's military protection against the French. The gathering proved to be a small step toward a colonial confederation, yet several influential men, and even important provinces like Virginia, avoided the proceedings, fearful of losing their sovereignty to an intercolonial council.

Franklin presented to the participants a detailed plan for a "general government" to manage national defense and westward expansion, while each colony would maintain control over its own affairs. He editorialized for this Albany Plan by equating French military successes in the West with "the present disunited state of the British colonies." On May 9, 1754, he also published America's first, and still one of its most famous, political cartoons. Franklin drew the sketch himself, a snake severed into eight pieces, each labeled with the name of a northern colony, and a caption reading: "Join, or Die."[15] (The snake cartoon became a rallying banner at the Albany Congress, and subsequent activists repositioned the image for their own purposes during the Stamp Act protests of 1765, the Revolutionary War, and the Civil War.)

Benjamin's arguments for a limited confederation failed, at least temporarily, since the colonial assemblies didn't want to give up any power and the English Parliament dreaded any unity among the provinces. Franklin couldn't even get the Pennsylvania legislature to embrace his Plan of Union; "by the management of a certain member," Benjamin complained, "the House took it up when I happened to be absent, which I thought not very fair, and reprobated it without paying any attention to it at all, to my no small mortification."[16]

(Thirty-five years later, Benjamin reflected that the Albany Plan "was judged to have too much of the *democratic*." Still, he felt that if it, "or something like it, had been adopted and carried into execution, the subsequent separation of the colonies from the mother country might not so soon have happened.")[17]

TENSIONS REACHED A HEAD IN 1755, MARKING THE BEGINNING OF the French and Indian War, the North American theater for the Seven Years' War between the British and the French. Fighting took place mostly along the frontiers between New France and the English colonies, with each side supported by different Native American tribes. Franklin procured 259 horses and 150 wagons to help Edward Braddock and his two regiments of regular English troops push the French out of the Ohio valley. Benjamin also tried to warn the headstrong general about the dangers of Indian ambushes: "The slender line near four miles long, which your army must make, may expose it to be attacked by surprise in its flanks, and to be cut like a thread into several pieces." To which the arrogant aristocrat huffed: "These savages may indeed be a formidable enemy to your raw American militias, but upon the king's regular and disciplined troops, sir, it is impossible they should make any impression."[18]

After the French and their Indian allies routed and killed the general, two-thirds of his officers, and over half his soldiers, increased calls for military spending prompted a temporary "compromise," whereby the Penns agreed to make a "voluntary" contribution to Pennsylvania's defense efforts.

Still embittered by the proprietor's selfishness, the fifty-year-old Benjamin—along with William, who acted as his father's aide-de-camp—helped form a new provincial militia of fifty cavalrymen and some three hundred rangers. The Franklins joined the troops and marched in inclement weather, slept on hard wooden floors, and built three stockades along the western frontier. Thus, Benjamin embarked on another career, this time in the military. Noting Benjamin's analytic and organizing skills, the regiment chose him to be their colonel.

The Pennsylvania Assembly, meanwhile, grew ever more frustrated by Thomas Penn's actions, which they viewed as "inconsistent not only with the privileges of the people, but with the service of the crown." Feeling themselves to be loyal Englishmen faithful to George II, the colonial legislators petitioned the king to change Penn's charter, and in 1757 they appointed Franklin—well-known from his frontier exploits and scientific accomplishments—to be their agent, travel to London, and lobby ministers and Parliament to shift Pennsylvania's fate from the proprietors to the monarch. Although prospects for success must have seemed low, assemblymen offered a substantial 1,500 pounds for Benjamin's services, plus 714 pounds for expenses.[19]

Franklin's Atlantic voyage was dangerous. Several French privateers chased his ship, and a strong and unexpected indraft almost blew it aground on the approach to St. George's Channel, the strait that connects Ireland on the west and Wales on the east. Only at the last moment did the captain spot a lighthouse upon the rocks, prompting Franklin to later write: "This deliverance impressed me strongly with the utility of lighthouses and made me resolve to encourage the building of more of them in America if I should live to return there."[20]

During that trip, Franklin returned to the study of science and technology. He watched the captain continuously adjust his ship's ballast and measure its speed, and he listened to the sailor's concerns "that it can never be known till she is tried, whether a new ship will or will not be a good sailor; for that the model of a good-sailing ship has been exactly followed in a new one, which have proved, on the contrary, remarkably dull."[21] Benjamin lamented this lack of rules for the construction of effective hulls, masts, rigs, and sails, or even instructions on how captains can best trim those sails sharper or flatter. "This is the age of experiments," the scientist declared, "and I think a set accurately made and combined would be of great use." Benjamin predicted "that ere long some ingenious philosopher will undertake it, to whom I wish success."[22]

Another shipboard observation would obsess Franklin for years. When he questioned why the ocean behind two of the convoy's vessels appeared calm, the captain explained that "the cooks have been emptying their oily water through the scupper, which has greased the sides of those ships." Recalling a passage about the oil-on-water phenomenon from Pliny the Elder, a first-century Roman philosopher, Benjamin promised to devise his own experiments.

Some three decades after visiting London as a fledgling printer, Franklin returned there as a noted scientist but fledgling diplomat. He was fifty-one years old, and his physique had evolved from a broad-shouldered swimmer to, in his words, "a fat old fellow."[23] He was accompanied by his twenty-six-year-old son William as well as two enslaved people, King and Peter, who worked as servants.

Father and son settled on Craven Street, not far from the coffee-houses and taverns of the Strand and the ministries of Whitehall. The home also was close to Middle Temple, where William would study law. Commenting on their lodgings, Franklin reported, "Everything about us pretty genteel."[24]

The four-story row-house was owned by Margaret Stevenson, a widow the same age as Benjamin. With her eighteen-year-old daughter, Mary, known as Polly, Stevenson offered Franklin a mirror of his Philadelphia family, with the two adults often going together to dinners and events. Franklin's friendly relations with Polly, whom he called "my little philosopher," have prompted some scandalous suggestions among scholars; those seem unlikely, and for our purposes, it is useful to simply note that their numerous letters over many years focused extensively on science, with Franklin offering tutorials about electricity, tidal basins, silkworms, and barometers.

Since his last trip across the Atlantic, Benjamin had gained renown as an experimenter among many of Britain's leading scientists and writers. Yet whether fame and contacts would help him lobby patrician decision-makers remained uncertain. The aristocratic, and arrogant, Thomas Penn confidently asserted: "There are very few of any consequence that have heard of his electrical experiments, those matters being attended to by a particular set of people, but it is quite another sort of people who are to determine the dispute between us."[25] Highlighting a crucial fact about the British hierarchy—scientists were not as important as gentry—Penn wrote: "Mr. Franklin's popularity is nothing here. He will be looked very coolly upon by great people." With self-serving bravado, Penn added that the set of people "of the greatest consequence, I know well."[26]

While Penn's assessment rang true, he underestimated Franklin's connections. William Strahan, for instance, was a key contact who owned the *London Chronicle*, which had printed thirty-two of Benjamin's articles, and he held substantial shares in the *Public Advertiser*, which published a similar number of Franklin's essays. A supporter of Pennsylvania in general and Franklin in particular, Strahan also encouraged other journals—including *The Citizen*, *The Gentleman's Magazine*, *Public Ledger*, and *Lloyd's Evening Post*—to run Benjamin's writings, thereby expanding the American's reach and influence.[27]

Despite sympathetic media, Franklin was asking England's elite to overturn their arrangements with Pennsylvania's well-connected proprietors. That was a hard sell. Benjamin quickly realized how hard when Lord Granville—chair of the King's Council, composed of Britain's senior ministers—delivered a blunt introduction to English politics. Peter Collinson, the London-based merchant who had circulated Franklin's letters on electricity among Royal Society members, arranged their meeting, which began "with great civility," but Granville soon declared, "You Americans have wrong ideas of the nature of your constitution." The minister dismissed the power of a colony's elected assembly, defined the king's instruction to his governors as the "law of the land," and labeled the monarch the "legislator of the colonies." Granville essentially said North Americans had no power to make or amend their own laws, and that they could be taxed, without representation, by the king and Parliament. Franklin's responses fell on deaf ears; as he wrote, his lordship "assured me I was totally mistaken."[28]

Granville's lashing, which Benjamin understatedly described as "having a little alarmed me," offered a clear outline of what would become the representation-taxation conflict between British ministers and a growing number of colonists. Benjamin lamented that he would obtain little support for amending the Penn's charter, wryly noting that Granville just happened to be married to Thomas Penn's sister-in-law.[29]

Through another science colleague, Franklin obtained a meeting with Thomas Penn at his London home in Spring Garden. That discussion also started cordially, but the parties quickly outlined their complaints, causing Franklin to comment that "(we were) so far from each other in our opinions as to discourage any hope of agreement." Penn ended the session by asking Franklin to outline his concerns in writing, which he did quickly, labeling the proprietors' demand to avoid taxation as "unjust and cruel." Penn sent Benjamin's reply to his solicitor, Ferdinand John Pris, knowing he would stall. Franklin had dealt with Pris on previous Pennsylvania business and found him "a proud, angry man." The feeling was mutual.[30]

Despite obtaining access to aristocrats through his Royal Society contacts, Franklin's temperament and interests differed from those of Britain's governing class. He favored industry, while aristocrats demonstrated at least the appearance of leisure. He advocated frugality, while Englishmen enjoyed showing off their accomplishments and wealth. He practiced science, to which most lords expressed indifference. He worked a trade, they managed estates.

While Pris procrastinated, Franklin returned to natural philosophy and technology. He obtained as well as constructed more electrical equipment, including a powerful generator that Lord Charles Cavendish estimated threw a nine-inch spark. He forwarded to John Pringle, the military doctor who was to become president of the Royal Society, a lengthy note on his new experiments in using electricity to battle paralysis. He also devised a curious clock, with three wheels and two gears, which an independent observer described as "economical but not quite practical."[31]

Benjamin continued to experiment with heat and to adjust his stove. He devised a damper, what he called a "sliding plate," to seal off drafts when a fire was not lit. He reduced smoke and improved airflow by cutting the size of the Craven Street stove to three feet by two feet and installing rear baffles. William, impressed with his father's continuous focus on science, commented, "It is surprising how you could find time to attend to things of that nature amid all your hurry of public business."[32]

Both science and diplomacy had to wait, however, when Franklin in late 1757 became seriously ill. What lingered for about eight weeks began with "a violent cold and something of a fever" and then accelerated to a "great pain in my head, the top of which was very hot and, when the pain went away, very sore and tender."[33] When well enough to venture outside the Craven Street house, Benjamin attended a Royal Society banquet, gatherings at coffeehouses, and the British Museum's opening at Montague House.

After more than a year of delays, Pris in November 1758 sent to the Pennsylvania Assembly what Franklin felt was "a flimsy justification" for Penn's positions, suggesting the family's social status should shield them from taxation. The proprietor's lawyer stingingly added, according to Franklin, that the Penns "should be willing to accommodate matters if the Assembly would send out *some person of candor* to treat with them for that purpose, intimating thereby that I was not such."[34]

There was no diplomatic congeniality at Franklin's next meeting with Thomas Penn, who argued that he could veto the Assembly's appointment of Indian affairs commissioners and that his esteemed father, William Penn, had never granted any powers to the colony's elected legislators. A livid Franklin wrote to Assembly Speaker Isaac Norris: "[Penn spoke] with a kind of triumphing, laughing insolence, such as a low jockey might do when a purchaser complained that he had cheated him in a horse. I was astonished to see him thus meanly give up his father's character and conceived at that moment a more cordial and thorough contempt for him than I have ever before felt for any man living."[35]

Franklin's letter leaked, prompting Thomas Penn, predictably, to label Benjamin "a malicious villain." The proprietor added that "from this time I will not have any conversation with him on any pretense."[36]

Benjamin's negotiations in tatters, he could have gone home to his family. Instead, he decided to travel around Britain, in part to introduce William to his Franklin ancestry and in part to meet and be feted by English scientists. As noted in an earlier chapter, he visited Cambridge University to work for several weeks with John Hadley on refrigeration experiments. He also attended the college's commencement ceremonies, later admitting that "my vanity was not a little gratified by the particular regard shown me by the chancellor and vice-chancellor of the university and the heads of colleges."[37]

The Franklins then headed to Ecton, some sixty miles north of London, where Benjamin showed William evidence of his industrious and ingenious paternal ancestors. Father and son met one of Benjamin's first cousins, reviewed birth-and-death records at the parish church, and copied information from the cemetery's gravestones. The rector's wife told extensive stories about Benjamin's uncle Thomas, who, she said, was "a very leading man in all county affairs and much employed in public business." Such presentations on his family's prudence reflected Benjamin's growing fear of William's profligate ways and social aspirations. The twenty-eight-year-old had enrolled in an elite law school, dated well-born debutantes, and favored fancy clothes. As biographer Walter Isaacson put it, William "liked to frequent the fashionable homes of the young earls and dukes instead of the coffeehouses and intellectual salons favored by his father."[38]

———

THE FRANKLINS' RETURN TO LONDON RESURRECTED BENJAMIN'S quarrels with the Penns, particularly their mistreatment of Indians and the subsequent dangers that tribes posed to frontier settlers. He tried again to assert the Assembly's power, but the Privy Council in June 1759 bluntly described Pennsylvania's legislature as an "inferior" body that "must not be compared in power or privileges to the House of Commons."[39] Benjamin, however, did enjoy a minor victory when the Board of Trade ruled that the proprietors' unsettled lands were subject to an assessment "no higher than similar land owned by others." Although Franklin boasted about winning on the principle of taxation, the Penns in the next year paid fifty times less in levies than the colonists.[40]

Seeing little substantive progress with the Penns, even Benjamin admitted, "a final end is put to all further negotiations between [the Penns] and me." Still, he decided against setting sail for home, preferring instead to spend another summer meeting friends and admirers.

So, in 1759 Benjamin and William headed to Ireland and then Scotland, where they mingled at length with distinguished leaders of the Scottish Enlightenment, including philosopher David Hume, economist Adam Smith, and writer Lord Kames. Hume became particularly charmed, saying of Franklin: "America has sent us many good things— gold, silver, sugar, tobacco, indigo. But you are the first philosopher, and indeed the first great man of letters, for whom we are beholden to her."[41]

Benjamin referred to these Scottish visits as "six weeks of the densest happiness I have met with in any part of my life."[42] He grew particularly close to Lord and Lady Kames who agreed with Franklin's current loyalist assessment "that the foundations of the future grandeur and stability of the British Empire lie in America."[43] While in Scotland, he received a doctorate degree for his scientific work from the esteemed University of St. Andrews, a substantial honor that prompted many to subsequently refer to him as Dr. Franklin.

Benjamin certainly welcomed meeting, and being feted by, other scientists, so he headed in the summer of 1761 to Holland and Flanders, where Prince Charles of Lorraine proudly showed him the equipment he had purchased to conduct the sentry-box experiment. In Leyden, Franklin talked at length with perhaps the world's other great electrician, Pieter van Musschenbroek, the Dutch inventor of the Leyden jar, the first device that could store substantial amounts of electric charge. Musschenbroek said of Franklin: "Nobody has discovered more recondite mysteries of electricity."[44]

Franklin returned to London earlier than planned to attend the September 1761 coronation of the twenty-two-year-old King George III, whom Benjamin hoped would embrace North Americans. Yet it was William who was invited to march in the official parade, while Benjamin had to purchase his own ticket to sit in the bleachers. English aristocrats simply liked William, whose temperament and style were like theirs. According to his biographer, he "was handsome, easy-going, and more agreeable than his father by all accounts, politically shrewd, and extremely capable. Well dressed and groomed, this new barrister had the manners of a courtier and all the advantage of his father's contacts without the obligations, private or political."[45]

Such attributes certainly helped William win his unexpected appointment as royal governor of New Jersey. Benjamin could have assisted, particularly with his friend John Pringle, a Scottish scientist who was then physician to the Earl of Bute, the new king's confidant, yet it seems the father did not seek the favor for his son.[46] Such reticence is telling since Benjamin demonstrated a fascination with the Earl, a botanist with an extensive garden and collection of scientific instruments. Franklin, according to a colleague, "speaks much of Lord Bute" and had even hung the aristocrat's portrait in his parlor.

Some ministers assumed Bute advanced William to temper Benjamin's political activism; that strategy, if true, failed. The assignment certainly surprised and displeased Benjamin's enemies; John Penn, Pennsylvania's new governor, later remarked, "I am so astonished and enraged at [William's appointment] that I am hardly able to contain myself at the thought."[47]

Franklin seemed unfazed by the royal snub at the king's coronation, maybe because the closing of diplomatic doors gave him time to explore music, what he called "that charming science." He long had demonstrated talent—having learned to play the harp, harmonica, guitar, and violin—and he greatly enjoyed singing with the Junto, particularly Scottish ballads. Yet in 1762, he went further and invented a new instrument, which he called the armonica. It was based on the common parlor game of rubbing wet fingers across the tips of different-sized glasses filled with water to indicated levels, as each note required. Franklin designed thirty-seven hemispheric glasses, ranging from three to nine inches in diameter, and he mounted them on an iron spindle within a five-foot-long case, which resembled a harpsichord. A foot-pumped treadle, as used in a spinning wheel, rotated the glasses, whose brims the player touched with her fingers, moistened on a sponge, to produce "three octaves with all the semi-tones."[48] Franklin praised the armonica's "incomparably sweet" tones that "may be swelled and softened at pleasure by stronger or weaker pressures of the finger."[49] William Stukeley, the pioneering English archaeologist, lauded the device's "glass balls that warble like the sound of an organ."[50] Mozart and Beethoven composed music for it, Marie Antoinette learned to play it, and the instrument became particularly popular in Germany. Yet interest gradually fell because the device proved expensive to make, hard to move, and difficult to play nicely.

With diplomatic and musical efforts stalled, Benjamin's interests finally shifted back to his home and life in the colonies. His five-month assignment in London had become a five-year slog. In this second trip to England's capital, he again failed in his mission—to convince English ministers to restrict the Penns' authority in Pennsylvania (although, not insignificantly, they did impose a small tax on some of the proprietor's land). Putting the best light on his efforts, Benjamin emphasized his meeting prominent scientists, inventing devices, and conducting experiments.

Benjamin set sail for Pennsylvania on August 24, 1762. It was odd timing since he left on the very day ministers formally announced his son's appointment as the royal governor of New Jersey, and it was just two weeks before William's scheduled London-based wedding to Elizabeth Downes, the daughter of a rich sugar planter from Barbados. Although Benjamin wrote of his pleasure with William's assignment and bride, calling the lady "so amiable a character,"[51] his absence from both the royal commissioning and marriage ceremony suggests a detachment, if not outright disapproval. As one biographer put it, "William's marriage to an upper-class woman was a declaration of independence, and his appointment as governor meant he was no longer subservient to his father."[52]

Onboard, Franklin again investigated the interactions of oil and water, paying particular attention to a lantern hung from his cabin's ceiling. Viewed from above, the surface layer of oil seemed to still the churning water beneath, yet from the side, Franklin observed, "the water under the oil was in great commotion, ... rising and falling in irregular waves."[53] The continued turbulence confused him, and, after reading Franklin's report, John Pringle added, "We are all agog about this new property of fluids."[54]

While Benjamin promised to pursue these properties, he arrived in Philadelphia to face a new form of turbulence.

# 7

### ⤫

# FRUSTRATION IN
# THE COLONIES

Franklin received a warm welcome home from family and friends. "My house has been full of a succession of them from morning to night ever since my arrival," he wrote, "congratulating me on my return with the utmost cordiality and affection."[1]

While Benjamin had been in London, his Philadelphia supporters elected him every year as their representative in the Assembly. Yet Franklin's enemies had expanded and grown more vocal, in large part because he increasingly alienated associates of the proprietor.

Thomas Penn hoped Benjamin might mellow when William Franklin obtained a royal appointment. "I am told you will find Mr. Franklin more tractable, and I believe we shall," he commented. "His son must obey instructions, and what he is ordered to do the father cannot well oppose in Pennsylvania."[2] Yet Benjamin was less swayable—and far more provocative—than Penn hoped.

During this period (1754–1763), Britain battled France for global primacy in the Seven Years' War (as it was known in Europe) and the French and Indian War (as it was called in the colonies). William Pitt, England's virtual leader and known as "the great commoner," had masterfully revived his nation's army, reorganized its navy, built alliances with Prussia, and crafted a military campaign that defeated French strongholds at Louisburg (near the mouth of the St. Lawrence River), Fort Duquesne (at the confluence of the Allegheny and Monongahela Rivers, which is now Pittsburgh), and finally Quebec and Montreal. France's defeat at Quebec prompted the previously neutral Iroquois to side with the English, thus turning the tide of the war. Through the Treaty of Paris, signed in February 1763, France lost to Britain all claims to Canada, the region east of the Mississippi River and west of the Appalachian Mountains, as well as several West Indian islands.

Two consequential, and unexpected, long-term impacts of that war were as follows: First, France's bitterness over these empire-crushing treaty terms would several years later help Franklin obtain foreign assistance for the American Revolution.[3] Second, Britain's subsequent breaking of William Pitt's promise—that the war's costs would be borne "at his majesty's expense"—saddled colonists with new taxes, just as a postwar depression crippled the economy, and prompted their calls for independence.

Franklin had been a colonel in the militia and served as Pennsylvania's representative in England. In the war's immediate aftermath, he became something of a local hero. Some twelve hundred men celebrated peace by marching past Benjamin's Market Street home, playing drums, and firing volleys. The militia's loud support, wrote a flattered Franklin, "shook down and broke several glasses of my electrical apparatus." A few weeks later, about forty uniformed horsemen of his regiment escorted him to the Lower Ferry, with their swords ceremoniously drawn the entire route. While Franklin feigned humility, suggesting he was "a good deal chagrined at their appearance" and "naturally averse to the assuming of state," he went out of his way to note that "no such honor had been paid [the London-based proprietor] when in the province, nor to any of his governors." Not surprisingly, the proud Penn took offense and, according to Benjamin, "greatly increased his rancor against me . . . and he instanced this parade with my officers as a proof of my having an intention to take the government of the province out of his hands by force."[4]

As the war wound down, Franklin weighed in on the peace negotiations to suggest that England assume control over Canada rather than Guadeloupe, arguing that the British Empire needed to secure North America's northern and western frontiers. He asserted that settlements in the Mississippi valley and Quebec would offer substantial benefits to the mother country, providing "an immense outlet for British industry." His so-called Canada pamphlet further argued that England should not fear North America's expansion, that the "growth of the children [meaning the colonies] tends to increase the growth of the mother [Britain]."[5] Such positions now seem obvious, but at the time many Englishmen viewed Canada as a bleak backwoods and Guadeloupe as a well-developed and prosperous sugar plantation in the Caribbean. *The London Chronicle* called Franklin's piece a "masterly performance" which "shows the writer to be perfectly acquainted with his subject and possessed of the happy talent of expressing himself with clearness, strength, and precision."[6]

Although they fought together to defeat the French, some British ministers feared that colonists—their numbers expanding, and their confidence emboldened by victories over the French and Indians— would unite against England, but Franklin asserted that a "union amongst them for such a purpose is not merely improbable, it is impossible." He boasted that Britain "has laid a broad and strong foundation [in the colonies] on which to erect the most beneficial and certain commerce, with the greatness and stability of her empire." He continued to assert that Americans would not "unite against their own nation [England], which protects and encourages them, with which they have so many connections and ties of blood, interest, and affection, and which 'tis well known they all love very much more than they love one another." Yet Franklin offered a prescient note of caution, writing that an American confederation would not arise "without the most grievous tyranny and oppression."[7]

At this stage, Franklin saw no conflict between an alliance with Britain and colonial expansion. Accurately sensing Americans' hunger to settle "our vast forests," he intended to profit personally from expansion. He had long proposed new settlements to the west of the Appalachian Mountains, and his Albany Plan called for two new colonies between the Great Lakes and the Ohio River. Franklin highlighted the "many thousands of families that are ready to swarm, wanting more land."[8] Before returning to Philadelphia, he had worked on his own land-speculation schemes with a member of Parliament, a director of the Bank of England, a principal in the East India Company, and holders of royal land grants. British officials granted him tracts of land in Nova Scotia totaling about 11,500 acres. Even more ambitious, he was one of twenty partners who formed the Walpole Company (later renamed the Grand Ohio Company), in which each offered to pay two hundred pounds to the Crown as "the first adventurers who have proposed to purchase from your majesty lands in the continent of America and to make a settlement there."[9] This real-estate scheme set out to acquire twenty million acres that would include all of what is now West Virginia and land north to Lake Erie.

Although often ignored or downplayed by biographers, Franklin's private land interests would influence his public diplomacy and statecraft in the coming decades. His desire for property and profit underlaid his efforts to expel France from the frontier and Canada, while England's later attempt to close western lands to American settlers accelerated his calls for independence.

Shortly after returning to Philadelphia, Benjamin, still deputy postmaster general for North America, prepared for an inspection tour of postal operations from New Hampshire to Virginia. Motivated also by his desire for North American scientists to share test results and spur new experiments, Franklin sought to improve communications within the colonies.

With Canada now under English control, Benjamin also developed communication routes between New York and Montreal and Quebec, as well as expanded the schedule across the Atlantic for packet ships, the medium-sized boats that carried mail, passengers, and freight. He accelerated the pace of mail delivery within the colonies, in part by hiring riders to travel at night. He extended daily deliveries to Boston, oversaw new routes to emerging cities, and upgraded service over the most popular routes. After these improvements, a Philadelphian could mail a letter to a friend in New York City and receive a response within two days.

Improved communications, however, did not guarantee cooperation within the colonies, pushing Franklin to play a diplomatic role within North America. The Treaty of Paris of 1763, which ended the French and Indian War, did little to resolve skirmishes among Indians and westward-expanding settlers. To protect their hunting lands, Indian tribes destroyed several English forts along the frontier, while some settlers, wanting to expand their farmlands, hunted down the natives. Scotch-Irish residents of the Paxton and Donegal townships, calling themselves Paxton Boys, went so far as to attack the peaceful village of English-supporting Conestoga Indians, murdering six unarmed residents. Pennsylvania authorities moved the remaining villagers for their protection to a workhouse in nearby Lancaster, but two days after Christmas, about one hundred Paxton Boys arrived, overwhelmed the sheriff, hacked fourteen Indians to death, and according to an outraged Franklin, "mounted their horses, huzza'd in triumph as if they had gained a victory, and rode off—unmolested!"[10]

Benjamin responded to the carnage with a hard-hitting pamphlet, *A Narrative of the Late Massacres, in Lancaster County*. He reminded readers that the Conestogas had welcomed colonists when they first arrived in Pennsylvania, sending them venison, corn, and animal skins. He explained that "Indians are of different tribes, nations, and languages, as well as the white people. In Europe, if the French, who are white people, should injure the Dutch, are they to revenge it on the English because they too are white people?"[11] Franklin then described the attacks as riotous and murderous. What, he asked, had the oldest tribesman done to deserve being cut to pieces in his bed? "What could children a year old do that they too must be shot and hatcheted? And in their parents' arms!"[12]

In perhaps his most emotional writing, Franklin declared, "This is done by no civilized nation in Europe. Do we come to America to learn and practice the manners of barbarians?" He added, "The blood of the innocent will cry to heaven for vengeance."[13]

Benjamin's pamphlet of January 1764 provoked the western settlers, whom he called "barbarous men," but it also rallied Philadelphians who did not want a mob invading their city and murdering innocent Indians who sought refuge there. In addition to revealing racial hatreds, these rising tensions played out on economic, ethnic, and religious lines, with "the frontier farmers against the merchants and tradesmen of Philadelphia, Germans and Scots against sons of old England, Presbyterians against Quakers and Anglicans."[14] Angry westerners also felt provincial officials in the capital had long neglected them, and they criticized passivist Quakers for being too kind to the natives.[15]

Pennsylvania's relatively new governor—John Penn, a cousin of the proprietor—ordered the rioters arrested but did nothing to enforce his directive, hoping to avoid alienating a political constituency. The Paxton Boys, however, grew to several hundred angry men eager to destroy Indians, including those sequestered in Philadelphia. As the mob approached the capital, Governor Penn scurried to Franklin's home at two o'clock in the morning. He claimed to be seeking "advice," but, according to Benjamin, "his counselors (were) at his heels and (he) made (the house) his headquarters for some time."

Franklin helped assemble artillery and three companies of regular troops, the Royal Americans, to block the Paxton Boys from crossing the main ford over the Schuylkill, but the rioters turned north and crossed the river at Germantown, about eight miles from Philadelphia. Franklin and three other brave men, at the governor's pleading, rode out to meet them. "The fighting face we put on and the reasonings we used with the insurgents," wrote Franklin calmly, but proudly, "turned them back and restored quiet to the city."[16]

The mob crisis dissipated, but a political one festered over who would control the colony—the Penns, the Assembly, or the Crown. Rather than hold the Paxton Boys accountable, John Penn formed closer ties with the frontiersmen, Scotch-Irish, and Germans—all offended by Franklin's pamphlet. The governor even met secretly with Paxton representatives, agreed to withdraw charges against them, and issued a bounty for the scalp of any Indian, male or female.

Such actions accelerated the already frosty relations between Franklin and Penn. Benjamin wrote, "All regard for him in the Assembly is lost. All hopes of happiness under a proprietary government are at an end."[17] The governor, despite recently having sought refuge in Benjamin's home, responded tartly, "There will never be any prospect of ease and happiness while that villain has the liberty of spreading about the poison of that inveterate malice and ill nature which is deeply implanted in his own black heart."[18]

Franklin maintained supporters within the Assembly, where he was unanimously elected speaker after Isaac Norris resigned from that office. Although his partial term did not last long, Benjamin pushed through a series of twenty-two resolutions attacking the Penns, whom he labeled "tyrannical and inhuman." He further charged the Penns with being tax avoiders unwilling to defend and support the colony, while he considered, at least for now, the king to be the benevolent leader of all Englishmen. The final Assembly-backed resolution called for citizens to sign a petition rejecting the proprietorship and asking the king "to take the people of this province under his immediate protection and government."[19]

With this petition, Benjamin vastly overestimated his popularity and leverage. Friends of the governor, as well as Pennsylvania's comfortable gentry, increasingly opposed any loss of control. Germans had not forgiven Franklin for calling them "Palatine boors," and the Scotch-Irish of Paxton County disliked being labeled "Christian white savages." Benjamin and his followers, as a result, could obtain only thirty-five hundred signatures on their antiproprietor petition, while their opponents garnered an impressive fifteen thousand on their pro-Penn declaration.

Attentions turned to the pending election in October 1764, when Franklin hoped to retain his Assembly seat and lead his party, called the Old Ticket or the Quaker Party, to continued dominance. It was one nasty campaign, with allegations that Franklin bedded a "kitchen wench" named Barbara to sire his bastard son, now the royal governor of New Jersey. Opponents also accused Benjamin of plagiarizing other scientists' writings, buying honorary academic degrees, and hypocritically enjoying a royal appointment while talking up the rights of colonists.

Election Day attracted large turnouts and proved to be volatile. Franklin's supporters forced the polls to stay open until the following afternoon, hoping they could use litters and chairs to transport more of their older supporters to the polls. Yet the postponement backfired as the proprietors' New Ticket used the extra time to obtain even more votes from Germantown and other outlying areas. In the end, Franklin lost his own position by twenty-five votes out of nearly four thousand cast, yet the Old Ticket maintained control of the Assembly.

Although he was no longer a legislator, Franklin's allies arranged for a new assignment, allowing him to return to cosmopolitan London and his English friends and admirers. The Assembly voted nineteen to eleven for Benjamin to again advance its pleas for the Crown, rather than the Penns, to appoint Pennsylvania's governor.

Benjamin departed with flair, as some three hundred supporters on horseback accompanied him for the sixteen miles to his ship, the *King of Prussia*, docked at Chester. Benjamin had told Deborah he'd be away only a few months, but he stayed in England an entire decade. Their farewell in Philadelphia, in fact, would be the last time husband and wife saw each other.

As he set sail in November 1764, Franklin held a blinding hated of the Penns, as well as an unwavering devotion to George III, asserting that the king's "virtue and the consciousness of his sincere intentions to make his people happy will give him firmness and steadiness in his measures."[20] Benjamin might have hoped this combination would open diplomatic opportunities, but, in this case, he underestimated the ferocity of British politics.

The difficult winter crossing—Franklin referred to the *King of Prussia* as "a miserable vessel improper for these northern seas"[21]—was nothing compared to the political storms in England, whose relatively new prime minister, George Grenville, proposed taxing the colonies and restricting their trade. How much abuse could Parliament dish out to make Franklin abandon his loyalty to the king and become an American patriot?

# 8

## FRUSTRATION IN LONDON

The Privy Council expressed no interest in Franklin's appeals to remove the Penns from the Pennsylvania colony, claiming the king had no legal authority to mediate between the proprietors and the colonists. A more pressing issue for England's key ministers was raising revenue to cover the costs of the French and Indian War, which had increased Britain's national debt from 70 million to 150 million pounds, almost twenty times the country's annual budget.

Even before advancing taxes on colonists, the king and Parliament tried to limit their autonomy. The Proclamation of 1763, for instance, forbade settlements to the west of the Appalachian Mountains, running from the Great Lakes to the Gulf of Mexico. Purportedly to appease Native American tribes and avoid the costs of more Indian uprisings, George III's order blocked colonists from cheap and fertile lands. It was an impossible policy to implement since more than a thousand settlers had already crossed that invisible border, and the number would grow as land-hungry Irish and Scottish immigrants flowed into America. Noting that ten thousand troops would have been needed to enforce such a policy, historian Joseph Ellis observed that the Proclamation was "a wholly arbitrary and presumptive attempt to impose an unprecedented level of British control over the colonies."[1]

Such royal impositions began to appear regularly, much to the dismay of North Americans. England, for instance, dispatched convicted felons to the colonies, supposedly to provide needed labor. In a biting protest, Franklin proposed a swap: American rattlesnakes for British convicts; "rattlesnakes," he wrote, "seem the most suitable returns for the human serpents sent us by our mother country."[2]

Colonists also complained that the British Iron Act restricted their iron and steel production, forcing Americans to depend on British manufacturers and their monopolistic charges. In protest, Benjamin again argued, without much success, that North American industrialization should be seen as strengthening the empire.

The most obvious expressions of imperial control came in the form of taxes, including the Sugar Act of 1764, Stamp Act of 1765, and Townshend Acts of 1767. The high-profile Stamp Act charged duties, represented by a revenue stamp on the colonies' newspapers, legal documents, and even decks of cards. As the tax was long-standing in Great Britain, Benjamin initially did not oppose the proposal outright. Instead, he and other colonial agents met with George Grenville in February 1765 and suggested duties be imposed in the "usual constitutional way" in which colonial legislatures responded to appeals from the king. Since Franklin could not guarantee American officials would approve the requested revenue, the prime minister quickly dismissed his suggestion.

Colonial patriots also rejected Benjamin's initial acquiescence, complaining the levies would cost more to collect than they would raise. Even the British Board of Trade admitted as much: the Stamp Act's taxes would total less than half their collection costs, and the Townshend Acts' duties would support only a few customs officials, when a multitude were needed. Americans viewed the measures as little more than punitive attempts to impose the war's costs on colonists.

As an alternative to duties and taxes, Benjamin encouraged Parliament to issue more paper currency, allowing the colonies to enjoy a larger supply of money and the English to obtain 6 percent interest on the new bills of credit. But Grenville, according to Franklin, remained "besotted with his stamp scheme" and again rejected Benjamin's proposal.[3]

Parliament, after little debate, approved the Stamp Act on March 22, 1765. Trying to minimize opposition throughout the colonies, Grenville cleverly encouraged Franklin and other agents to nominate New World–based stamp officers to collect this expensive tax. Benjamin, displaying cronyism, advanced his friend John Hughes to be Pennsylvania's tax representative. "Your undertaking to execute it may make you unpopular for a time," an unrealistic Franklin wrote to Hughes, "but . . . a firm loyalty to the Crown and faithful adherence to the government of this nation will always be the wisest course for you and I to take, whatever may be the madness of the populace."[4]

Benjamin wildly misjudged the anger among colonists toward both the tax and him. Predicting violence, a very nervous Hughes responded: "A sort of frenzy or madness has got such hold of the people of all ranks that I fancy some lives will be lost before this fire is put out."[5] David Hall, Benjamin's printing partner, further cautioned: "The spirit of the people is so violently against everyone they think has the least concern with the Stamp law."[6] Even his good friend Benjamin Rush wailed, "O Franklin, Franklin, thou curse of Pennsylvania and America, may the most accumulated vengeance burst speedily in thy guilty head."[7]

The threats became real when a drunken and angry mob ransacked the Massachusetts governor's house on Beacon Street and ruined the residence of the lieutenant governor; both British officials narrowly escaped with their lives. A Philadelphia horde even tried to burn Franklin's new home, but sixty-six-year-old Deborah met them at the door, armed with a flintlock musket and supported by gun-toting relatives and supporters nicknamed the White Oak Boys. Demonstrating fortitude, she declared, "If anybody came to disturb me, I would show a proper resentment, and I should be very much affronted."[8]

The ferocity of opposition frightened the order-seeking Franklin. When Patrick Henry advanced defiant resolutions against the Stamp Act in the Virginia House of Burgesses, Benjamin responded: "The rashness of the Assembly in Virginia is amazing. I hope, however, that ours (in Pennsylvania) will keep within the bounds of prudence and moderation, for that is the only way to lighten or get clear of our burdens."[9]

Franklin tried to defend himself from colonial criticism. The report that "I offered to desert my constituents," he wrote, "is an infamous falsehood. . . . I would not accept the best office the king has to bestow while such tyrannic measures are taken against my country."[10] Yet in a letter that became public and used by Benjamin's political opponents to question his commitments, Franklin wrote cavalierly: "We might well have hindered the sun's setting. That we could not do. But since it is down, my friend, and it may be long before it rises again, let us make as good a night of it as we can. We may still light candles."[11]

A growing number of colonists wanted a fight rather than a good night. With cries of "no taxation without representation," they organized as Sons of Liberty and rioted up and down the Atlantic seaboard. Slightly calmer delegates from nine colonies gathered in October in New York's city hall as the Stamp Act Congress, declaring "that it is inseparably essential for the freedom of a people, and the undoubted right of Englishmen, that no taxes be imposed on them, but with their own consent, given personally, or by their representatives."[12] British officials viewed the gathering and statement as evidence of mutiny.[13]

The opposition of colonial merchants accelerated when they refused to import English goods, which reportedly cut American-English trade in half and motivated British manufacturers and marketers to become Stamp Act critics. Such resistance did not extend to the West Indies, which relied on sugar crops, making them more desirous of British protection from slave rebellions than angry at English taxes.[14]

Faced with growing colonial protests, Franklin slowly shifted ground to argue against the Stamp Act, which he eventually referred to as "the mother of mischief."[15] To impress Pennsylvania officials who paid him as their representative in London, he claimed to be lobbying actively for the tax's repeal: "I was extremely busy attending members of both Houses, informing, explaining, consulting, disputing, in a continual hurry from morning to night."[16] His core argument was that Americans covered the war's costs in North America and didn't need to suffer extra fees: "The colonies raised, paid, and clothed near 25,000 men during the last war; a number equal to those sent from Britain, and far beyond their proportion; they went deeply into debt in doing this, and all their taxes and estates are mortgaged for many years to come for discharging that debt."[17]

Unrelated to the Stamp Act or Franklin's new rhetoric, the Grenville ministry fell in July 1765, and the new prime minister, Lord Rockingham, wanted to evade the growing controversy. No doubt George III continued to view colonial opposition as threatening his rule, and wealthy landowners liked the law because it reduced their own taxes, but traders and tradesmen increasingly felt the boycott's effect and demanded the measure be overturned.

Parliament scheduled hearings from December 1765 through February 1766 and invited Franklin, the best-known colonist, to argue for repealing the Stamp Act. Standing on his feet for more than four hours, Benjamin answered 174 queries. Although he considered himself a poor orator, one biographer wrote, "His dramatic appearance was a masterpiece of both lobbying and theater."[18] When asked if Americans pay taxes, Franklin responded cogently, "Certainly many, and very heavy taxes." Questioned if the colonies could afford the new taxes, he said, "In my opinion there is not gold and silver enough in the colonies to pay the stamp duty for one year." When queried how Americans felt about Great Britain before the Stamp Act, Franklin responded diplomatically, "The best in the world. They submitted willingly to the government of the Crown, and paid, in all their courts, obedience to acts of Parliament."[19]

British legislators repealed the Stamp Act in late February and the king grudgingly assented a week later. When news made it across the Atlantic, colonists rejoiced, but few paid attention to the provision lords added to save face—a pronouncement that Parliament had the right to enact laws binding on the colonies "in all cases whatsoever."[20] That Declaratory Act would spur new controversies, as when English ministers dissolved local assemblies for New York refusing to quarter British soldiers as well as for Massachusetts and Virginia circulating letters defending colonial rights.

The Stamp Act's reversal improved Franklin's reputation, at least in North America. One friend wrote: "Your enemies at last began to be ashamed of their base insinuations and to acknowledge that the colonies are under obligation to you."[21] Views of Benjamin's performance before Parliament were so positive that Georgia and New Jersey added him as their official agent, making Franklin the de facto ambassador for all of the colonies. His reputation even soared in France, where his testimony was translated and published in five separate editions.

Franklin diplomatically acknowledged that a variety of factors and players led to the tax's nullification. "There are claimers enough," he admitted, "of merits in obtaining the repeal." He even added, "I will let you know what an escape we had in the beginning of the affair, and how much we were obliged to what the profane would call luck and the pious, providence."[22]

DESPITE THE REPEAL, THE DIVIDE BETWEEN BRITAIN AND HER COLonies widened again in June 1767 when Parliament approved the Townshend import duties—on seemingly everything from paper to tea. That act outraged Americans, particularly in Massachusetts where the Sons of Liberty, led by Samuel Adams, famously riled up tea-loving rioters.[23]

London-based Benjamin, again misreading American public sentiment, responded with little more than a call for "civility and good manners."[24]

To some extent, Franklin's awkward public positions resulted from his conflicting personal ambitions. He walked a fine line between protecting colonial interests and hoping to obtain a land grant from the king and maintain his royal postmaster appointment, with its annual salary of about three hundred pounds, the loss of which he claimed, with some exaggeration, "would make a very serious difference in my annual income."[25] He even expressed interest in becoming a minister within the Board of Trade that oversaw relations with the colonies, writing to a friend, "I am told there is talk of getting me appointed undersecretary to Lord Hillsborough." Benjamin acknowledged the odds were against him, saying, "It is a settled point here that I am too much of an American,"[26] yet he continued lobbying, even coyly writing to the chancellor of the exchequer that "I should stay [in London] with pleasure if I could any ways be useful to the government."[27] Hillsborough in August 1768 squashed Benjamin's hopes, however, when he announced an alternative candidate for the Board of Trade and rejected any further discussions about removing the proprietors from Pennsylvania.

Franklin turned to his publishing contacts and wrote a series of letters and articles claiming colonists "were not quite so unreasonable as they appeared to be."[28] Trying to change public opinion in England, he argued Americans were willing to tax themselves, but not without consultation, a doctrine he called "essential to English liberty." He maintained that colonists remained loyal to the king "by principle and by affection," but he drew a distinction to Parliament, "in which there is not a single member of our choosing" but they think "fit to grant [our properties] away without our consent."[29] British legislators, he continued, "are undoubtedly the only proper judges of what concerns the welfare of that state, but the Irish legislature are the proper judges of what concerns the Irish state, and the American legislatures of what concerns the American states respectively."[30]

Unfortunately for Benjamin, his public-relations writings neither convinced Englishmen nor calmed Americans. "I do not find that I have gained any point in either country, except that of rendering myself suspected by my impartiality," he wrote. "In England of being too much an American, and in America of being too much an Englishman."[31]

Tattered politically, Franklin began expressing concerns about his battered body. "I am now myself grown so old as to feel much less than formerly the spur of ambition," the sixty-five-year-old wrote to his son.[32] He increasingly moaned about intermittent colds and regular spells of gout, a form of arthritis that suddenly inflames joints, particularly in big toes. Yet some vigor, and pride, remained: "If it were not for the flattering expectation that by being fixed here, I might more effectually serve my country, I should certain determine for retirement, without a moment's hesitation."[33] Benjamin decided to stay fixed in London for what turned out to be another four, even more contentious, years.

Franklin's diplomatic job became noticeably harder on March 5, 1770, when the British Parliament reversed all the Townshend duties— except the one on tea. The taxes on this popular drink had raised little money, but English legislators, pushed by the king, wanted to maintain some semblance of authority. In Boston on that same day, British soldiers, hectored by a mob that hurled ice and oyster shells, fired into a crowd in front of the Town-House, and killed five colonists. Americans referred to that event as the Boston Massacre.

London-based Benjamin, not yet aware of the violence, protested Parliament's continued taxation of tea, calling it "bad policy when they attempted to heal our differences by repealing part of the duties only; as it is bad surgery to leave splinters in a wound which must prevent its healing or in time occasion it to open afresh."[34] He urged Americans to be "steady and persevere in our resolutions," specifically pushing for the continued boycott of British manufactured goods.[35] When news arrived about the massacre in Massachusetts, Franklin notched up his angry rhetoric, labeling the British soldiers "detestable murderers."[36]

Such statements mark the growth of Franklin's patriot leanings, but this reluctant revolutionary still called for uniting England, at least her monarch, with the colonies. "Let us therefore hold fast our loyalty to our king," he wrote, "as that steady loyalty is the most probable means of securing us from the arbitrary power of a corrupt parliament that does not like us and conceives itself to have an interest in keeping us down and fleecing us."[37]

Benjamin's relations with Parliament deteriorated. After Lord Hillsborough sided with the Penns, Franklin described privately the colonial secretary's character as made of "conceit, wrong-headedness, obstinacy, and passion."[38] His evaluation worsened on January 16, 1771, when Hillsborough rejected Franklin's additional appointment as Massachusetts's representative. "You're not agent," the secretary declared, and he claimed to "have a letter from Governor Hutchinson (who) would not give his assent to the bill." Franklin tried to clarify that "there was no bill, my lord; it was a vote of the House." Even after Hillsborough's assistant embarrassingly admitted the governor wrote no such correspondence, the minister grew angrier and announced: "The (Massachusetts) House of Representatives has no right to appoint an agent. We shall take no notice of any agents, but such as are appointed by acts of Assembly to which the governor gives his assent."[39]

Franklin responded tartly: "It is, I believe, of no great importance whether the appointment is acknowledged or not, for I have not the least conception that an agent can at present be of any use to any of the colonies. I shall therefore give your lordship no further trouble."[40] Benjamin left the room abruptly.

Franklin later heard "that his lordship took great offense at some of my last words, which he calls extremely rude and abusive. He assured a friend of mine that they were equivalent to telling him to his face that the colonies could expect neither favor nor justice during his administration. I find he did not mistake me."[41]

Benjamin wasn't advocating independence from England, but he was getting closer. He saw in Hillsborough's words and actions "the seeds sown of a total disunion of the two countries." While still praising the monarch, Franklin began predicting that "the bloody struggle will end in absolute slavery to America, or ruin to Britain by the loss of her colonies."[42]

Portrait of Benjamin Franklin by Anne-Rosalie
Bocquet Filleul, 1778 or 1779.  *Philadelphia Museum of
Art: Gift of the Honorable Walter H. Annenberg and Leonore
Annenberg and the Annenberg Foundation.*

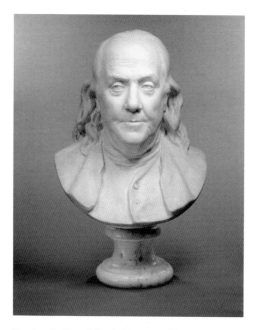

Benjamin Franklin (1706–1790) by Jean
Antoine Houdon, 1778.  *The Metropolitan
Museum of Art, New York, Gift of John Bard, 1872.*

*Benjamin Franklin Drawing Electricity from the Sky* by Benjamin West, circa 1817.   *Philadelphia Museum of Art: Gift of Mr. and Mrs. Wharton Sinkler.*

BELOW: *Franklin's Experiment, June 1752,* Currier & Ives, 1876.   *MET/BOT/Alamy Stock Photo.*

Deborah Reed Franklin by Benjamin Wilson, circa 1759. *American Philosophical Society.*

William Franklin by Mather Brown, circa 1790. *Courtesy of the Frick Art Reference Library.*

Sarah "Sally" Franklin Bache by John Hoppner, 1793. *Courtesy of The Metropolitan Museum of Art, New York, Catharine Lorillard Wolfe Collection, Wolfe Fund, 1901.*

Benjamin Franklin, age 42, by Robert Feke, circa 1746. *Harvard University Portrait Collection, Bequest of Dr. John Collins Warren.*

Benjamin Franklin, age 53, by Benjamin Wilson, circa 1759. *White House Collection/White House Historical Association.*

Benjamin Franklin, age 61, by David Martin, 1766. *White House Collection/White House Historical Association, Gift of Mr. and Mrs. Walter H. Annenberg.*

Franklin in France, age 67, by Mason Chamberlin, 1762. *Philadelphia Museum of Art: Gift of Mr. and Mrs. Wharton Sinkler.*

Benjamin Franklin, age 72, by Workshop of Joseph Siffred Duplessis, 1779. *The Metropolitan Museum of Art, New York. Gift of George A. Lucas, 1895.*

Benjamin Franklin, age 81, by Charles Wilson Peale. *Metropolitan Museum of Art, Bequest of Charles Allen Munn, 1924.*

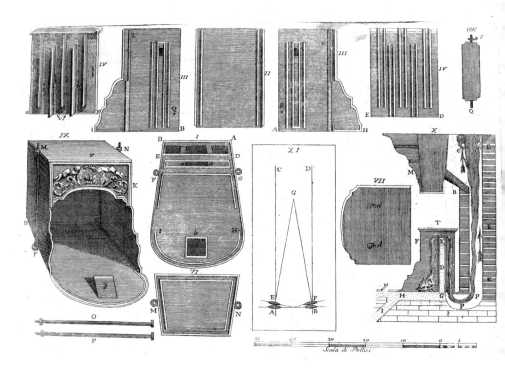

Franklin Stove. Benjamin Franklin, *Descrizione della stufa di Pensilvania inventata dal signor Franklin americano*, trans. Antonio Graziosi (Venice: Nella stamperia graziosi a S. Apollinare, 1778). *Internet Archive, courtesy of John Carter Brown Library, Brown University.*

Franklin's Electric Battery, Battery of Leyden Jars, Pieter van Musschenbroek. *American Philosophical Society.*

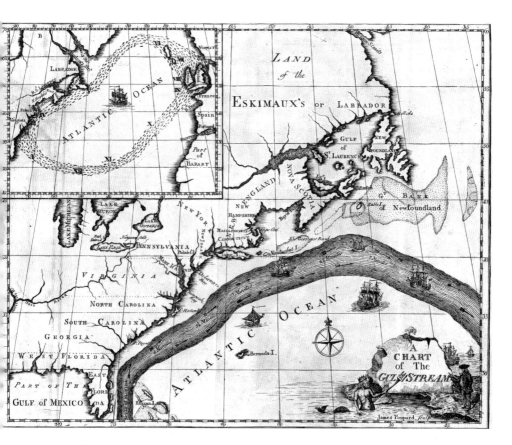

Chart of the Gulf Stream Detail, Benjamin Franklin, "A Chart of the Gulf Stream."    Transactions of the American Philosophical Society *(Philadelphia, 1786).*

"Benjamin Franklin & His Armonica."    *Courtesy Architect of the Capitol.*

Alexander Hamilton, James Wilson, James Madison, and Benjamin Franklin, by
Allyx Cox.    *Courtesy Architect of the Capitol.*

Benjamin Franklin's Fur Cap by an unidentified
artist, circa 1777–1780.    *© Tallandier/Bridgeman
Images.*

# 9

## EVERY KIND OF SCIENCE

As London politics grew more stressful, Franklin found a respite in science. He conversed with natural philosophers in coffeehouses, wrote about his observations in pamphlets and letters, and traveled to see experiments and receive accolades.

Among Benjamin's disparate contacts were Joseph Priestley, who wrote a history of electricity and explained to Franklin how he isolated oxygen; Henry Cavendish, the renowned chemist, discussed isolating hydrogen, what he called "inflammable air"; and Marquis de Condorcet, perhaps France's leading mathematician, described his probability theories. Christian VII, king of Denmark and first cousin of George III, claimed Benjamin to be the world's greatest natural philosopher, prompting Franklin to boast, "Learned and ingenious foreigners that come to England almost all make a point of visiting me."[1]

Benjamin served on several of the Royal Society's committees that tested or verified the new research of other members, giving him a first-hand view of fresh experiments and evolving scientific knowledge. For instance, he changed his belief that liquids could not be compressed after he and others confirmed John Canton's claim that compressibility varied according to the surrounding temperature and barometric pressure; they successfully promoted the British physicist to receive the prestigious Copley Award.

The gregarious Franklin dined frequently at the Royal Society Club, London's most prestigious science-focused social organization, as well as the Mitre Tavern, frequented by literary lights such as author Samuel Johnson. Those conversations ranged widely, as did Franklin's proposals, even if some were not successful. To simplify spelling, for instance, he created a new alphabet based on phonetics. Arguing that English letters do not match their sounds, Benjamin substituted six new characters for ones he found unnecessary (including $c, j, q, w, x, y$). Even the ever-supportive Polly Stevenson, the daughter of his London landlady, found the system baffling, and, years later, Benjamin forwarded his scheme to Noah Webster, who labeled the effort "deeply interesting" but ignored it.

Science even pervaded Franklin's London home. Benjamin, as noted before, gave numerous tutorials to Polly, and she married William Hewson, a doctor who brought to the house his medical equipment, skeletons, and "prepared fetuses." When Henson died about four years later, in May of 1774—from sepsis he contracted while dissecting a cadaver—he left behind in a basement pit some 1,200 bones, remnants of bodies he probably used for anatomy classes and experiments.[2]

Traveling, however, seemed to provide the most relief from politics. In the summer of 1767, Franklin and John Pringle went to Paris, where they enjoyed acclaim as scientific celebrities. Benjamin learned that electricians called themselves *franklinistes*, and he engaged with a new breed of economists, known as "physiocrats," who applauded his extrapolations of population growth. The pair also were presented by French ministers at Versailles to Louis XV, who, Benjamin wrote, "spoke to both of us very graciously and cheerfully."[3]

The touring scientists grew close during their joint ventures, yet they were an odd couple. According to James Boswell, the celebrated

Scottish author, "Sir John, though a most worthy man, has a peculiar sour manner. Franklin is all jollity and pleasantry. I said to myself: Here is a prime contrast: acid and alkali."[4]

Franklin found travel "one of lengthening life, at least in appearance. It is but about a fortnight since we left London, but the variety of scenes we have gone through makes it seem equal to six months living in one place."[5] According to Benjamin, "The time I spent in Paris and in the improving conversation and agreeable society of so many learned and ingenious men seemed like a pleasing dream from which I was sorry to be awakened by finding myself again at London."[6] This particular trip also enlightened Benjamin's political perspective—displaying the contrasts between science-indifferent British ministers and Enlightenment-embracing French royals.

Vacations, of course, do not last forever, and Franklin quickly resumed his oft-frustrating efforts to explain Americans to Englishmen. Yet his wide-ranging curiosity continued to find joy in a growing breadth of experiments, observations, and theories. In 1769, he published in England a "revised, methodized, and improved" fourth edition of his *Experiments and Observations on Electricity* that also explored "population, smallpox, whirlwinds and waterspouts, geology, evaporation, salt mines, Scottish tunes and modern music, the origin of north-east storms in America, sound, tides in rivers, insects, the absorption of heat by different colors."[7] Depending upon his mood, Franklin described these disparate inquiries as "philosophical studies" or "amusements."

Intrigued by technology, Benjamin and two colleagues in May 1771 set out again, this time to survey the machines responsible for an industrial revolution. They toured a tin factory in Rotherham, metalworking plants in Birmingham, and a silk mill with 63,700 spinning reels in Derby. They descended into a British coal mine, ending up 160 yards under the Irish Sea's surface; explored Scotland's Carron ironworks; watched James Watt test his innovative steam engine; and took a horse drawn boat onto an aqueduct that traversed a river.[8]

When the expedition brought Franklin to Wales, he stayed at the Twyford manor of Joseph Shipley, a natural philosopher and Anglican bishop of St. Asaph. Taking advantage of the estate's quiet, Benjamin, now sixty-five years old, began writing his *Autobiography*, originally conceived as a letter to his son about their ancestors. Recall that William was New Jersey's royal governor with aristocratic airs, while his more democratic father wanted him to appreciate the Franklin family's humble origins and the benefits of thrift and industriousness. As the memoir writing progressed, Benjamin expanded his audience to include "young readers" who he felt needed to appreciate "the effects of prudent and imprudent conduct in the commencement of a life of business."[9] The piece ultimately became a description, in his words, of "my success in emerging from poverty," the importance of science, and "the advantages of certain modes of conduct which I observed." Franklin drafted the first eighty-six pages over two weeks in Wales but would not finish the now-famous manuscript until he reached his eighties.

When back in London, Franklin kept in touch with numerous colonial researchers, who, even in his extended absence, continued to elect him president of the American Philosophical Society (APS). Those letters addressed diverse topics. To John Winthrop, he described his pulse-glass experiments. For physician Cadwalader Colden, he described the threat of lead poisoning among tradesmen who handled the heavy metal,[10] and he discussed the management of silkworms, calling silk "the happiest of all inventions for clothing" and noting that, compared to the large amounts of land needed for sheep to make wool, "mulberry trees may be planted in hedgerows on walks or avenues, or for shade near a house, where nothing else is wanted to grow."[11] To John Bartram, the Pennsylvania-based botanist and farmer, he forwarded several plants and seeds never seen before in America, including the medicinal Chinese rhubarb, cabbage turnip, and Scotch kale.[12] With James Logan, the Philadelphia-based bibliophile, he reviewed science (particularly botanical) books for the Library Company. Other Franklin letters touched on sunspots, magnetism, new ways to produce carriage wheels, the purification of air by vegetation, and a census in China.

A continuing interest was the interaction of oil and water, which raised fundamental questions about membranes, fluid dynamics, and adhesion and cohesion. When Franklin sailed to England in 1757, he had noticed the still wakes of ships from which cooks had dumped their grease. He also observed that "when put on water [oil] spreads instantly many feet around, becoming so thin as to produce the prismatic colors for a considerable space, and beyond them so much thinner to be invisible."[13] Over the next two decades, he designed experiments aimed to address those two puzzling factors—oil's calming of waves and its rapid spread across the water's surface.

Benjamin wasn't the first to make either observation; St. Aidan, an Irish monk living in the seventh century, commented on the spreading phenomena. Initially foreseeing no practical application of either factor—calming or spreading—Franklin simply sought to satisfy his curiosity about the dramatic effects. He also had fun, sometimes playing tricks on friends. For example, one afternoon while walking with two friends along a small stream in Wycombe, about thirty-five miles to the northwest of London, he proposed to still the waves whipped up by the wind. He proceeded alone some two hundred paces ahead and dramatically waved his bamboo cane three times over the water, and then, for additional effect, three times over his head. To his colleagues' amazement, the waves subsided, and the stream smoothed. Only after basking for several moments in their accolades did Franklin reveal his hollow cane had contained oil, drops of which he released on the water.

Benjamin went south to Portsmouth for further tests in Spithead Bay, which separates the British mainland from the Isle of Wight. He hired a long boat to spread oil beyond the surf but—because of the tiny amount of oil compared to the huge quantities of water within the large inlet—he observed no material difference in the height or force of the surf upon the shore. "The experiment," he wrote, "had not the success we wished."[14] Yet those in the long boat, he later learned, "could observe a tract of smoothed water. . . . I call it smoothed, not that it was laid level, but because, though the swell continued, its surface was not roughened by the wrinkles, or small waves and none, or very few white caps (or waves whose tops turn over in the foam) appeared in the whole space."[15]

Franklin's explanation of the experiment's failure reveals much about his approach to science. First, he freely admitted disappointment and argued that setbacks, if critically examined, benefit future experimenters. Second, he considered new factors, suggesting, in this case, that "waves once raised, whether by the wind or any other power, have the same mechanical operation by which they continue to rise and fall, as a pendulum will continue to swing a long time after the force ceases to act."[16] Third, he questioned the design of his own experiment, wondering that "perhaps we did not pour oil in sufficient quantity," and we should not have "expected that those waves should be instantly levelled." He also commented that spreading oil close to shore might not have allowed enough space for the oil to impact the waves; he added, "If we had begun our operations at greater distance the effect might have been more sensible."[17]

Franklin decided to try his experiment in a smaller body of water and proceeded to the pond at Clapham Common, just a few miles to the southwest of London. There on a slightly windy day, he noticed that a teaspoon of fish oil produced "an instant calm . . . [that made] a quarter of the pond, perhaps half an acre, as smooth as a looking glass." He hypothesized that "the wind blowing over water thus covered with a film of oil cannot easily catch upon it so as to raise the first wrinkles" that lead to waves.[18]

"With particular surprise," he also discovered a "sudden, wide, and forcible spreading of a drop of oil on the face of the water."[19] To explain how the oil dispersed, Franklin suggested, "It seems as if a mutual repulsion between its particles took place." He guessed, correctly, the repulsed fragments were extremely thin, but he lacked the tools to measure their actual thickness.[20]

According to Charles Tanford, a biochemist who in 1989 wrote a book on macromolecules, "Franklin sensed the importance of the spreading of the oil, that it could reveal crucial facts about molecules and the forces between them. He was able to perceive these questions only dimly, for the time was not quite ripe to do more." Some forty years passed before subsequent researchers repeated Franklin's experiment—admittedly in controlled laboratories with sophisticated equipment—and calculated the size of molecules, learned about their shapes, and revealed their segregation and partitioning.[21]

Modern scientists also expanded on Franklin's observations about smoothing. Using advanced measuring tools, they found that a thin layer of oil on a small body of water causes a rapid change in tangential stresses near the water's surface, leading to energy dissipation, which tempers the buildup of wave energy.[22]

Franklin launched another water-based experiment after hearing in Holland that canal boats moved more slowly in shallow waterways. Upon returning to London, he learned the same was true of vessels on the Thames. Benjamin theorized that shallows forced more water to pass by the sides of a boat, retarding her movement. As was his way, he put this hypothesis to a test. "I provided a trough of planed boards fourteen feet long, six inches wide, and six inches deep, in the clear, filled with water within half an inch of the edge, to represent a canal," he wrote. He also devised little wedges to depict different depths, and he built a small boat that drew one inch of water. He then tied a long silk thread to the vessel's bow and its other end through a pulley to which he attached a shilling as the weight that would draw the boat across the trough. Through numerous runs at varying depths, he counted the seconds it took for the boat to make it across the "canal." The time differences, he remarked, were "considerable. Between the deepest and shallowest it appears to be somewhat more than one-fifth." Only after making these calculations did Franklin consider a practical application for his findings, suggesting that "whether this difference is of consequence enough to justify a greater expense in deepening canals is a matter of calculation which our ingenious engineers in that way will readily determine."[23]

Franklin also charted the Gulf Stream, the warm ocean current flowing north from the Gulf of Mexico and then eastward across the north Atlantic.[24] He became aware of the phenomenon from sailors, particularly Nantucket-based whalers who remarked on "the dimensions, course, and swiftness of the stream" impacting their ships as they hunted leviathans along the eastern seaboard. When Benjamin himself crossed the Atlantic, he carefully tracked this flow by measuring ocean temperatures at various depths. In October 1769, to obtain deeper readings, he cleverly corked an empty bottle and attached it to a leaded rope that he dropped thirty-five fathoms (210 feet), where the greater water pressure pushed the cork into the bottle along with seawater; after he hauled up the bottle, he could measure the water's temperature and characteristics. Repeating this effort four times a day yielded temperature differences between submerged and surface waters of seventy degrees Fahrenheit, suggesting the Gulf Stream's warm waters flowed over the ocean's colder base.

Franklin also observed that this slightly submerged river "does not sparkle in the night" and included more of what sailors called "gulf weed." The warm and humid flow, he added, spurred thunderstorms, heavy rains, and strong winds. It also impacted shipping, and Franklin sent notes and maps to the British post office explaining how mail packets could shorten their voyages from America to England by "catching" the current.[25]

Although Juan Ponce de León in 1513 commented on an undertow his ships confronted while trying to explore to the south along the Florida coast, and sailors in the seventeenth and eighteenth centuries referred to this flow as a "river in the sea," Franklin was the first to examine its direction and velocity at varying depths. A few years after Benjamin mapped its route, William Gerard De Brahm—a German cartographer who served with Franklin on a royal commission to set the border between New York and New Jersey—offered more complete observations of the current moving in a circle around the North Atlantic, and he noted how the stream's path and temperature varied depending upon wind, lunar cycles, and storms.

As others noted the breadth of his interests, Benjamin sometimes got credit for things he did not invent. Consider daylight savings time. The closest he came was a satirical essay entitled "An Economical Project," published in the spring of 1784 in the *Journal de Paris*, in which he argued Parisians should rise early in the spring and summer to take advantage of longer days. Suggesting the French would save "an immense sum" by "using sunshine instead of candles," he cheekily proposed taxing every window shutter that blocked sunlight; placing guards at tallow-chandler shops; and ringing church bells and firing cannons to awaken the populace at sunrise. "For the great benefit of this discovery," he flippantly continued, "I demand neither place, pension, exclusive privilege, nor any other reward whatever. I expect only to have the honor of it."[26]

Despite Franklin's ongoing arguments with British officials, they repeatedly called upon him for technical advice. He installed lightning rods on the massive St. Paul's Cathedral and concocted a hot water system to warm the large (and drafty) chamber of the House of Commons. He even helped the English military protect its Purfleet munition warehouses from lightning. Yet little did Franklin know that the gunpowder he shielded would, in just a few years, be loaded into English muskets and deployed against American colonists.

# 10

## THE CATALYST

Franklin's transition from British loyalist to American patriot accelerated in 1772, not long after his tense meeting with Lord Hillsborough. Maintaining a glimmer of hope for reconciliation, Benjamin thought he could put the blame for rising political tensions on a couple of English officials whose private letters revealed anticolonial sentiments. Being oblique about how he obtained the thirteen messages, he wrote: "There has lately fallen into my hands part of a correspondence that I have reason to believe laid the foundation of most if not all our present grievances."[1]

Franklin—who was by now the appointed agent in London for Pennsylvania, Massachusetts, Georgia, and New Jersey—identified the authors as Thomas Hutchinson, a Massachusetts merchant at the time the letters were written and its royal governor at the time of their release, and Andrew Oliver, Hutchinson's brother-in-law and the king's appointed lieutenant governor.

Boston partisans had long disliked Hutchinson and Oliver—mobs wrecked their homes during the Stamp Act riots—and their leaked letters clearly showed these influential politicians supporting British-imposed taxes and trade restrictions. Oliver in his own hand wrote that officers of the Crown, such as himself and the governor, should be "in some measure independent" of the elected Assembly. Hutchinson added: "There must be an abridgment of what are called English liberties [in the colonies]; I doubt whether it is possible to project a system of government in which a colony 3,000 miles distant shall enjoy all the liberty of the parent state."[2] The two loyalists, although raised and schooled in Massachusetts, called for British troops to keep order within the province.

Hutchinson and Oliver must have expected their letters to become public—they were written to Thomas Whately, a well-known gossiper who would become a member of Parliament. The pair probably calculated that their criticisms of the Massachusetts Assembly would garner appreciation from British ministers in London.

Franklin asked the Assembly speaker, Thomas Cushing, not to publish the notes, and then he mischievously suggested that their contents "be seen by some men of worth in the province for their satisfaction only." Surely he understood that revolutionaries—including Sam Adams, Patrick Henry, and Paul Revere—would circulate widely the inflammatory letters in order to accelerate popular rage against the governor and England.

Benjamin tried to justify his action by claiming he had received the letters with an understanding that "there was no restraint proposed to talking of them, but only to copying."[3] The patriots, not surprisingly, both discussed and duplicated the notes. Samuel Adams read them aloud to the entire legislature, and the city's printers distributed copies. In response, angry throngs hanged and burned the royal officials in effigy, and Ebenezer Kinnersley, Franklin's science partner, is said to have started at least one of the bonfires with an electrical spark. John Adams referred to Hutchinson as a "vile serpent."[4]

Hutchinson, meanwhile, forwarded to Lord Dartmouth, the colonial secretary, what he described as one of Benjamin's inflammatory letters. That communique encouraged the colonies "to engage firmly with each other that they will never grant aid to the crown in any general war. . . . Such a step, I imagine, will bring the dispute to a crisis; and whether our demands are immediately complied with, or compulsory means are thought of to make us rescind them, our ends will finally be obtained."[5] Dartmouth labeled Franklin's note treasonous.

Ignoring his own obvious provocations, Benjamin claimed he distributed the Hutchinson-Oliver letters to promote a "tendency towards a reconciliation," which, he asserted, "I earnestly wished."[6] He implied that the notes showed that England's hostilities toward the colonies resulted from the bad advice of Americans like Hutchinson and Oliver rather than any inherent animosity from the king and Parliament.

If appeasement with London-based officials was Benjamin's intention, his actions backfired. If his hypothesis was that the letters would direct the colonialists' anger toward the governor rather than the king, the experiment failed. His release of the Hutchinson-Oliver letters only prompted patriots to increase their fury toward the English, and British ministers to intensify their distrust of colonists, particularly Franklin for misappropriating private letters, even while he served as deputy postmaster. The affair also furthered the split between Franklin and his son; "I think those letters more heinous than you seem to think them," Benjamin wrote to William.[7]

A riled-up Massachusetts Assembly proclaimed the colony would no longer comply with English orders, to which Lord Dartmouth snapped, "It is impossible that Parliament can suffer such a declaration to pass unnoticed."[8] Although he started the letters controversy, Franklin preached caution, advising the Brits: "Parliament would do well to turn a deaf ear and seem not to know that such declarations had ever been made. Violent measures against the province will not change the opinion of the people. Force could do no good."[9] And to the colonists, he called for peace: "That as between friends every affront is not worth a duel, between nations every injury not worth a war, so between the governed and the governing every mistake in government, every encroachment on rights, is not worth a rebellion."[10] Benjamin further observed: "Nothing is more wished for by our enemies than that by insurrection, we should give a good pretense for increasing the military among us, and putting us under more severe restraints."[11]

Franklin struggled to explain British politics to Americans. "We have many friends and well-wishers," he wrote to the Massachusetts House of Representatives. In addition to the growing number of merchants and manufacturers hoping to do business in the colonies, "there seems to be, even among the country gentlemen, a general sense of our growing importance, a disapprobation of the harsh measures with which we have been treated, and a wish that some means may be found of perfect reconciliation."[12] Yet Benjamin admitted that many ministers—and the king himself—viewed colonists as upstarts and adversaries. He warned, "There was no chance of any sudden change in the feelings or the policy of Britain." Colonists, he advised, must bear "a little with the infirmities of her government, as we would with those of an aged parent."[13]

Resorting to satire, Franklin anonymously wrote *Rules by Which a Great Empire May Be Reduced to a Small One* in September 1773. He offered twenty realm-destroying guidelines Britain had already adopted toward Americans, including:

- Suppose [the colonies are] always inclined to revolt and treat them accordingly. Quarter troops among them, who by their insolence may *provoke* the rising of mobs. . . . By this means like the husband who uses his wife ill from suspicion, you may in time convert your suspicions into realities.
- Take special care the provinces are never incorporated with the mother country, that they do not enjoy the same common rights, the same privileges in commerce, and that they are governed by severer laws, all of *your enacting*, without allowing them any share in the choice of the legislators.

- To make your taxes more odious and more likely to procure resistance, send from the capital a board of officers to superintend the collection composed of the most *indiscreet, ill-bred* and *insolent* you can find.[14]

Franklin notched up his sarcasm with *An Edict by the King of Prussia*, a hoax asserting that since Germans had come to England's aid during its recent war with France, they were imposing a 4.5 percent duty on all British imports and exports. The "Prussian king" further ordained and commanded "that all the thieves, highway and street robbers, housebreakers, forgers, murderers (and) sodomites . . . shall be emptied out of our gaols [jails] into the said island of Great Britain, for the better peopling of that country." Franklin had the German monarch "claim" that the English would accept these "just and reasonable" regulations since they were copied from "resolutions of both [British] houses entered into for the good government of their own colonies in Ireland and America."[15]

The anonymous pamphlets sold well in both England and the colonies and were reprinted in the *Chronicle, Gentleman's Magazine,* and the *Advertiser*. It seems many readers, including a group breakfasting with Franklin, were taken in by the ruse. When a guest began reading aloud the edict, he shouted, "Here's the King of Prussia claiming a right to this kingdom!" while another barked, "Damn his impudence." Franklin stayed silent, yet as the reading progressed, one guest pointed to Benjamin, smiled, and announced, "I'll be hanged if this is not some of your American jokes upon us." By the end of the meal, according to Franklin, there was an "abundance of laughing and a general verdict that it was a fair hit."[16]

The two documents reflected Franklin's growing willingness, even if anonymously with satire and sarcasm, to mock George III and English ministers. "Rules" and "Edict" further marked Benjamin's break with William. "Parliament has no right to make any law whatever binding on the colonies," the increasingly patriotic father wrote to his loyalist son. "I know your sentiments differ from mine of these subjects. You are a thorough government man."[17]

During this stressful period, Franklin tried to soothe himself with science, finding time to challenge conventional wisdom about the common cold, arguing that aches and fevers had "no relation to wet or cold." Instead, he maintained that "people often catch cold from one another when shut up together in small close rooms, coaches, etc. and when sitting near and conversing so as to breathe in each other's transpiration." In notes to a physician, he defined a cold as "a siziness [viscousness] and thickness of the blood, whereby the small vessels are obstructed and the perspirable matter retained," which then "offends [the body] both by its quantity and quality."[18] Several years later, when Benjamin and John Adams were forced to share a small room at an inn, Benjamin went on at length about how an open window on a winter night would not cause a cold, but, rather, prevent one by circulating air; a chilly Adams fell asleep as Franklin lectured.

PARLIAMENT ENFLAMED TENSIONS IN 1773 BY EXTENDING THE TARiff on tea and giving the corrupt East India Company a virtual monopoly over all tea trade. The latter move particularly angered (and radicalized) American merchants who had been handling sales within the colonies. In mid-December, those traders joined rebels to block three tea ships from docking in Boston, while the increasingly despised Governor Hutchinson responded by ordering English war vessels to stop those ships—the *Dartmouth, Beaver,* and *Eleanor*—from leaving the harbor before unloading their cargo.[19] Samuel Adams and Sons of Liberty held rallies at the Old South Church and on the evening of the sixteenth prompted about two thousand to swarm Griffin's Wharf. That mob cheered on some fifty to eighty patriots—painted, dressed, and whooping (not very convincingly) as Mohawk Indians—to board the boats and throw into the cold

Boston harbor 342 chests of tea, valued at about ten thousand pounds (some $1.5 million in today's dollars).

Franklin had been willing to mock the king and British ministers, but he disapproved of mobs. He referred to the Boston Tea Party as "an act of violent injustice" and declared it wrong "to destroy private property."[20] Such sentiments did not endear Benjamin to the partisans, who found him, again, to be "too much of an Englishman," nor did his admonitions elicit any appreciation from outraged British ministers.

Franklin continued to avoid talk of independence. While increasingly critical of English policies, he regularly appealed for moderation and tried to convince British ministers that colonists had no interest in breaking ties. "Having more than once traveled almost from one end of the [American] continent to the other, and kept a great variety of company, eating, drinking and conversing with them freely," he wrote, "I never had heard in any conversation from any person drunk or sober, the least expression of a wish for a separation, or hint that such a thing would be advantageous to America."[21] Benjamin was not alone in this sentiment. George Washington in 1774 wrote: "I am well satisfied as I can be of my own existence that no such [independence] is desired by any thinking man in North America."[22] Thomas Jefferson almost a year later added: "We have not raised armies with ambitious designs of separating from Great Britain. We still wish for reunion with the parent country and would rather be dependent on Great Britain, properly limited, than any other nation on earth."[23]

The king, in contrast, was not feeling moderate. "The die is now cast," George III declared, "and the colonies must either submit or triumph."[24] In response to the Tea Party, he and English ministers adopted in 1774 three Coercive Acts (which Americans would refer to as the Intolerable Acts); the Boston Port Act closed the harbor to all exports, blocking trade and effectively slashing the province's economy; the Massachusetts Government Act enhanced the power of the royally appointed governors while diminishing that of locally elected legislators; and, finally, the Administration of Justice Act took away the authority of colonial juries to try British officials or soldiers charged with crimes.

English politicians justified these restrictions and tariffs by arguing that Americans needed to pay more taxes since Britons contributed some twenty-six shillings per capita compared to only one shilling from Massachusetts residents.[25] While the specific figures were challenged, historian Jill Lepore observed, "The tax burden against which the colonists were protesting was laughably small, and their righteousness was grating."[26] From an English minister's perspective, Americans selfishly refused to pay for their own defense, assaulted the king's soldiers, and dumped expensive tea into the water. British officials also embraced mercantilism, the belief, as Professor Leo Lemay put it, "that the colonies and colonists existed for the good of England."[27]

Meanwhile, the Hutchinson affair became a riveting scandal as gossip swirled about who leaked the letters. Two gentlemen accused each other and tried to settle their differences in a bungled duel in Hyde Park, where one was injured. Franklin remained silent, and only when both men demanded another fight with pistols and swords did he issue a statement saying the two were "totally ignorant and innocent" of the affair, and that "[I] alone am the person who obtained and transmitted to Boston the letters in question."[28]

Benjamin's London-based enemies pounced. The Privy Council in mid-January 1774 summoned him to appear in "the Cockpit," its octagonal-shaped hearing room in Whitehall Palace so named because Henry VIII had used the space for cockfights. The official agenda—to consider Massachusetts's motion to remove Hutchinson as governor—was a ruse, as would soon become clear: the king's ministers wanted to focus on how Franklin obtained and distributed the Hutchinson-Oliver letters. Leading the charge would be the solicitor general, Alexander Wedderburn, considered to be an ambitious, brilliant, and nasty prosecutor; one historian referred to him as "the government's master of abuse"[29] who had lost his Scottish law license for insulting the lord president in open court. To buy time and prepare for the expected assault, Benjamin said to the assembled ministers: "I thought that this had been a matter of politics and not of law, and I have not brought any counsel." They gave him three weeks to find a lawyer.[30]

Franklin expected Wedderburn's main argument—against making private letters public—would be a pretext for discrediting him and colonial patriots. He prepared responses, some of which he issued before the hearing in a letter to the *London Chronicle*, arguing that these were not "private letters between friends" but were "written by public officers to persons in public station." He further claimed that Hutchinson and Oliver crafted their correspondence to "incense the Mother Country against her colonies."[31] Benjamin's lawyer, however, advised him to avoid all defensive responses in the Cockpit and to endure whatever scorn and abuse the solicitor general threw at him.

In an hour-long tirade, Wedderburn harangued Franklin, labeling him the "first mover and prime conductor"—a jab at Benjamin's electrical experiments—of challenges to the king and Parliament. The aristocratic solicitor mockingly claimed the American tradesman "moves in a very inferior orbit," and had obtained the now-infamous letters "by fraudulent or corrupt means, for the most malignant of purposes." Pounding the table, Wedderburn—described as short, delicate, and hawk-nosed[32]—declared that nothing could be more sacred than "the private letters of friendship," and he asked the assembled lords to "mark and brand this man" for "he has forfeited all the respect of societies and of men."[33] Although Franklin's own letters had long been opened by British spies, Wedderburn railed on: "Will Dr. Franklin avow the principle that he has a right to make all private letters of your lordships his own and apply them to such uses as will best answer the purposes of party malevolence?"[34]

The solicitor enjoyed a receptive audience of British ministers protective of their own correspondence and outraged that Bostonians had destroyed some forty-five tons of tea. As Franklin subsequently noted:

"All the courtiers were invited, as to an entertainment, and there never was such an appearance of privy councilors on any occasion."[35]

Amid this jeering crowd, Franklin stood stiff, not revealing the slightest emotion. He appeared, said an observer, "as if his features had been made of wood."[36] The stoic sixty-eight-year-old wore an old-fashioned wig and a plain suit of Manchester velvet. He placed his left foot forward, his right hand behind his back, and his left hand on his lapel. Franklin's silence, according to one biographer, "would be taken for both contempt for Wedderburn, which it was, and magnanimity, which it was no less."[37]

After the show, Wedderburn received triumphant acclaim in an anteroom, while Franklin walked home alone. The next day, after twenty years of service, Benjamin was stripped of his appointment as deputy postmaster general. The Privy Council also rejected Massachusetts's request to remove the governor, it censored the colony's assembly, and it bestowed honors on Hutchinson and Oliver.

For British ministers, the Cockpit allowed them to vent their frustrations and proclaim their dominion over colonists. Lord Sandwich subsequently castigated Benjamin as "one of the bitterest and most mischievous enemies" England had ever known.[38] They didn't realize that their grilling and name-calling alienated the one American who might have been able to sustain their empire.

The vicious and personal attacks, in fact, pushed Franklin to finally accept that a peaceful union could not be maintained between England and the colonies. They also heightened his standing among patriots; Sons of Liberty who once thought Benjamin too moderate in his relations with British officials now considered him a man of courage. In a subsequent letter printed in the *Boston Gazette*, Franklin played up his role as a partisan, warning, "Behold Americans where matters are driving!"[39]

Another consequence of Franklin's public rebuke was the acceleration of a civil war in the colonies between patriots and loyalists, even within families. Jabbing his son's work as a royal official, Benjamin derisively encouraged him to become a farmer: "It is honester and more honorable, because a more independent employment."[40] But William Franklin, the reigning governor of New Jersey, doubled down on this commitment to the Crown and wrote to British ministers: "His majesty may be assured that I shall omit nothing in my power to keep the province quiet. Let the event be what it may, no attachments or connections shall ever make me swerve from the duty of my station."[41]

Benjamin's censure by English politicians notably did not extend to the nation's scientists. Just weeks after Wedderburn's grilling, William Brownrigg read Benjamin's paper about oil-on-water experiments to great interest at the Royal Society's regular meeting. Thomas Percival reported to the same group that he repeated Franklin's test in Manchester, while Matthew Boulton "astonished our rural philosophers exceedingly by calming the waves a la Franklin" in Birmingham.[42]

Franklin, however, had stirred up more waves than he could calm in London.

AFTER THE COCKPIT REBUKE, BENJAMIN FACED FEW OFFICIAL DUTIES in London. Nine months passed, and he wrote, "I have seen no minister since January, nor had the least communication with them."[43] He entertained himself mostly with science, examining in February David Hartley's equipment for making houses fireproof; suggesting in March a new electrical experiment to Giovanni Beccaria, the mathematics professor from Turin; and communicating in April with Joseph Priestley about marsh gas.

Franklin could only watch powerlessly as British ministers closed Boston's port to all but coastwise ships bringing fuel and food, and they blocked the delivery of any tools that colonists could use to manufacture cotton, linen, wool, or silk. They made Gen. Thomas Gage, the British Army's commander-in-chief, Massachusetts's new governor and deployed "so many soldiers in the town that there was one of them to every five inhabitants."[44] All Benjamin could muster were biting, albeit anonymous, satires, including an exaggerated dare for England to "without delay introduce into North America a government absolutely and entirely military" that would "intimidate Americans" to accept virtually any tax or regulation.[45]

Acknowledging such frustrations, as well as the fact that his wife five years earlier had suffered a stroke and was "growing very feeble very fast," Franklin promised Richard Bache, his son-in-law, that he would return to Philadelphia in May 1774. But as that date neared, he hesitated for fear "I shall find myself a stranger in my own country; and leaving so many friends here, it will seem leaving home to go there."[46]

Benjamin's sick partner pined for his company and complained that her poor health resulted from her "dissatisfied distress" due to his long-term absence.[47] Yet Franklin, as one biographer reported, "was enjoying a flirtatious series of chess matches with a fashionable woman he had just met in London."[48] The well-connected widow was Caroline Howe, whom Franklin found to be "of sensible conversation and pleasing behavior," as well as skilled at board games. She also happened to be the sister of Richard and William Howe, who would become the commanders of England's naval and land forces and who wanted to find some last-gasp way to avoid the colonies' becoming independent states. Probably at their request, she eventually asked Benjamin to draft a plan for reconciliation. Despite Franklin's diplomatic ostracism at the Cockpit, he suggested to the Howes and the House of Lords that armed conflict could be avoided under three conditions: Massachusetts would pay for the dumped tea if England repealed the duty on such merchandise; British troops would withdraw from the colonies at the request of local legislatures; and the provinces, not Parliament, would hold all powers of taxation.[49]

Franklin returned to suggesting his favorite, even if undemocratic, way for negotiating such terms—to allow two or three reasonable men to work it out. "The two countries," he argued unconvincingly, "have really no clashing interest to differ about. It is rather a matter of punctilio."[50] Displaying a remarkable lack of political sensitivity, he failed to recognize the growing anger in both the streets of colonial cities and the halls of Parliament. Rather than seek reconciliation, the First Continental Congress, meeting in Philadelphia in September 1774, called for an expanded boycott of British goods, the repeal of coercive acts and taxes, and the withdrawal of British troops and ships. Parliament's upper chamber, at about the same time, quietly rejected all of Franklin's terms.

On the personal front, Deborah died "without a sound" on December 19, 1774, at the age of sixty-six after suffering another stroke. (News did not reach England until about a month later.) William, the out-of-wedlock son she informally adopted and sometimes attacked, rode through "wind and storm" from New Jersey to attend her funeral in Philadelphia. Wanting to admonish his absent father, he wrote acidly, "I heartily wish you had happened to have come over in the fall, as I think her disappointment preyed a good deal on her spirits."[51] William added a poignant push for Benjamin's return to Philadelphia: "You are looked upon with an evil eye in (England) and are in no small danger of being brought into trouble for your political conduct.... You had certainly better return while you are able to bear the fatigues of the voyage to a country where the people revere you."[52]

There's no record of Franklin reacting to the death of his wife of forty-four years, but he did express his growing frustration with England, writing bluntly, "When I consider the extreme corruption prevalent among all orders of men in this old rotten state, and the glorious public virtue so predominant in our rising country, I cannot but apprehend more mischief than benefit from a closer union."[53] His judgment colored, he even drafted an insolent petition demanding reparations from the British, but a friend, he acknowledged, "looked at it and me several times alternately, as if he apprehended me a little out of my senses."[54]

Aware of his ostracism and eager to be revered, Franklin boarded the Philadelphia-bound packet ship in late March 1775. Not understanding how tempers were flaring in America, he wasn't sure if he'd thrown oil on the waves or on the fire.

# 11

**REVOLUTION**

F ranklin's westbound boat in April 1775 enjoyed weather "constantly so moderate that a London wherry might have accompanied us all the way."[1] During the first half of the six-week voyage, he, with the experience fresh in his mind, wrote a two-hundred-page account of his troubles with the British ministry. He spent the second half conducting more measurements of the Gulf Stream.

Benjamin increasingly connected those two activities, finding a link between patriotism and science. He had launched the American Philosophical Society thirty-two years before to advance scientific dialogue and cooperation among the colonists. Now he argued that science and technological advances in North America would bring international respect, economic development, and political freedoms.

Benjamin mocked European philosophers who, like numerous public officials, looked down on colonists as unsophisticated. The Comte de Buffon, for instance, wrote extensively about the "degeneracy" of American flora, fauna, and civilization, and Abbé Guillaume Raynal charged that "America has not produced one able mathematician, one man of genius in a single art or a single science."[2] Thomas

Jefferson joined in the defense of New World science by responding: "In physics, we have produced a Franklin, for whom no one of the present age has made more important discoveries, nor has enriched philosophy with more, or more ingenious solutions to the phenomena of nature."[3] At a dinner party in Paris, Raynal, according to Franklin, "got on his favorite theory of the degeneracy of animals, and even in men, in America, and urged it with his usual eloquence." Benjamin observed that the Americans and French happened to sit on different sides of the table and that the Americans happened to be tall and stout, while the French, particularly Raynal, were short and slender. Benjamin asked everyone to stand and "we will see on which side nature has degenerated"; pleased with his impromptu demonstration, he later referred to Raynal as "a mere shrimp."[4]

Franklin and Jefferson were not alone in bristling at the disdain from their rich and titled counterparts. John Bartram, as noted above, complained that England's "expert" botanists simply wanted him to forward North American specimens but reserve for themselves their cataloging according to appearance and attributes. Alexander Garden, a South Carolinian naturalist, lamented the "dictatorial power" applied by Old World natural philosophers.[5]

Even science, much to Franklin's dismay, was becoming politicized. Since Benjamin favored pointed lightning rods, for instance, George III ordered blunt ones for British buildings. Sir John Pringle objected and stated: "The laws of nature were not changeable by royal pleasures," but the king's ministers responded by forcing Pringle from his presidency of the Royal Society and his position as physician to the queen. Benjamin replied impertinently: "If I had a wish about [pointed or blunt conductors], it would be that [the king] had rejected them altogether as ineffectual. For it is only since he thought himself and family safe from the thunder of heaven that he dared to use his own thunder in destroying his innocent subjects."[6]

BENJAMIN ARRIVED IN PHILADELPHIA IN MAY 1775 TO A JITTERY public. He learned that during his journey home blood had spilled at Lexington and Concord, and he stepped ashore into a frenzied environment of militia riding, bands playing, church bells ringing, and thousands gathering for martial parades. The day after his arrival, Pennsylvania elected him a delegate to the Second Continental Congress, scheduled to meet in town later that week.

Nearing seventy years old (at a time when the average American lived to only about forty), Franklin initially spoke little at the congressional committee meetings, and he tended to skip the alcohol-fueled tavern sessions afterward in favor of quiet evenings at his Market Street home with his daughter, her husband, and their two young children. He reported each morning to the Congress, and the oft-critical John Adams complained that he "from day to day (sat) in silence, a great part of the time fast asleep in his chair."[7] According to James Madison, concerned younger delegates "began to entertain a great suspicion that Dr. Franklin came rather as a spy than as a friend, and that he means to discover our weak side and make peace with the ministers."[8]

Few of those legislators appreciated that Franklin, rebuked by English ministers, had evolved from advancing the British Empire to challenging its authority.[9] Revealing a new patriotism in his newspaper writings, he declared that Americans "have no favors to expect from the Ministry; nothing but submission will satisfy them." Only a "spirited opposition," he continued, could save the colonies from "the most abject slavery and destruction."[10]

Yet as late as July 1775, part of Benjamin's prose could be seen as a pose. To convey his patriotic fervor, he distributed among delegates a letter he wrote to William Strahan, in which he called his old friend "now my enemy" and blasted him for being "a member of Parliament and one of that majority which has doomed my country to destruction." But that's not the letter he sent to Strahan! Instead, he secretly crafted his usual warm note to the Scottish printer, demonstrating perhaps his higher allegiance to friends and fellow tradesmen.[11]

Despite the rise of passionate speeches attacking British tariffs and violence, moderate representatives advanced one more deferential petition to the king. Franklin unenthusiastically joined the unanimous decision to send this so-called Olive Branch Petition, but he was writing to friends that "the breach between the two countries is grown wider, and in danger of becoming irreparable."[12] Across the ocean, George III proclaimed colonists to be rebels and warned against giving aid to them. Moreover, the English attacked America's coastal towns, enlisted colonial-based slaves as well as foreign mercenaries into the British military, and formed alliances with Ohio Indians to harass frontier settlements. As if Americans needed more proof of English intentions, Massachusetts-based British troops in June burned Charlestown and in October did the same to Falmouth.

Having fully come over to the patriots' side, Franklin in July 1775 responded assertively with a blueprint for confederation, an expansion of his Albany Plan from twenty-one years before. His thirteen principles began: "The said United Colonies hereby severally enter into a firm League of Friendship with each other, binding on themselves and their posterity, for their common defense against their enemies, for the security of their liberties and properties, the safety of their persons and families, and their mutual and general welfare."[13] While supportive of this preamble, most delegates fretted about Franklin's call for a strong central government.

Benjamin turned his attentions toward the military challenge, and in October he led a delegation to meet in Massachusetts with General Washington, whose 19,000 motley militia paled in comparison to 32,000 disciplined British soldiers. Franklin evaluated the army's funding needs, which he estimated at a substantial 1.2 million pounds annually. As was his way, he appealed for frugality: "If 500,000 families will each spend a shilling a week less, they may pay the whole sum without otherwise feeling it. Forbearing to drink tea saves three-fourths of the money, and 500,000 women doing each three pence worth of spinning or knitting in a week will pay the rest."[14] With his usual attention to detail and procedures, Benjamin also prescribed a list of military punishments, including up to thirty-nine lashes for sleeping sentries, the loss of a month's pay for officers—and seven days' confinement for enlisted men—absent without permission, and a firing squad for mutineers.[15]

Franklin tried using mathematics and demographics to convince Englishmen that their military costs were unsustainable. "Britain, at the expense of three million, has killed one hundred and fifty Yankees this campaign, which is twenty thousand pounds a head," he wrote. "During the same time sixty thousand children have been born in America. From these data [your] mathematical head will easily calculate the time and expense necessary to kill us all."[16]

Not all Americans wanted conflicts that might lead to such an end. By one estimate, about one-third were patriots, one-third loyalists, and one-third undecided.[17] In Franklin's family, Benjamin increasingly demanded acquiescence from his son: "There are natural duties which precede political ones and cannot be extinguished by them."[18] Yet William was unmoved and encouraged New Jersey's General Assembly to break with the Continental Congress and remain loyal to the Crown. "You have now pointed out to you, gentlemen, two roads," the loyalist governor declared. "One evidently leading to peace, happiness, and a restoration of the public tranquility—the other inevitably conducting you to anarchy, misery, and all the horrors of civil war."[19]

Benjamin remained taciturn during Congress's public debates, but behind the scenes he assertively prepared the colonies for revolution. He took over and restructured the postal system, arranged for the printing of paper money, and oversaw the stockpiling of saltpeter, a key component of gunpowder. As president of Pennsylvania's Council of Safety, he devised a pike for infantrymen that would counter the British bayonet, as well as "machines for the interruption of navigation," essentially large logs and iron balls planted in shipping channels to block English vessels from American towns. That committee also oversaw the selection of military officers and the stowing of medicines for the troops. Franklin, moreover, joined a five-person secret panel charged with finding European allies who would provide arms and ammunition, and beginning in March 1776 he participated in an arduous trip to Canada, an ultimately fruitless mission to gain support from French Canadians. That late winter expedition wore Franklin out, prompting him to complain: "I find I grow daily more feeble."[20]

A travel-weary Franklin informed George Washington that his gout had flared and "has kept me from Congress and company . . . so I know little of what has passed except a declaration of independence is preparing."[21] A great deal, in fact, had passed recently. On New Year's Day the British burned Norfolk, Virginia, and nine days later, a forty-seven-page pamphlet titled *Common Sense* was published in Philadelphia, with hard-hitting, clearly written arguments for America's separation from Britain. The author remained anonymous for several months, and many thought they recognized Franklin's hand. In fact, Benjamin had met the real author, Thomas Paine, in England, where he had worked as a corset maker and tax clerk, a job he lost for demanding higher wages. Impressed with Paine's maverick ways and sharp writing style, Franklin arranged passage to America for this "ingenious young man." He also encouraged his son-in-law to find Paine a job with a Philadelphia printer, pushed the essayist to craft "a history of the present transactions," and reviewed the writer's draft. Franklin particularly applauded Paine's promise to "offer nothing more than simple facts, plain arguments, and common sense."[22]

Deriding England's occupation of America, Paine wrote: "Small islands, not capable of protecting themselves, are the proper objects for kingdoms to take under their care; but there is something absurd in supposing a continent to be perpetually governed by an island." Attacking hereditary rule, he continued: "Men who look upon themselves born to reign, and others to obey, soon grow insolent; selected from the rest of mankind their minds are early poisoned by importance; and the world they act in differs so materially from the world at large, that they have but little opportunity of knowing its true interests, and when they succeed to the government are frequently the most ignorant and unfit of any throughout the dominions." Paine referred to George III as the "Royal Brute."[23] Colonists within a few months purchased a remarkable 120,000 copies, which proportionately would today be approximately 50 million.[24]

The war had been waged for about a year, having begun when shots were fired outside Boston, but Paine's popular pamphlet galvanized public sentiment toward independence. On June 7, 1776, Virginia's Richard Henry Lee introduced a resolution stating that "these United Colonies are, and of right ought to be, free and independent states." Congress appointed a special committee to draft a declaration expanding on that motion; legislators selected Virginia's Thomas Jefferson, then thirty-three, to be chief writer, with support from Franklin of Pennsylvania, John Adams of Massachusetts, merchant Roger Sherman of Connecticut, and lawyer Robert Livingston of New York.

It's probably fair to say that team did not appreciate the historic significance of their task. Jefferson holed up in a second-floor room within a boarding house at the intersection of Market and Seventh Streets. Poised in front of a small lap desk of his design, he drew ideas, particularly about natural rights, from a variety of sources, including John Locke's *Second Treatise of Government* and George Mason's *Declaration of Rights*.

Written poetically and in cadences, most of Jefferson's draft presented a list of grievances, or charges against the king. "The history of the present king of Great Britain," he wrote, "is a history of repeated injuries and usurpations, all having in direct object the establishment of an absolute tyranny over these states."[25]

Rumors suggested Franklin was not selected as lead for fear the witty writer would conceal taunts within the text, but Benjamin was happy to allow Jefferson to craft the first draft. Bedridden with boils and arthritis, he later told the Virginian: "I have made it a rule, wherever in my power, to avoid becoming the draughtsman of papers to be reviewed by a public body."[26] Jefferson, however, wanted Franklin's review and forwarded the draft on June 21 with a note: "Will Doctor Franklin be so good as to peruse it and suggest such alternations as his most enlarged view of the subject will dictate?"[27]

Benjamin's edits seemed minor but were telling. While Jefferson wrote, "We hold these truths to be sacred and undeniable," Franklin tightened the wording and declared them to be "self-evident." That small change reflected a shift from Jefferson's poetic philosophy to Franklin's fact-based science.[28] While "sacred" implied truths supplied by god, "self-evident" verities were observable and required no faith. In other adjustments, Franklin strengthened Jefferson's language by substituting "absolute despotism" for "arbitrary power." Adding the single word "only," Benjamin also bolstered the line that America's petitions were "answered *only* by repeated injury." To protest Parliament's invalidating several acts of Pennsylvania's Assembly, he inserted a complaint about England "abolishing our most valuable laws."

Members of Congress made their own revisions, deleting approximately 20 percent of the draft; the most significant changes came from southern delegates removing any mention of slavery, including Jefferson's extensive lines that criticized George III for supporting the slave trade. Officials approved the revised version on July 4, 1776; a Philadelphia printer released a broadside copy that afternoon, and four days later, the Declaration was read to a crowd gathered before the Pennsylvania State House. Not until August 2, however, did members begin signing the engrossed copy. John Hancock, as president of the Congress, acted first and declared: "We must be unanimous; there must be no pulling different ways; we must all hang together." Despite no contemporary confirmation, Franklin seems to have added a now-famous quip: "Yes, we must indeed all hang together, or most assuredly we shall all hang separately."[29]

Legislators then began to draft Articles of Confederation that would set the rules for governing this independent nation, to be called The United States of America. Yet they also asked Franklin, Adams, and Edward Rutledge of South Carolina to explore with Lord Howe any last-minute means to avoid more bloodshed. The English general in September 1776 arranged for a barge to meet the United States delegation at Perth Amboy in New Jersey. Howe went out of his way at the Staten Island meeting to suggest that Britain and America were like brothers and that he would be saddened if this relationship faltered. With a smile and slight bow, Franklin responded: "My lord, we will use our utmost endeavors to save your lordship that mortification."[30] Not unexpectedly, the pleasant discussions produced no tangible results, and revealed that Howe's only authority was to grant pardons if colonists surrendered.[31]

With more war imminent, Americans desperately needed money and arms to combat British forces who were poised to overwhelm Washington's troops on Long Island and cut off New England from the other states. France was the most likely source, noting its anger toward Britain for the strict terms within the Treaty of Paris. Although aged and ailing, Franklin was the most logical choice to pursue such assistance since he was the American whom the French revered for his science experiments, catchy maxims, and folksy persona. He also was the most prepared, having held secret talks with several French agents while Congress edited the Declaration.

When approached about a Paris assignment, Benjamin initially played coy, writing that he was "old and good for nothing,"[32] but this happy traveler who loved Europe, especially Paris, quietly embraced the assignment, even if it meant crossing the stormy Atlantic controlled by the British Navy. Congress added Silas Deane of Connecticut and Arthur Lee of Virginia to America's negotiating team.

He set sail on October 27, 1776, aboard the American warship *Reprisal*, an appropriate name for the tasks ahead.

# 12

## SCIENCE OPENS
## THE DOOR

L ouis XVI ascended the French throne in May 1774 when he was only nineteen years old, and Franklin had only recently been admonished in the Cockpit. The young king's first international priority was to weaken Britain and reverse its harsh terms from the Seven Years' War. He and his powerful foreign minister, Count of Vergennes, shared a particular interest in the growing unrest of American colonists against England.

Although Benjamin felt France was his best possible source of munitions and money, he knew the diplomacy would be delicate. Before leaving for Paris and while editing the Declaration, he had met three times with Achard de Bonvouloir, a cadet of a noble Norman family who claimed to understand French interests and intentions. Bonvouloir wanted to profit from private arms deals with Americans, but he couldn't get too far ahead of Vergennes, who sought to punish England but was not about to risk another costly war if Americans were not organized and committed to independence.

Americans divided into their own factions. Franklin didn't want to push Louis XVI too hard, commenting "that a virgin state should preserve the virgin character and not go about suitoring for alliances but wait with decent dignity for the applications of others." Yet Deane and Lee, his delegation partners, sought immediate financial and military assistance. Another contingent within America's Congress[1] simply distrusted France, feared its Catholicism, and recalled their grisly battles against that country and its Indian allies.

Franklin sought advice and help from his Paris contacts, including Jacques Barbeu-Dubourg, a well-connected physician who had translated several of Benjamin's scientific papers. He also tested the waters with Spain, an ally of France; in a note thanking Prince Don Gabriel de Bourbon for forwarding a valuable physics book, he slyly added that "the late proceedings of our American Congress, just published, may be a subject of some curiosity to your court," and he claimed to see "a powerful dominion growing up here, whose interest it will be to form a close and firm alliance with Spain."[2]

Such outreach required strict secrecy since English spies seemed to roam freely throughout American states and European capitals. In Philadelphia, Franklin always met with Bonvouloir at night, each arriving separately after having taken multiple coaches. He sent his sensitive letters with apolitical, but trusted, merchants who had business relations in Paris and Madrid.[3]

The *Reprisal*'s four-week crossing in late 1776 exhausted the seventy-year-old Franklin, still suffering from the boils that had developed during his Canadian trip.[4] Dogged psoriasis also covered his arms and legs, leaving his clothes and sheets covered in blood. He subsisted "chiefly on salt beef"—which only exacerbated those rashes—"the fowls being too hard for my teeth."[5] In addition to bad weather and discomfort, Benjamin rightly feared roaming English warships that might imprison or hang him for signing the Declaration of Independence.

As the *Reprisal* approached Europe, the winds turned, and an impatient Franklin alighted in southwestern France, about three hundred miles by land to Paris. Wanting his diplomatic mission to remain secret, he quietly entered Nantes, the closest large town. Yet since Benjamin's image had been on coins, medallions, and even chamber pots, admirers spotted the famous scientist and spread the word. Scores of visitors stopped by the country house where he had tried to rest, and town dignitaries hosted a grand dinner on his behalf. It took another three weeks for him and his entourage to reach the outskirts of Paris, where larger crowds lined the streets and applauded his carriage into the capital.

In hindsight, Benjamin's task should have seemed overwhelming: to convince a Catholic king to provide money, trade, weapons, and ships to English-speaking Protestants wanting to overthrow another monarch. To make it worse, France was experiencing food shortages, and Louis XVI faced mass protests by his hungry subjects, some calling for the very independence Franklin advanced for the North American colonies.

The American revolution's fate seemed to lie on Franklin's shoulders, a weight perhaps comparable only to what George Washington shouldered. Yet Benjamin confidently felt himself to be the right man for the job. His science accomplishments had made him well-known, with French ministers and intelligentsia vying for audiences. The previous king had blessed Frenchmen conducting Franklin's electricity experiments, and the Académie des sciences elected Benjamin to be its initial American foreign associate. His fame expanded among everyday people in 1758 when *La Science du Bonhomme Richard*, the French edition of Poor Richard's *The Way to Wealth*, was published, and went through four printings in the next two years. Condorcet, the respected mathematician, accurately observed that Benjamin's writings appealed to the nation's average men and women as much as his science opened doors to the continent's aristocrats and literati. And never forget that the engaging Franklin spun entertaining tales, with his affability being an asset. He was that rare politician, let alone scientist—or American—with whom the French might want to share a bottle of wine.

According to one observer, Franklin's "reputation was more universal than that of Leibniz, Frederick, or Voltaire, and his character more loved and esteemed. There was scarcely a peasant or a citizen, a valet de chambre, coachman or footman, a lady's chambermaid or a scullion in the kitchen who was not familiar with Franklin's name."[6] Another added that Franklin's foreignness enhanced his popularity; he was a "man of a very different universe; he could have had no idea of how to enter a French drawing room or hold his glass or arrange his sword. And his French was, to say the least, rudimentary."[7] Yet another commentator later referred to Benjamin as "America's first rock star."[8]

Paris experienced a Franklin craze. Ladies wore wigs, called *coiffures a la Franklin*, styled after the martin fur cap which he obtained in Canada, and his countenance appeared on virtually everything from snuffboxes to rings. Benjamin himself admitted his face had become "as well-known as that of the moon."[9]

Franklin proved to be in the right place at the right time. He arrived in Paris just as French ministers had become interested in alliances that would challenge Britain and overturn France's humiliation from the Treaty of Paris. He appealed to a new king and French intellectuals appreciative of reason, experimentation, and other Enlightenment ideals. The witty researcher from the rising middle class who called for American independence also exemplified the French population's growing interest in both science and democracy. He seemed to enjoy perfect timing.

A few ministers remained dubious of Benjamin's diplomacy. Although no friend of the British, the controller general of finance believed France could not afford another war, and prospering merchants did not want to disrupt the economy. Several noblemen feared any effort to overthrow hereditary monarchs, and Queen Marie Antoinette outright opposed aid to the rebellious colonies. Noting the French exempted nobles from land taxes, road expenses, and military conscription, historian Ronald Clark commented: "Few societies differed more from that which Franklin and his supporters were trying to build along the eastern seaboard."[10]

Yet Franklin's scientific celebrity garnered political cachet. Most government ministers, leading intellectuals, and aristocratic ladies sought out Benjamin's company at cafés, seminars, and the court's frequent parties. He used those opportunities to advance America's interests, and his admiring supporters in turn lobbied the French government to support the colonies.

As evidence of his influence, Franklin on his first night in Paris was feted at the Académie des sciences, where he met Voltaire, the revered French philosopher who shared Benjamin's wit and skepticism toward orthodoxy. The two Enlightenment heroes embraced and kissed each other's cheeks, prompting "noisy acclamation" from the assembled scientists and government officials. As historian Joseph Ellis observed, "What Voltaire was to France, Franklin was to America, the symbol of mankind's triumphal arrival at modernity."[11]

Fearing Franklin's effectiveness in garnering French support, British imperialists worried greatly about his presence in Paris; the London stock market fell on word of his arrival. While publicly dismissing Benjamin's diplomacy, Lord Rockingham, then an opposition leader, admitted that "inwardly (Englishmen) will tremble at it."[12] Lord Stormont, the imposing English ambassador to Paris, went further, complaining that Franklin "will use every means to deceive," that he was "a dangerous engine," and that some British ministers were "very sorry that some English frigate did not meet with him by the way."[13]

Franklin fashioned his style to advance his notoriety, purposely reinventing himself since his first trip to France in 1767 when he wore a "little bag wig" and a suit that, he said, "transform(ed) me into a Frenchman."[14] Now almost a decade later and seeking to stand out for his frontier modesty and wisdom, he became, in his own words, "very plainly dressed, wearing my thin, gray straight hair that peeps out under my only coiffure, a fine fur cap, which comes down to my forehead almost to my spectacles. Think how this must appear among the powdered heads of Paris."[15]

The public also admired Franklin's spectacles, particularly his modifications to them, revealing the popular interest in his practical science. As he aged, Benjamin complained he could no longer "distinguish a letter even of large print,"[16] and he tired of juggling two pairs of spectacles, one for reading and another "to regard the prospects." As he put it, "Since my being in France, the glasses that serve me best at table to see what I eat not being the best to see the faces of those on the other side of the table who speak to me." Thus, he invented what he called "double spectacles": "I had the glasses cut and half of each kind associated in the same circle." The bifocals allowed him to see his food as well as the lips of speakers; acknowledging his rudimentary foreign language skill, he claimed to "understand French better by the help of my spectacles."[17] And he boasted, "I have only to move my eyes up and down, as I want to see distinctly far or near, the proper glasses being always ready."[18]

Benjamin focused his full diplomatic attention on the Count of Vergennes, the key member of Louis XVI's council. This captivating foreign minister, as noted above, despised the English for the Treaty of Paris that stripped France in 1763 of several possessions in Africa, the Caribbean, and its empire between the Appalachian Mountains and the Mississippi River. At fifty-eight years old, he appeared to be a classic diplomat—handsome, tall, and with piercing blue eyes within a chiseled face. In response to the English ambassador's threat to leave Paris if Franklin remained, this French minister embraced the American and replied diplomatically: "The government, notwithstanding its desire to comply as far as possible with the views of the Court of London, would not like to send (Franklin) away because of the scandalous scene this would present to all France, should we respect neither the laws of nations nor of hospitality."[19]

Even before Benjamin arrived in Paris, Vergennes had approved several measures to help the colonies. He opened French ports, including those in the West Indies, to ships of any flag, including the United

States, and he directed French warships to block any British vessel trying to retard such commerce. He also arranged with Spain to secretly provide two million francs and establish fictitious trading companies that could move military equipment into the colonies. Still, Vergennes fell far short of declaring war on England, since he remained unconvinced of America's probable success.

One of Franklin's first Paris meetings, therefore, was to inform Vergennes that the American commissioners were "fully empowered by the Congress of the United States of America to propose and negotiate a treaty of commerce between France and the United States. The just and generous admission into the ports of this kingdom, with other considerations of respect, has induced the Congress to make this offer first to France."[20] Vergennes used the occasion to acknowledge Franklin's fame and respect among the French people, observing him as "intelligent, but very circumspect; this did not surprise me."[21]

Complicating their complex diplomatic task, the American delegation bickered among themselves. Arthur Lee, for instance, grew bitter toward Silas Deane's work in London and tried to expel him on suspicion of stock speculation. Envious of Benjamin's celebrity in Paris and desirous of more authority, Lee also consistently undercut Franklin within the American Congress. Arthur's brother, William Lee—who stayed in Paris since Berlin and Vienna would not accept his diplomatic appointment—increasingly complained that Franklin did not give him the attention and respect he desired.

Also troubling, Edward Bancroft—the group's Massachusetts-born secretary whom Franklin had sponsored for membership in the Royal Society—became a spy for England and regularly passed secrets and smuggled documents to British ministers. Bancroft practiced classic espionage, crafting letters in invisible ink, and depositing them on Tuesday evenings in sealed bottles within the hollow of a tree's root on the grounds of the royal Tuileries Palace. He and other English spies provided valuable and damaging information, including details about

American ships—their names, their captains, and the timings of their sailings; they even stole dispatches to Congress that revealed details about the commissioners' activities and plans.[22]

Yet some informants fell for ridiculous claims. One exaggerating agent asserted that Franklin planned to assemble on the cliffs of Calais "a great number of reflecting mirrors" that would concentrate the sun's rays and destroy the British fleet. Another suggested Benjamin intended to send a powerful shock across the channel and incinerate English cities, and yet another alleged that he possessed an explosive device, "the size of a toothpick case," that could blow up St. Paul's Cathedral into "a handful of ashes."[23]

Aware of "pretended friends" but not of Bancroft's role, Benjamin imposed one rather cavalier rule on himself: "To be concerned in no affairs that I should blush to have made public, and to do nothing but what spies may see." Adding reckless levity to this advice, he wrote, "If I was sure, therefore, that my *valet de place* was a spy, as probably he is, I think I should not discharge him for that, if in other respects I liked him."[24]

Caring little about secrecy and believing publicity would advance America's interests, Franklin openly engaged the French public. To discredit Britain, he translated and reprinted a few of his most popular political pamphlets, including *Edict* from the Prussian king and *Rules* for dismantling powerful empires. To obtain French support, he crafted new pieces, including one arguing that "from the general industry, frugality, ability, prudence, and virtue of America, she is a much safer debtor than Britain; to say nothing of the satisfaction generous minds must have in reflecting that by loans to America they are opposing tyranny and aiding the cause of liberty, which is the cause of all mankind."[25]

Diplomatic efforts stalled, however, as bad military news poured in from America—Gen. William Howe had forced George Washington out of Long Island and then advanced toward Philadelphia, while

John Burgoyne's large army had captured Ticonderoga on its march south from Canada. Franklin did his best to celebrate small victories; he applauded, for instance, the 28 percent rise in London's shipping insurance rates after French-supported privateers and cruisers destroyed several British ships.[26]

The American delegation received endless requests from European military officers wanting to join the American army; these pleas, Franklin wrote, "are my perpetual torment.... You can have no conception how I am harassed."[27] To answer most pleas, Franklin crafted a humorous form letter that read: "The bearer of this, who is going to America, presses me to give him a letter of recommendation, though I know nothing of him, not even his name."[28] He and Deane made a few noteworthy exceptions for the Marquis de Lafayette of France, Baron von Steuben of Prussia, and Count Pulaski of Poland, all of whom became valuable American officers.

Despite the depressing military updates and boring bureaucratic tasks, Franklin enjoyed living in Passy, which he called "a neat village on a high ground, half a mile from Paris."[29] He set up a separate room with his scientific instruments and cleared space for a small printing press, finding satisfaction in experimenting and publishing his writings. He also met daily with visiting philosophers, economists, and "his small tribe of humble friends in the literary way."[30] According to his grandson Temple, "I never remember to have seen my grandfather in better health. The air of Passy and the warm bath three times a week have made quite a young man out of him. His pleasing gaiety makes everybody in love with him, especially the ladies, who permit him always to kiss them."[31]

Franklin particularly enjoyed engaging natural philosophers. He visited Antoine Lavoisier in his laboratory and attended his lectures on oxygen before the Académie des sciences. He talked with Alessandro Volta, when the Italian came to Paris, about storing electricity and generating it chemically. He participated regularly in meetings of the Royal

Society of Medicine, where he read his paper about infection remaining in dead bodies, and he frequently joined his friend Jean-Baptiste LeRoy for electricity tests at the royal laboratory in Passy. Among his incredibly varied letters to scientists in Europe and America, he contrasted the Leyden jar to Volta's new electrophorus (which reliably produced static electricity); examined the impact of a lightning strike in Cremona; commented on the aurora borealis; described a revised smoke-retarding stove; and opined on the linguistics of different Indian tribes.

One of Benjamin's more perceptive studies addressed England's geology. Coal veins under the sea at Whitehaven and oyster shells in the Derbyshire mountains, he observed, were "unlikely to happen if the earth were solid to the center." He theorized insightfully that the earth's hot inner core might be "more dense and of a greater specific gravity than any of the solids we are acquainted with, which therefore might swim in or upon that fluid. Thus, the surface of the globe would be a shell, capable of being broken and disordered by the violent movements of the fluid on which it rested."[32]

The honorary doctor, feeling old but still enthusiastic about the future, commented, "It is impossible to imagine the height to which may be carried in a thousand years the power of man over matter." He even offered visionary predictions: "We may perhaps learn to deprive large masses of their gravity and give them absolute levity for the sake of easy transport. Agriculture may diminish its labor and double its produce."[33]

Amidst Franklin's science and socializing, he regularly appealed to Vergennes for France's recognition and resources. Yet the French minister kept Benjamin's requests in his large rosewood desk for some fourteen months, unwilling to advance them to the king until the colonies demonstrated more potential for victory. He felt American military setbacks, particularly General Howe's capture of Philadelphia in September 1777, made French support a bad investment. That defeat also delivered a personal jolt to Franklin because a British captain took over his home on Market Street. The Baches managed to escape to the countryside, but English soldiers stole Franklin's scientific tools, books, musical devices, and even his portrait that hung in the dining room.

While appearing to be a conciliatory diplomat, Franklin could be a ruthless warrior. He pushed American ship captains, for instance, to invade England's coastal towns and seize "ready money and hostages," and he paid French privateers to grab British seamen from merchant vessels and villages.[34] Benjamin justified his aggressive actions by complaining about Britain's "wanton barbarity and cruelty," and by claiming the English "burnt our defenseless towns in the midst of winter, excited the savages to massacre our peaceful farmers and our slaves to murder their masters, and [are] even now bringing foreign mercenaries to deluge our settlements with blood."[35] Yet such acts further enraged English officials, particularly Lord Stormont, who, when Franklin proposed an exchange of prisoners, huffed: "The king's ministers receive no applications from rebels, unless when they come to implore his majesty's clemency."[36]

In early October 1777, military momentum began to shift when English general Burgoyne surrendered his entire army after the Battles of Saratoga. News of that turning point reached Paris on December 4, prompting a buoyant Franklin to boast to Vergennes: "We have the honor to acquaint your Excellency with advice of the total reduction of the force under General Burgoyne." Two days later, Louis XVI formally invited American negotiators to resubmit their proposal for a commercial alliance between France and the United States.

Vergennes offered generous terms. While wanting economic trade in exchange for military assistance, he did not require exclusive privileges. Careful to avoid criticism from other Europeans, he also demanded no territory within North America. Franklin emphasized these points in a note to Congress: "No monopoly of our trade was granted. None are given to France but what we are at liberty to grant to any other nation."[37]

To avoid surveillance, Benjamin and his colleagues negotiated with Vergennes at a private home half a mile from Versailles, where they arrived after taking a series of coaches. Despite such precautions, spies, including Bancroft, used news about the talks to speculate on stock price changes.

Aware of the negotiations and fearful of an ongoing French-American partnership, English officials tried to launch their own discussions with the United States' team. Britain's highly resourceful spy chief, Paul Wentworth, offered to repeal restrictive regulations, withdraw troops from everywhere but the New York islands, and return to the imperial status that existed before the war. According to Wentworth's spy-craft notes to his prime minister, Deane reiterated America's demand for full independence, and Franklin (identified as "72") blasted Britain for "the regular system of devastation and cruelty which every [English] general had pursued. Here [Franklin] lost his breath in relating the burning of towns, the neglect or ill-treatment of prisoners."[38]

Benjamin quietly alerted Vergennes to England's backdoor efforts, prompting, as Franklin had hoped, Louis XVI's council to finally approve military and economic assistance to the United States. It still took nearly a month to conclude the treaty's specific language, but the parties signed the coalition documents on February 6, 1778, at the office of the ministry for foreign affairs in the Hotel de Lautrec in Paris. When asked about his wearing an old velvet coat for the occasion, Franklin recalled what had happened four years before in the Cockpit and commented: "To give it a little revenge. I wore this coat on the day Wedderburn abused me at Whitehall."[39]

Although British spies already had obtained copies of the treaties, France's ambassador to London in mid-March formally informed the British government of his country's new alliance with the United States. France and England recalled their emissaries and declared war.

Hoping to avoid additional conflicts and expenses, Lord North,

England's prime minister, pushed Parliament to repeal many of the laws that had angered Americans. Yet George III rejected American independence, repeated his support for a British Empire, and expressed his distaste for Franklin, whom he called "that insidious man."[40]

Louis XVI embraced the alliance by inviting America's envoys to Versailles. As Benjamin's carriage arrived, crowds outside the palace gates strained to see the famous man and shouted, "Vive Franklin!" Benjamin arranged to stand out at the French court. While others wore stiff coats, ceremonial swords, and large wigs, Franklin dressed like a plain Quaker. In what some viewed as republican simplicity, he allowed his hair to hang loose and his glasses to rest on his nose. "I should have taken him for a big farmer," wrote one admirer, "so great was his contrast with the other diplomats, who were all powdered, in full dress, and splashed all over with gold and ribbons."[41]

After rising from his noon prayers, the French king pronounced, "Firmly assure Congress of my friendship. I hope that this will be for the good of the two nations." Louis XVI then turned to Franklin and stated, "I am very satisfied with your conduct since you arrived in my kingdom."[42]

Historians of the American Revolution have compared Benjamin's diplomatic achievement to Washington's military victories.[43] Edmund Morgan labeled Franklin's efforts "the greatest diplomatic victory the United States has ever achieved."[44] Yet despite such success, America's delegation in Paris remained fractured. Lee felt left out of key discussions and whined to Franklin, "Had you studied to deceive the most distrusted and dangerous enemy of the public you could not have done it more effectively. I trust, Sir, that you will think with me that I have a right to know your reasons for treating me thus."[45] Benjamin immediately expressed his growing impatience, but decided not to send his first draft: "My pity for your sick mind, which is forever tormenting itself with its jealousies, suspicions, and fancies that others mean you ill, wrong you, or fail in respect for you.

If you do not cure yourself of this temper it will end in insanity."[46] In a separate letter to Deane, Franklin explained his approach to Lee: "I bear all his rebukes with patience for the good of the service, but it goes a little hard with me."[47]

Lee did not help his cause by asking that a special ship send word to Congress of the envoys' meeting with the king. Deane and Franklin thought the vain proposal expensive and unnecessary, particularly since the signed treaties already had been transmitted across the Atlantic. Lee's criticisms of Deane, however, gained traction within Congress, where Lee's brother, Richard Henry, advanced the view that the delegate from Connecticut defrauded the colonies.[48] Legislators eventually recalled Deane from France to face a long and bitter audit of his expenses. Franklin remained an ally, writing, "I had an exceeding good opinion of him when he acted with me, and I believe he was then sincere and hearty in our cause,"[49] yet Congress replaced Deane with John Adams.

"Loathing" is a term sometimes used to describe the complex relations between Franklin and Adams. The two shared a passion for American independence, and both recognized the need to work together toward that goal. Adams even once called Franklin a "great and good man," while Benjamin referred to Adams as "always an honest man,"[50] yet they differed in so many ways that tensions flared regularly. Adams was thirty years Franklin's junior, and even five years younger than William Franklin. Puritanical in his judgments and lifestyle, Adams abhorred Franklin's flirtations, irregular schedule, and oblique opinions.[51] Adams felt Franklin became too deferential to the French, and he was repeatedly jealous of his colleague's renown, arguing that Benjamin did little of the hard work but enjoyed "a monopoly of reputation here and an indecency in displaying it." The volatile Adams further complained, "If I were in Congress, and this gentleman and the marble Mercury in the garden of Versailles were in nomination for an embassy, I would not hesitate to give my vote for the statue, upon the principle that it would do no harm."[52] The usually patient Franklin countered that Adams was "sometimes, and in some things, absolutely out of his senses."[53]

Adams, Lee, and Franklin agreed on one matter—that a single commissioner in France was enough. Lee lobbied for the job, but French ministers made it clear they wanted to deal only with Franklin, so in September 1778, Congress revoked the three-person delegation and appointed Benjamin minister plenipotentiary.

One of Franklin's first official acts was to provide safe passage for British captain James Cook as he completed his surveying throughout the Pacific. Demonstrating respect for another scientist, Benjamin instructed American commanders not to consider the HMS *Resolution* "an enemy, nor suffer any plunder to be made of the effects contained in her, nor obstruct her immediate return to England . . . but you would treat the said Captain Cook and his people with all civility and kindness."[54] Franklin had been unaware that Cook was killed in a skirmish on the Big Island of Hawaii, but his directive held and the English ship returned to London safely with its maps and specimens.

Science was never far from Benjamin's mind. He coauthored a report on lightning conductors for the Académie des sciences, prepared pamphlets on Native American language and orthography, composed a history of the compass, and described how atmospheric pressure could further cut smoke within his stove.[55]

He also turned his scientific lens toward politics, issuing a pamphlet supporting the use of paper money rather than gold and silver coins. That position certainly would benefit Franklin and other shopkeepers and tradesmen, who felt it would lower interest rates, increase wages, accelerate construction, and decrease reliance on imports. Yet Benjamin in 1779 provided a philosophical spin, arguing with statistics that hard currency did not accurately measure an economy's wealth; instead, "the riches of a country are to be valued by the quantity of labor its inhabitants are able to purchase and not by the quantity of silver and gold they possess."[56] About a century later, Karl Marx would credit Franklin with being "one of the first" to advance the labor theory of value, which determines the worth of a good or service by the total amount of labor needed to produce it.[57]

Despite, or maybe because of, the stress of wartime negotiations, Franklin periodically turned to his wry wit. Mocking pretentious scientists, in 1780 he prepared a proposal for the Royal Academy of Brussels to study the causes and cures of farts. He suggested "immortal honor" would flow to the researcher who determined how different foods alter the odor and frequency of a person's bodily emissions, claiming that such research would be far more "useful than those discoveries in science that have heretofore made philosophers famous." He further suggested the findings would empower scientists, asking, "What comfort can the vortices of Descartes give to a man who has whirlwinds in his bowels?"[58]

Returning to his warrior role, Benjamin instructed John Paul Jones to attack English vessels off the coast of Britain. The captain's *Bonhomme Richard*, named as a tribute to one of Franklin's aliases, captured more than seventy-five British ships in a single year, with his most famous battle being in September 1779 against the warship *Serapis*. After suffering considerable damage and being told to surrender, Jones responded, "I have not yet begun to fight." Three more hours of fierce conflict later, during which half of Jones's crew were killed or wounded, Americans won their first major victory over the vaunted British Navy.

The plenipotentiary's tasks varied widely. When Americans captured British vessels, for instance, Franklin had to judge whether to condemn or sell their goods. But his main task, which he dreaded, was to plead for more money from Vergennes. The French minister in 1778 approved a new loan of three million livres, but additional payments to America had to compete against France's internal challenges, including peasant protests over skyrocketing bread prices.

Even Congress complicated Franklin's money-raising efforts. Not only did the states refuse to tax themselves, but legislators consistently pressured Benjamin for more foreign support and then tried to draw on those requested monies before amounts had been approved. "The anxiety I have suffered and the distress of mind lest I should not be able to pay them has for a long time been very great indeed," complained Franklin. "To apply again to this court for money for a particular purpose, which they had already over and over again provided for and furnished us, was extremely awkward."[59] He further criticized American officials for spending his hard-won funds on "gewgaws, and superfluities."[60] He even expressed "disgust" with his own daughter's extravagance for requesting black pins, lace, and feathers, admonishing Sally that "feathers, my dear girl, may be had in America from every cock's tail."[61]

French support continued to be Franklin's only option. Holland, despite being at war with England, offered no assistance to the United States. Spain's loans remained small, with larger sums dangled only if America would cede control of the Mississippi River. That very proposition, Franklin wrote, "can only give disgust at present. Poor as we are, yet, as I know we shall be rich, I would rather agree with them to buy at great price the whole of their right on the Mississippi than sell a drop of its waters. A neighbor might as well ask me to sell my street door."[62]

Franklin's challenges shifted along with battle lines in America. They rose when British army general Charles Cornwallis in 1780 routed the larger US forces outside Camden, South Carolina; Benedict Arnold's treason almost gave control of the Hudson to the English; and American and French forces lost Savannah, Augusta, and Charleston. Yet the colonies' prospects looked a bit brighter in early 1781 when Nathanael Greene started winning battles in the Carolinas and Lafayette harassed Cornwallis in Virginia.

Despite these fluctuations of war, Franklin somehow convinced the French to send more ships and to grant another 6 million livres. In all, he obtained the equivalent of more than $16 billion in aid, as well as most of the gunpowder used by the Continental Army.[63] The skillful negotiator felt that "an expression of gratitude is not only our duty but our interest."[64] Yet gratitude was not a sentiment shared by other Americans, particularly John Adams, who, according to Franklin, "seems to think a little apparent stoutness and greater air of independence and boldness in our demands [of France] will procure us more ample assistance." Benjamin railed against these "ravings of a certain mischievous madman here in France," and Paris officials took offense, cut off further discussions with Adams, and refused to answer any of his letters. In barely diplomatic terms, the French minister wrote to Adams: "The King did not stand in need of your solicitations to direct his attentions to the interests of the United States."[65]

Although pleased with his own diplomatic efforts in France and Adams's eventual departure to Holland, Franklin grew weary. "I have passed my seventy-fifth year," he wrote in a resignation letter to Congress, "and I find that the long and severe fit of the gout which I had last winter has shaken me exceedingly, and I am yet far from having recovered the bodily strength I before enjoyed." He added, "I do not know that my mental faculties are impaired; perhaps I shall be the last to discover that; but I am sensible of great diminution in my activity, a quality I think particularly necessary in your minister for this court. I am afraid, therefore, that your affairs may some time or other suffer by my deficiency. I find also that the business is too heavy for me and too confining."[66]

Benjamin's resignation letter allowed his critics to accelerate their expressions of disapproval. Ralph Izard, appointed to be commissioner at the Court of Tuscany but stuck in Paris, blamed Franklin for not allowing his large family to live in the manner to which they had been accustomed, and wrote venomously to his congressional allies: "The political salvation of America depends upon the recalling of Dr. Franklin."[67] Arthur Lee, a bitter but brilliant lawyer, joined in by accusing Benjamin of financial mismanagement, prompting Franklin to refer to the two politicians as "unhappy gentlemen; unhappy indeed in their tempers and in the dark uncomfortable passions of jealousy, anger, suspicion, envy, and malice."[68]

Outsiders observed the tension. A French diplomat commented that "neither of the two parties has in Dr. Franklin the confidence that his intelligence and his integrity deserve."[69] Lafayette added: "If Mr. Franklin sends the treaty, his enemies in Congress will attempt to belittle it and will defeat the treaty itself in order to harm a single person."[70]

Still, enough American legislators blocked Franklin's critics, rejected Benjamin's resignation, and denied Izard's recall resolution. In fact, legislators in June 1779 recalled Izard and in August 1781 authorized Benjamin—along with John Adams and John Jay of New York, who had served as ambassador to Spain—to negotiate a hoped-for peace agreement with Britain.[71] Congress set only two foundational conditions: that America's independence be acknowledged and that the alliance with France be upheld.

Vergennes praised Americans for requiring French approval of any peace settlement, and he embraced Franklin's continued diplomatic leadership, arguing his manner "is as zealous and patriotic as it is wise and circumspect."[72] On the other hand, Arthur Lee—who increasingly despised Franklin, found him unduly biased toward Paris, and considered him dishonest and incapable—grumbled that Benjamin got appointed only "by the absolute order of France."[73]

Prospects for the new negotiating team improved greatly after October 19, 1781, when the Continental Army—led by Washington, Lafayette, and Comte de Rochambeau—defeated Cornwallis at the battle of Yorktown. Word of the British surrender took a month to reach France. When that news arrived in Paris at about eleven o'clock at night on the nineteenth of November, Vergennes informed Franklin that the aged diplomat now had the opportunity to attain peace.

# 13

# PEACEMAKER

Franklin, despite his aches, relished the new assignment, writing, "For in my opinion there never was a good war or a bad peace."[1] Yet he understood the associated challenges: "The public is often niggardly, even of its thanks, while you are sure of being censured by malevolent critics and bug-writers, who will abuse you while you are serving them, and wound your character in nameless pamphlets, thereby resembling those little dirty stinking insects that attack us only in the dark, disturb our repose, molesting and wounding us while our sweat and blood are contributing to their subsistence."[2]

As he had with the French, Benjamin enjoyed an extensive network among British scientists and publishers. His Paris-based contacts also proved to be useful across the Channel, as evidenced by Madame Anne Louise Brillon de Jouy. The two met in the spring of 1777; she was thirty-eight to his seventy (and her rich, philandering husband was in his sixties). Madame Brillon was regarded as "one of the most beautiful women of France" and lived in a grand estate at Passy. Franklin referred to her "sweet habit of sitting on my lap," and she called him "Cher Papa." A talented musician, Madame Brillon composed songs for

Franklin about America's independence. He wrote reflections on paradise for her, and many evenings after dinner the pair played lengthy games of chess, at least once, if Franklin's account is accurate, while she sat naked in her covered bath. More relevant to Franklin's pending peace negotiations, Madame Brillon happened to be good friends with Lord Cholmondeley, who offered to renew Franklin's relations with Lord Shelburne. In early 1782, Shelburne was named England's home secretary, the equivalent of America's secretary of state, and soon he would be prime minister and responsible for Britain's negotiating. Franklin commented on the serendipity, "Great affairs sometimes take their rise from small circumstances."[3]

Welcoming the reintroduction, Lord Shelburne dispatched to Franklin in Paris his confidant, Richard Oswald, a crusty, one-eyed Scottish trader of military equipment and enslaved people. Franklin and Oswald were the same age, and Oswald knew America, having lived there, and still maintained property and relatives in the states. Perhaps as important, Oswald understood how to flatter the US negotiator, with Benjamin boasting that "he repeatedly mentioned the great esteem the ministers had for me."[4] The two talked at length about recognition for America's independence, the future control of Canada, and reparations for Indian attacks on the colonies. They parted their first discussions, wrote Franklin, "exceedingly good friends."[5]

Internal English politics, however, complicated negotiations. After Cornwallis's surrender, Prime Minister Lord North, whom Franklin despised, lost a vote of no confidence, and was replaced by the more sympathetic Marquess of Rockingham. Trying to satisfy different wings of his government, that Whig leader appointed overlapping ministers to craft peace treaties: Lord Shelburne and Foreign Secretary Charles Fox. At least in theory, Shelburne was to negotiate with the United States, leaving Fox to deal with European allies, yet the two officials fought frequently over diplomatic turf.

While Oswald continued to represent Shelburne, Fox advanced

twenty-seven-year-old Thomas Grenville, whose father had promoted the hated Stamp Act of 1765. The novice negotiator, moreover, impressed neither Franklin nor Vergennes. While at Versailles, Grenville suggested that if "England gave America independence," then France should in turn give back to Britain several Caribbean islands it had recently captured. Vergennes mocked the offer, saying, "America did not ask [independence] of you," to which Franklin added, "We do not consider ourselves as under any necessity of bargaining for such a thing that is our own and which we have bought at the expense of much blood and treasure."[6]

At least from Benjamin's perspective, discussions became smoother after Rockingham died in early July 1782 and Shelburne became prime minister. The new government did not reappoint Fox as foreign secretary and recalled young Grenville, allowing Franklin to deal with Oswald and the new prime minister, both of whom he respected and was respected by.

In addition to cordial discussions, Franklin added abrasive propaganda to his diplomatic arsenal. His *Supplement to the Boston Independent Chronicle* condemned British abuses and featured a disturbing letter from a so-called Captain Gerrish of the New England militia claiming that Seneca Indians had delivered eight boxes of American scalps to the Canadian governor. To bring home the point of England's cruel and gruesome involvement in the killing of American patriots, Franklin invented quotes from the Seneca chief encouraging the governor to "send these scalps over the water to the great king, that he may regard them and be refreshed; and that he may see our faithfulness in destroying his enemies and be convinced that his presents have not been made to ungrateful people."[7] Franklin tried to make the broadsheet believable by including a mock advertisement that offered a reward for a strayed or stolen horse.

Not long after John Jay (who had been America's diplomat in Spain) and John Adams (who had tried to obtain a loan from Holland) arrived in Paris to join Franklin's peace-negotiating team, the

Americans quickly disagreed among themselves about France, with Adams and Jay wanting to distance the colonies from this ally now that the war was ending. They reflected the sentiments of a growing number of American-based patriots, including General Washington, who embraced the myth, as historian Stacy Schiff put it, "of self-realization and self-actualization, of having sprung fully formed from her own high-blown ideals."[8] Franklin, however, protested: "It is our firm connection with France that gives us weight with England, and respect throughout Europe. If we were to break our faith with this nation, on whatever pretense, England would again trample on us, and every other nation despise us."[9]

The American team did agree to more face-to-face negotiations with Britain, which seemed willing, unlike France, to cede to the United States the vast lands east of the Mississippi, north of Florida, and south of Canada. Paris-based officials certainly wanted American independence from Britain, but to moderate the new nation's clout and ensure its continued reliance on France, they sought to confine the United States to an area bordered by the Appalachian Mountains to the west, the Ohio River to the north, and Florida to the south.

While being coy with Vergennes about his talks with Oswald, Franklin demanded that Britain remove its troops from the United States, as well as provide joint navigation privileges on the Mississippi and fishing rights off Newfoundland, in the Grand Banks, and within the Gulf of Saint Lawrence. On the second tier of his list, Benjamin asked for Canada to become part of the United States, for England to pay reparations associated with American property damaged during the war, for Britain to admit guilt of wartime abuses, and for the two countries to sign a free trade agreement.

Formal peace negotiations began in the spring of 1782. In return for agreeing to Franklin's top priorities, British prime minister Shelburne hoped to split the United States from France and obtain an economic partnership with the fast-growing country. Discussions stalled briefly because of Franklin's "cruel gout" and kidney stones, what he referred to as "the gout and the gravel," but when everyone returned to the table, the most contentious issue was compensation for the lost property of British loyalists. The most prominent British loyalist, of course, was William Franklin, once the royal governor of New Jersey. Benjamin's animosity toward his son, as well as his belief that American patriots suffered great losses from British troops—his own library and scientific equipment had been destroyed—led to uncharacteristic belligerence. Even John Adams, who previously suspected Benjamin of being soft on loyalists because of William, commented, "Dr. Franklin is very staunch against the Tories, more decided on this point than Mr. Jay or myself."[10]

A few years earlier, in September 1778, William had been part of a prisoner exchange, was released from his Connecticut jail, and moved to British-occupied New York. Much to his father's outrage, he became president of the Board of Associated Loyalists that financed and organized raids, one of which lynched a captain of the New Jersey militia. George Washington threatened to hang the hangman, whose rich and influential parents convinced the prime minister to appeal for mercy to Benjamin, who flatly refused. When an English court released the hangman, saying he simply had followed William Franklin's orders, Americans demanded William's arrest. Realizing his tenuous circumstance, Benjamin's son fled to London in August 1782.

Further complicating matters, Shelburne, then a new and politically vulnerable prime minister, wanted to appease the many well-connected Tories now living in England; thus, he met with William and promised to support loyalists during the peace negotiations. An angry Benjamin threatened to scuttle the entire treaty unless it rejected reparations for loyalists. The British eventually caved and offered a toothless provision calling for the Congress to "earnestly recommend" that the states make whatever restitution they felt appropriate. Still, Franklin demanded an amendment, targeted at William, specifically blocking payments to any Tories who had "borne arms against the said United States."[11]

To maintain at least the appearance of an alliance with France, Franklin inserted a provision that stated the pact with England would not become binding "until terms of a peace shall be agreed upon between Great Britain and France." When Benjamin arrived at Versailles to explain the provisional treaty—and, with temerity, to request another French loan—Vergennes expressed his displeasure. Noting their clear agreement that America would not negotiate separately, the French minister reminded Benjamin: "You have all your life performed your duties. I pray you to consider how you propose to fulfill those which are due to the [French] king."[12]

Franklin tried to apologize, expressed his respect for Louis XVI, and admitted, "We have been guilty of neglecting a point of propriety." He pleaded that this "single indiscretion of ours" be "excused" and not ruin "the great work, which has hitherto been so happily conducted, is so nearly brought to perfection, and is so glorious to his reign."[13]

Vergennes did not buy Franklin's puffery. "You can imagine my astonishment," he wrote to the French ambassador in Philadelphia. "I think it proper that the most influential members of Congress should be informed of the very irregular conduct of their commissioners in regard to us." Feeling deceived and neglected, he further complained, "We shall be but poorly paid for all that we have done for the United States, and for securing to them a national existence."[14]

Franklin tried to convey further contrition . . . and change the subject. He called Vergennes's observation "apparently just," yet quickly turned the discussion toward a critique of the English, hoping to find common ground with the French minister. "The English, I just now learn," he wrote, "flatter themselves they have already divided us. I hope this little misunderstanding will therefore be kept a secret, and that they will find themselves totally mistaken."[15]

Vergennes, although probably not swayed by Franklin's words, had few options. Since further French complaints might push the Americans even closer to the British, he decided against filing an official protest with the Congress, and he settled for France negotiating its own peace treaty with Britain.

Franklin admitted his embarrassment over begging France for an additional loan. He privately criticized some members of Congress for believing that "France has money enough for all her occasions and all ours besides."[16] He mocked Americans for failing to levy taxes: "Our people certainly ought to do more for themselves," he wrote. "It is absurd, the pretending to be lovers of liberty while they grudge paying for the defense of it."[17] Yet while Vergennes understood well the limits on France's treasury, he appreciated the dangers of withholding aid when military hostilities might resume. In the end, he approved another $6 million livres loan.

Representatives of Britain and the United States signed the Peace Treaty of Paris at the Hôtel d'York on September 3, 1783, just a few hours before France and England approved their armistice agreement at Versailles.[18] Historians tend to contend that Franklin outmaneuvered the French negotiator. "Two great diplomatic duelists had formally crossed swords," wrote Carl Van Doren, "and the philosopher had exquisitely disarmed the minister."[19] Walter Isaacson, referring to Franklin's love of chess, commented, "Franklin mastered a three-dimensional game against two aggressive players by exhibiting great patience when the pieces were not properly aligned and carefully exploiting strategic advantages when they were."[20] Even the oft-critical John Adams admitted Benjamin had "behaved well and nobly."[21]

Franklin simply expressed relief. "We are now friends with England and with all mankind," he wrote. "May we never see another war!"[22]

With treaties signed, Benjamin again informed Congress of his wish "for the little time I have left to be my own master."[23] Eager to return to Philadelphia and rebuild his laboratory and library, he found the new nation had new demands. Ultimately, Franklin could no more resist the pleas of his country than he could that of his curiosity.

# 14

## MORE TO DISCOVER

How to account for Franklin's lifelong zeal for wonder? What motivated his disparate and deep interests, as well as his consistent efforts to examine and explain the world about him?

His ancestors certainly possessed an abundance of ingenuity, and Enlightenment writers he read encouraged experiments and reason. His youthful creations and wanderings surely suggested a raw intelligence and innate independence. His vibrant energy, moreover, was motivated by his life's precariousness, having lost a son, a beloved uncle, and friends to disease, alcoholism, and poverty. And yet, Benjamin stands out even among the bright, restless, and driven young men of his time.

Examples galore may be the best means for demonstrating his distinctive curiosity and creativity. Take the frigid winter of 1783–1784, when Franklin idiosyncratically assumed a connection between smoke in the French air—what he called "dry fog"—and Iceland's Hecla volcano. To explain the pall's impact, he demonstrated that his magnifying glass could not concentrate the remaining rays sufficiently to ignite brown paper, and he proposed that the lack of sunlight hitting the earth's surface exacerbated the season's cold temperatures.

Another atmospheric wonder was hail, whose origins he'd wondered about, particularly in the summer months. "How immensely cold must be the original particle of hail which forms the center of the future hailstone," he asked, "since it is capable of communicating sufficient cold, if I may so speak, to freeze all the mass of vapor condensed round it and form a lump of perhaps six or eight ounces in weight!" In a 1784 paper, *Meteorological Imaginations and Conjectures*, submitted to the Literary and Philosophical Society of Manchester, he speculated on a hailstone's origin: "There seems to be a region high in the air over all countries where it is always winter, where frost exists continually."[1]

Like many before him, Franklin looked to the daytime sky and questioned the composition of light. "Universal space, as far as we know of it, seems to be filled with a subtle fluid, whose motion, or vibration, is called light," he wrote to the American Philosophical Society.[2] Those motions, Benjamin continued, cause the particles within bodies and objects to vibrate, and thus warm. He used the term *fire* to describe the various forms of energy that provoked vibrations, and then anticipated two fundamental concepts, which Albert Einstein about a century and a half later would expand and expound upon. First, Franklin suggested a relationship between fire (or energy) and matter; think $E=mc^2$. Second, he speculated on the conservation of mass and energy. "If fire be an original element, or kind of matter, its quantity is fixed and permanent in the world," Benjamin wrote. "We cannot destroy any part of it or make addition to it; we can only separate it from that which confines it, and so set it at liberty, as when we put wood in a situation to be burnt."[3]

Scientists and theologians are inveterate seekers of our celestial origins, and in a prescient series of questions in May 1788 to James Bowdoin—a collaborator on early electricity experiments—the eighty-two-year-old Benjamin essentially laid out the salient questions for the field that would become known as geophysics. "How came the earth

by its magnetism?" his queries began. "Is it likely that iron ore immediately existed when the globe was first formed, or may it not rather
be supposed to be a gradual production of time? Was the earth's magnetism related to the iron it contained? If so, had that iron ever been
nonmagnetic? And if that was so, how had it become magnetized? May
not a magnetic power exist throughout our system, perhaps through
all systems, so that if men could make a voyage in the starry regions, a
compass might be of use? . . . As the poles of magnets may be changed
by the presence of stronger magnets, might not, in ancient times, the
near passing of some large comet, of greater magnetic power than this
globe of ours, had been a means of changing its poles? Did not the presence of cold regions of the shells and bones of animals natural to warm
regions indicate that the earth's geographic poles had shifted? Does
not the apparent wrack of the surface of this globe thrown up into long
ridges of mountains, with strata in various positions, make it probable
that its internal mass is a fluid, but a fluid so dense as to float the heaviest
of our substances?"[4]

Despite such insights, Franklin made mistakes, as would be expected of any scientist considering the laws of nature. He maintained, like
other researchers, that the earth's magnetic field resulted from a magnetized core of iron ore, but he strayed from reality by suggesting such
magnetism derived from a field permeating all of space. He also failed
to understand ship stability, largely because he lacked an understanding
of mathematical concepts like metacentric height, which measures the
static stability of a floating body.

As Franklin aged, moreover, his science became dated. With more
sophisticated equipment, emerging researchers could examine nature
with increased precision and better control their experiments; science,
as a result, shifted from the realm of polymaths to specialists. Franklin
accepted, even embraced, such changes. "I begin to be almost sorry I
was born too soon," he wrote in 1783, "since I cannot have the happiness of knowing what will be known 100 years hence."[5]

INCREASINGLY FRAIL, FRANKLIN NONETHELESS STAYED ATOP SCI-entific discussions, particularly those focused on flight and hypnosis. In the summer and fall of 1783, when the Treaty of Paris was being finalized, the most popular topic in Paris was the hot air balloon. Ailments kept Franklin from visiting Lyons in June, but he read much about Joseph and Etienne Montgolfier launching the first unmanned craft, this one made of linen that the brothers inflated with the smoke from burning dried stalks of straw. In August, Benjamin witnessed in Paris a varnished-silk balloon lifted by hydrogen gas, which Jacques-Alexandre-César Charles, a respected physicist who had investigated how heated gases expand, generated by pouring sulfuric acid over blazing iron filings. It took four days to produce enough hydrogen, during which time public excitement grew; more than fifty thousand people watched the unmanned inflatable rise at five o'clock in the afternoon, as a cannon fired, and a band played. "Never before was a philosophical experiment so magnificently attended," Franklin declared.[6]

Benjamin watched the spectacle from his carriage, where, with a pocket-glass, he tracked Charles's balloon's rise "till it entered the clouds, when it seemed to me scarce bigger than an orange and soon after became invisible." The inflatable floated for forty-five minutes, rose three thousand feet, and traversed about fifteen miles, landing in a village where, according to Franklin, "the country people who saw it fall were frightened and attacked it with stones and knives so that it was much mangled."[7]

The king summoned the Montgolfier brothers to Versailles in mid-September to repeat the experiment, this time in a balloon adorned with rococo ornaments and a basket containing a duck, a cock, and a sheep. Two months later just outside Paris, on the first human flight, the scientist Pilatre de Rozier and the Marquis d'Arlandes burned straw in a grate beneath their inflatable. Although tree branches initially blocked their progress—prompting Franklin to fret, "I was then in great pain for the men, thinking them in danger of being thrown out or burnt"— they ascended five hundred feet, passed directly over Benjamin, safely crossed the Seine, and popped champagne bottles upon landing. The marquis and Montgolfiers visited Franklin at Passy that evening to continue their celebrations.

Benjamin preferred hydrogen gas to hot air, largely because such balloons didn't need to carry heavy and dangerous burners, and he helped finance a second effort by Charles in December that attracted 200,000 spectators. That physicist and his copilot took off from the Tuileries, the royal residence next to the Louvre, ascended almost two thousand feet, floated for more than two hours, traversed twenty-seven miles, and landed without frightening villagers. Charles brought along a barometer and thermometer to measure the atmosphere above the earth's surface, greatly advancing the emerging science of meteorology.

Benjamin argued that the launch of air travel would "pave the way to some discoveries in natural philosophy of which at present we have no conception."[8] When a skeptic questioned the new development's future value, he countered, "What is the use of a new-born baby?"[9]

Considering flight's personal impacts, Franklin felt this means of transport would relieve him of the painful jostling that accompanied his carriage rides over rough stones. Thinking bigger, "possibly (giving) a new turn to human affairs," he suggested aircraft might convince sovereigns "of the folly of war" since it would be impracticable to guard against thousands of balloons carrying two soldiers each.[10]

Franklin praised the American Philosophical Society for replicating balloon flights, and gently admonished the British for their hesitations. "I am sorry this experiment is so totally neglected in England, where mechanic genius is so strong," he wrote to the Royal Society. "Your philosophy seems to be too bashful. In (the United States) we are not so much afraid of being laughed at. If we do a foolish thing, we are the first to laugh at it ourselves."[11]

Benjamin, not surprisingly, found a humorous angle to the inflatable's momentous advance. Using the alias of a woman commenting on human relations, he crafted a parody for French newspapers. "If you want to fill your balloons with an element ten times lighter than inflammable air," "she" wrote, "you can find a great quantity of it, and ready-made, in the promises of lovers and courtiers."[12]

After ballooning, the next popular craze to hit Paris was animal magnetism, or the healing power of a "universal fluid" supposedly released by stars in the galaxy. Leading the fad's charge was Franz Anton Mesmer, who promoted early versions of hypnotism, séances, and curing by suggestion. A charismatic and colorful speaker, he "mesmerized" Marie Antoinette, Lafayette, and other members of the aristocracy, yet physicians denied him a doctor's license in Vienna, Berlin, and Paris. Claiming grand plans to build a hospital and academy, Mesmer launched a company that raised 340,000 livres; the amount was so substantial that it prompted Louis XVI to appoint a commission to judge the German doctor and evaluate animal magnetism.

Four representatives of the panel came from the Faculty of Paris, including Joseph-Ignace Guillotin, who later advanced the death machine that came to bear his name. Among the five from the Académie des sciences were Franklin, who expressed initial skepticism of a universal fluid but appreciated the power of suggestion. "Delusion may," he wrote, "in some cases be of use while it lasts. There are in every great rich city a number of persons who are never in health because they are fond of medicines and always taking them, whereby they derange the natural functions and hurt their constitutions. If these people can be persuaded to forbear their drugs in expectation of being cured by only the physician's finger or an iron rod pointing at them, they may possibly find good effects though they mistake the cause."[13]

The royal commission first gathered in Paris to witness a public healing, in which patients linked themselves around a wooden tub, filled with iron scraps and broken glass, that purportedly would condense and conduct the group's animal magnetism. As a pianoforte played soft music, a "healer" walked about the dimly lit room and pointed an iron rod at, or touched his hands to, each patient's ailing parts. The "treatment" lasted about two hours, during which time several patients broke into convulsions.

Franklin conducted subsequent tests at his Passy home during late April and early May of 1785. He and his grandsons felt nothing from the procedure, but a few sufferers noted some effect, such as one gentleman who sensed warmth when the healer moved his hand over the tumor on his knee. Yet when blindfolded, participants often claimed to feel the universal fluid even though they were not being magnetized and acknowledged no impact when they were.

The most dramatic—if unsuccessful—demonstration involved an apricot tree, which the healer "magnetized" and claimed a blindfolded twelve-year-old boy would be able to distinguish from others. As the lad moved away from the tree, however, he claimed to be getting closer, and he became more agitated until he fainted.

In reports to the king and Académie des sciences, commission members unanimously rejected the existence of animal magnetism, labeled Mesmer a fraud, and argued that any strange actions from patients resulted from the power of imagination, which they said "does everything, the magnetism nothing." The panelists added: "We discovered we could influence [the patients] ourselves so that their answers were the same, whether they had been magnetized or not." In an unpublished appendix, they warned against mesmerizing healers trying to treat young women with *"titillations delicieuses."*[14] Yet admitting the limited power of reason among the superstitious, Franklin concluded: "Some think (the royal commission's report) will put an end to Mesmerism, but there is a wonderful deal of credulity in the world, and deceptions as absurd have supported themselves for ages."[15]

Having made it to Paris in August 1784, Thomas Jefferson endorsed Franklin's report, calling animal magnetism a "compound of fraud and folly." It was one of many points on which the two scientists agreed, with Jefferson finding "more respect and veneration attached to the character of Dr. Franklin in France than to that of any other person, foreign or native."[16]

Congress had selected Jefferson to be a peace commissioner in 1781, but he declined to travel because his wife had been ill. Three years later, the forty-one-year-old widower technically arrived in France to replace Franklin as America's chief diplomat, but he responded tartly to such a suggestion, "No one can replace him, sir; I am only his successor." Later in his life, noting Benjamin's many accomplishments, Jefferson reflected, "The succession to Dr. Franklin at the court of France was an excellent school of humility."[17]

Benjamin had become a regular feature in French salons, and, according to Jefferson, the seasoned diplomat opened "a door of admission for me to the circle of literati."[18] In the eight months that their tenures overlapped, the two spent many evenings dining and playing chess together. During the day they negotiated commercial agreements with other European nations and met with numerous visiting politicians, which prompted Franklin to observe dryly: "It is amazing the number of legislators that kindly bring me new plans for governing the United States."[19]

Their personal interests overlapped. Both were skilled writers, even if Franklin displayed more wit and Jefferson more eloquence. Both were scientific polymaths, with Jefferson an avid agriculturist, botanist, and geologist. Both invented gadgets, with the Virginian introducing a dumbwaiter, revolving book stand, and macaroni-making machine. And both enjoyed social clubs and the company of women.

After nine years in Paris, Franklin did not want to leave his friends and admirers, and another trans-Atlantic voyage—when almost eighty years old and suffering gout and kidney stones—threatened a good bit of pain. Still, Franklin knew his remaining days were limited, and he longed to see his home and the new nation he helped create. "The

French are an amiable people to live with," he submitted, "yet I do not feel myself at home, and I wish to die in my own country."[20]

Benjamin's letters increasingly took on a tone of resignation. To one peace-negotiating colleague, he wrote: "I leave you still in the field, but having finished my day's work, I am going home to go to bed! Wish me a good night's rest, as I do you a pleasant evening. Adieu!"[21]

Amid his travel preparations, Franklin published in April 1785 one of his last pamphlets—*Observations on Mayz, or Indian Corn*— explaining the history and applications of this ubiquitous cereal grain. In his straightforward style, Benjamin discussed its various forms, including corn meal, hasty pudding, popcorn, and corn liquor.[22]

The retiring ambassador enjoyed widespread expressions of appreciation. Louis XVI provided a miniature portrait of himself surrounded by 408 diamonds. Vergennes sent a gracious tribute and declared that "the United States will never have a more zealous and more useful servant than M. Franklin."[23] Madame Brillon expressed her enduring love and smothered him with embraces, prompting Jefferson to wish "(Benjamin) could transfer these privileges to me [as the new ambassador], to which (Franklin) responded: 'You are too young a man.' "[24]

The queen, to cushion his road trip to the English Channel, made available her enclosed litter conveyed by surefooted Spanish mules. The wheelless vehicle arrived at Passy at four o'clock in the morning on July 12, but Franklin's last-minute activities kept him occupied until the late afternoon. "In the midst of a very great concourse of the people of Passy," recorded his grandson, "a mournful silence reigned around him, and was only interrupted by a few sobs."[25] Jefferson added: "When he left Passy, it seemed as if the village had lost its patriarch."[26]

During the early days of his eighth and final sail across the Atlantic, Franklin produced forty pages of notes and drawings about ocean currents and ship designs. He again took regular readings of air and water temperatures, and he devised a keg that obtained deep-ocean samples.

About halfway through the trip, Franklin considered relaxing, "but the garrulity of an old man has got hold of me, and, as I may never have another occasion of writing on this subject, I think I may as well now, once and for all, empty my nautical budget." So he added to his *Maritime Observations* discussions about the use of airtight compartments to prevent a ship's sinking; the design of Indian canoes, Chinese rowboats, Eskimo kayaks, and Pacific Island proas; optimal shapes for hulls to limit resistance; sail designs to catch the maximum amount of wind; swimming anchors to retard a ship's movement in water too deep for traditional anchorage; and sliced playing cards that measure the speed and direction of wind.[27]

Benjamin had other writing budgets to empty, as well. His *Description of a New Stove for Burning of Pitcoal, and Consuming All Its Smoke* explained, in far more detail than previous publications, how to curtail the dirty gases and soot that afflicted home furnaces in both Europe and America.[28]

Franklin landed at Philadelphia's wharfs on September 14, 1785, sixty-two years after his first arrival as a seventeen-year-old vagabond. Ships in the harbor, even British ones, showed their colors, and welcoming throngs lined the docks. Church bells rang and cannons boomed as Benjamin slowly proceeded up Market Street to his house, which he had not seen in nine years and the British Army had recently occupied. He wrote succinctly in his diary: "We were received by a crowd of people with huzzas and accompanied with acclamations quite to my door. Found my family well."[29]

# 15

## THE CONSTITUTIONAL EXPERIMENT

F ranklin enjoyed one night of rest before being swarmed by notables from the General Assembly, militia, library, and university, each offering tributes and making requests. Pennsylvania's biggest celebrity was embraced by both major political blocs—the populists, including tradesmen and farmers, as well as the conservatives, composed largely of landowners. As Benjamin Rush, surgeon general of the Continental Army, put it, "To borrow an allusion from one of his discoveries, his presence and advice, like oil upon troubled waters, have composed the contending waves of faction."[1]

Almost unanimously, the blocs elected Franklin to Pennsylvania's executive council and then to its presidency (analogous to a governor, although the post lacked veto powers). Feigning reluctance, he wrote, "Though I apprehend they expect too much of me and that without doing the good proposed I shall find myself engaged again in business more troublesome than I have lately quitted."[2] But of course, he was won over, later admitting, "This universal and unbounded confidence of a whole people flatters my vanity much more than a peerage could do."[3] He wrote to a relative, "Old as I am, I am not yet grown insensible with respect to reputation."[4] And to a friend, he acknowledged being susceptible to "the remains of ambition from which I had imagined myself free."[5]

Despite his pledge to enjoy a quiet retirement, Benjamin also never let up inventing. Unable to reach the higher shelves of his rebuilt floor-to-ceiling library, which contained more than four thousand books, he devised a mechanical arm to pluck publications. He improved James Watt's copying machine with a rolling press that pushed damp tissue paper against documents printed with a slow-drying ink. He constructed a chair with a hinged seat that converted into a ladder when the top was tipped back, as well as a large lounger with a pedal that swayed an overhead fan to provide a breeze and keep flies at bay.

Franklin even got the chance to express pride in his previous creations. When refurbishing his Market Street house, workmen replacing the lightning rod discovered that a powerful bolt had melted the copper point but been rendered harmless by the grounded conductor. "At length," Benjamin bragged, "the invention has been of some use to the inventor."[6]

On other fronts, members of the American Philosophical Society elected him chair, as they had done every year he lived in Europe, and they printed and distributed his various writings from the recent sea voyage. Franklin praised the group's "promotion of useful knowledge among us, to which I shall be happy if I can in any degree contribute."[7]

While that association examined natural science, Benjamin helped found the Society for Political Enquiries to study political science. As the group's first president, he commented, "The arduous and complicated science of government" had been too long "left to the care of practical politicians or the speculations of individual theorists."[8] To form a functioning United States, Franklin added, "We are making experiments in politics,"[9] so we need "a society for mutual improvement in the knowledge of government."[10] The new society initially met at the City Tavern, with subsequent sessions at Franklin's house. Its first discussion papers were Benjamin Rush's analysis of the "effects of public punishment upon criminals and upon others," and Tench Coxe's "principles on which a commercial system for the United States should be founded."[11]

Benjamin continued his active correspondence, often writing long letters of advice to friends. To obtain a good night's sleep, he advocated moderate eating, "a good conscience," and exercise (if it preceded, rather than followed, meals). Taking his own advice on temperate living, he gave up wine and began exercising every day with dumbbells. Yet Franklin the scientist oddly distrusted treatments, saying, "I am more afraid of the medicines than of the malady."[12] When not in excruciating pain, he added, "I flatter myself that the stone is kept from augmenting as much as it might otherwise do, and that I may still continue to find it tolerable."[13]

Although busy, his life in Philadelphia appeared comfortable. Once worried about household expenses, Franklin had become financially secure. Largely because property values increased as America's population rose and because the war inflated prices throughout the economy, his "estate more than tripled in value since the Revolution."[14]

Adding to his calm, Benjamin surrounded himself with family. Although "the companions of my youth are indeed almost all departed," he found "an agreeable society among their children and grandchildren."[15] News of such cheerfulness prompted Polly Stevenson and her three children to follow Franklin to Philadelphia. They joined a full house, including Sally, her husband Richard Bache, and their young children, who, according to Benjamin, "cling about the knees of their grandpapa and afford me great pleasure."[16]

Yet Franklin's schedule grew teeming when Pennsylvania named him a delegate to the Constitutional Convention being assembled in Philadelphia in May 1787 to revise what many felt were weak Articles of Confederation that gave the federal Congress no power to levy taxes, no control over interstate or foreign commerce, and no ability to draft troops or coin money. The confederation of states, as a result, featured a more than cumbersome thirteen separate currencies and even different navies.

Benjamin entered the Assembly Room of the State House by eleven o'clock each day for the next four months, often arriving earlier to participate in meetings of Pennsylvania's Executive Council. To avoid aggravating Franklin's gout and kidney stones, his colleagues arranged for four prisoners from the Walton Street jail to carry him gently to and from work in a covered sedan chair.[17]

William Pierce, a representative from Georgia, offered one of the most balanced views of the convention's most-traveled delegate: "Dr. Franklin is well known to be the greatest philosopher of the present age.... But what claim he has to the politician, posterity must determine. It is certain that he does not shine much in public council; he is no speaker, nor does he seem to let politics engage his attention. He is, however, a most extraordinary man, and tells a story in a style more engaging than anything I ever heard.... He is eighty-two and possesses an activity of mind equal to a youth of twenty-five years of age."[18]

Franklin was of a different generation from other delegates. The hunched-over octogenarian with freckled hands was twenty-six years older than George Washington (even Benjamin's son, William, was born a year before the general) and nearly thirty years older than John Adams. Thirty-seven years separated him from Thomas Jefferson; John Hancock was thirty-one years and James Madison a full forty-five years his junior. As he had been in Paris for almost a decade, many delegates knew him mostly by his outsized reputation as scientist and diplomat.

Franklin also was less philosophical about politics than many of his colleagues. Madison, Alexander Hamilton, and John Jay, all groomed for statecraft, published the *Federalist Papers*, a series of essays outlining the ideal structure of government, while Adams and Jefferson independently offered their own detailed theories about public administration. In contrast, Benjamin's political writings tended to address specific challenges and offer practical solutions to them.

Although a revolutionary when it came to American independence, Benjamin could be quite cautious. He chafed at authority but dreaded emotional throngs. He wanted a strong central government but distrusted public-sector interventions, favoring actions by individuals and their civic associations. He displayed a conservatism when warning about reliance on the state, writing: "I fear that giving mankind a dependence on anything . . . tend[s] to flatter our natural indolence, to encourage idleness and prodigality, and thereby to promote and increase poverty, the very evil it was intended to cure." He even opposed a minimum wage, complaining that "if our manufactures are too dear, they might not vend abroad."[19]

Franklin failed to win support for most of his legislative proposals, including having a single body of Congress, creating a plural executive that would spread power among several elected leaders, and rejecting presidential vetoes. What may seem contrary to his pro-democracy nature, Franklin also wanted government officials to be well-to-do volunteers. "There are two passions which have a powerful influence in the affairs of men," he argued. "These are *ambition* and *avarice*—the love of power and the love of money. Separately, each of these has great force in prompting men to action; but when united in view of the same object, they have in many minds the most violent effect."[20] John Adams countered that Franklin's proposal would ensure all offices are "monopolized by the rich, the poor and middling ranks would be excluded, and an aristocratic despotism would immediately follow." Benjamin's motion failed to garner support and was tabled, with James Madison, the crafty parliamentarian, explaining that the proposal "was treated with great respect, but rather for the author of it than from any conviction of its expediency or practicability."[21]

Benjamin did weigh in successfully on a few issues advanced by others. He opposed a president being chosen for life, and he supported "the regular punishment of the executive when his misconduct should deserve it and for his honorable acquittal when he should be unjustly accused."[22] He rejected suffrage only for wealthy landowners and opposed a requirement for foreigners to live in America fourteen years before gaining rights. Recalling the many immigrants "who served us faithfully" during the Revolution, he argued for pluralism, affirming the value of diversity within a political system: "When foreigners after looking about for some other country in which they can obtain more happiness give a preference to ours, it is a proof of attachment which ought to excite our confidence and affection."[23]

Rather than pushing specific policies, Franklin's key roles during the convention were convening and conciliating. As one biographer put it, "He embodied a spirit of Enlightenment tolerance and pragmatic conciliation."[24] Benjamin's house and garden, only a block from the State House, became centers for after-session relaxation and friendly discussions that fostered conciliation. The importance of such assembling is revealed in one of the sixteen murals within the United States Capitol that highlight key events in American history; it features Franklin in his garden under a mulberry tree with Alexander Hamilton, James Madison, and James Wilson.

On one of the great controversies at the convention, Benjamin decided against advancing an antislavery provision, fearing it would tear apart the fragile union. Yet three years later, less than three months before he died and after being elected president of the Pennsylvania Society for Promoting the Abolition of Slavery, he petitioned Congress to end the practice, writing: "Mankind are all formed by the same Almighty Being, alike objects of his care, and equally designed for the enjoyment of happiness." His measure would grant "liberty to those unhappy men who alone in this land of freedom are degraded into perpetual bondage."[25] Not surprising, probably even to Franklin, slavery's supporters denounced and defeated the petition.

One Georgia legislator argued, religiously, that the Bible authorized slavery and, economically, that subjected Blacks were the only ones who would do the grueling work needed to cultivate cotton and tobacco. Franklin responded with his last, and perhaps most biting, satire. Claiming to have located a speech given years before by a legislator in Algeria, Benjamin invented a character he called Sidi Mehemet Ibrahim, who defended the capture and enslavement of European Christians to work in Algiers, arguing, "If we forbear to make slaves of their people, who in this hot climate, are to cultivate our lands? Who are to perform the common labors of our city, and in our families?" Mocking the Georgian's speech, Franklin's purported councilman claimed the Koran allowed slavery and that Islamists "take care to provide [the enslaved 'infidels'] with everything, and they are treated with humanity."[26]

Benjamin, however, was an effective mediator on the convention's other great argument—the division of votes among smaller and larger states. Rural areas, already enjoying equal representation under the Articles of Confederation, feared being overwhelmed by population centers. Large states, like Virginia with 420,000 residents, objected to having the same number of legislators as Delaware with only 37,000 people. Several delegates threatened to withdraw from the Constitutional Convention unless they prevailed on this key point of representation.

To explain the debate and the need for compromise, Franklin offered a further clarification and an analogy. "The diversity of opinions turns on two points," he said. "If a proportional representation takes place, the small states contend that their liberties will be in danger. If an equality of votes is to be put in its place, the large states say their money will be in danger. When a broad table is to be made, and the edges of planks do not fit, the artist takes a little from both and makes a good joint. In like manner here, both sides must part with some of their demands in order that they may join in some accommodating proposition."[27]

Soon thereafter, the delegates appointed a special committee, made up of one representative from each state, to craft a settlement. Pennsylvania elected Franklin. Although others had advanced a similar deal, it was on Benjamin's motion that the panel recommended the so-called Connecticut Compromise, what we now recognize as the basic three-part makeup of the United States Congress. First, it called for a House of Representatives to include delegates from each state based on population (at the time, the committee recommended one legislator for every thirty thousand inhabitants). Second, the House would originate all spending bills, while the Senate would confirm executive officers. And third, the states would hold equal votes in the Senate.

Such momentous political negotiations did not seem to monopolize Franklin's mind. When botanist Manasseh Cutler visited from Massachusetts, for instance, Benjamin gave a tour of his large library, paying special attention to the full *Systema Vegetabilium* by Carl Linnaeus. He also revealed to Cutler a reptilian marvel—a ten-inch snake having two identical heads. According to the botanist, Franklin "seemed extremely fond, through the course of the visit, of dwelling on philosophical subjects and particularly that of natural history; while the other gentlemen were swallowed up with politics."[28]

After months of intense debates, Franklin sealed support for the Constitution with a powerful statement conveying humility, reason, and tolerance. Too feeble to rise and speak, he sat beside James Wilson as the younger Pennsylvania delegate read Franklin's words: "I agree to this Constitution with all its faults, if they are such, because I think a general government necessary for us, and there is no form of government but what may be a blessing to the people if well administered. . . . I cannot help expressing a wish that every member of the Convention who may still have objections to it would, with me, on this occasion doubt a little of his infallibility, and, to make manifest our unanimity, put his name to this instrument."[29]

To Franklin, the United States was an experiment, and the Constitution was a set of hypotheses to be tested, and adjusted, over time. He appreciated the science of politics, which Alexander Hamilton acknowledged "like most other sciences has received great improvement."[30]

As representatives on September 17, 1787, signed the document—by delegation in geographical order, from New Hampshire to Georgia—Franklin commented to a few colleagues near him about the sun carved and painted on the back of the president's chair. "I have often in the course of the session, and the vicissitudes of my hopes and fears as to its issue, looked at that behind the president without being able to tell whether it was rising or setting," he said. "But now at length I have the happiness to know that it is a rising and not a setting sun."[31]

As Franklin left what's now known as Independence Hall, a lady, probably Elizabeth Willing Powel, a prominent society figure in Philadelphia, asked loudly whether the delegates created a republic or monarchy. Benjamin reportedly responded with the ominous quote: "A republic, if you can keep it."[32] It's a line that often gets referenced when the nation faces constitutional crises, such as insurrections and impeachments.

When Franklin added his name to the paper that begins "We the people," he became the only person to sign all four of the key documents forming the United States—the Declaration of Independence (1776), the alliance with France (1778), the peace treaty with Britain (1783), and the Constitution (1787). When it came to inventing a nation, he was present.

# 16

## CLOSING THE BOOKS

Franklin resigned from the Pennsylvania Council in October 1788, having promised himself "to engage no more in public business." He added, "I hope to enjoy the small remains of life that are allowed me in the repose I have so long wished for."[1]

Yet Benjamin continued to offer observations about technology and agriculture. He expressed particular interest in steam-powered thrust; John Fitch tried, unsuccessfully, to interest him in his own steamboat drawings, but Benjamin sided with James Rumsey, a protégé of George Washington, who devised apparatus that utilized steam in vessels, water pumps, and grain grinders. Franklin also was one of the first to propose crop insurance, writing: "I have sometimes thought that it might be well to establish an office of insurance for farms against the damage that may occur to them from storms, blight, insects, etc. A small sum paid by a number would repair such losses and prevent much poverty and distress."[2]

He maintained his offerings of practical advice. When a friend complained about his advancing deafness, Franklin proposed a ready remedy: "Putting your thumb and fingers behind your ear, pressing it outwards, and enlarging it, as it were, with the hollow of your hand." He claimed this "exact experiment," done at midnight when his house was quiet, allowed him to "hear the tick of a watch at forty-five feet distance by this means, which was barely audible at twenty feet without it."[3]

Benjamin also carried on with optimism for the new nation, even while acknowledging it would confront challenges. "We must not expect," he wrote, "that a new government may be formed, as a game of chess may be played by a skillful hand, without a fault.... (Yet) if any form of government is capable of making a nation happy, ours I think bids fair now for producing that effect."[4] Demonstrating a still-agile mind, he added his famous caveat, originally written in French to scientist Jean-Baptiste LeRoy: "Our new Constitution is now established, and has an appearance that promises permanency, but in this world nothing can be said to be certain except death and taxes."[5]

Despite his active intellect, Franklin's body was deteriorating. Pain from kidney stones and gout became extreme and he began taking opium, which slashed his appetite and impeded his digestion, prompting him to report that "little remains of me but a skeleton covered with a skin."[6] He appeared quite the contrast to the young man who swam every day and carried two sets of type up flights of stairs.

"Between the effects of both (pain and opium)," he complained, "I have but little time in which I can write anything." When he could no longer "bear sitting to write," he dictated additional passages for his autobiography. When he no longer trusted his memory, he appealed for reviews from friends, noting, "For I am now grown so old and feeble in mind, as well as body, that I cannot place any confidence in my own judgment." He finally broke off all efforts on his memoirs in early 1790, leaving it to others to describe his role with the Declaration and Constitution.

By April, according to his physician Dr. John Jones, Benjamin "was seized with a feverish indisposition, without any particular symptoms attending it, till the third day when he complained of a pain in the left breast, which increased till it became extremely acute, attended with a cough and laborious breathing." These sufferings lasted for ten days, but the symptoms subsided briefly, allowing him to rise slowly from his bed and have his daughter change his sheets "so that he might die in a decent manner."[7] When Sally expressed hope that her father was on the mend and would be active for many more years, he replied tersely: "I hope not."

Early in the evening of the seventeenth, the abscess in his lungs burst and "discharged a large quantity of matter, which he continued to throw up while he had sufficient strength to do it; as that failed, the organs of respiration became gradually oppressed—a calm lethargic state succeeded."[8] With grandchildren around his bed, the eighty-four-year-old Benjamin Franklin died quietly that night at about eleven o'clock.

The public grieving was Philadelphia's largest gathering to date. The funeral procession began on April twenty-first at the State House and featured clergy of all faiths, state and local officials of all parties, scientists, family members, printers and other tradesmen, firefighters, as well as leaders of the American Philosophical Society and the College of Philadelphia. An estimated twenty thousand mourners lined the procession route to Christ Church's burial grounds. Muffled bells tolled, and ships in the harbor flew their flags at half-mast. As pallbearers lowered Franklin's body into his grave at four o'clock in the afternoon, the militia, in which Franklin had been a colonel, fired their funeral guns. The flat gravestone, a heavy blue marble tablet measuring six feet by four feet, bore his specified engraving: "Benjamin and Deborah Franklin 1790."

International acclaim followed, with a French official calling Franklin "one of the greatest men who have ever been engaged in the service of philosophy and liberty."[9] The National Assembly, after hearing a stirring tribute from Lafayette, by acclamation agreed to wear mourning. Condorcet offered a eulogy before the Académie des sciences, and the Commune of Paris called for celebrations in the city's streets and cafés.

Among US politicians, the House of Representatives voted unanimously to wear mourning for a month, but the Senate refused, largely because of grudges from the Lees and Vice President (and Senate president) John Adams. Even the American Philosophical Society, which Franklin founded, took almost a year to hear a eulogium; one of the association's vice presidents had long despised Franklin, calling him an "inflammatory and virulent man."[10]

Perhaps the most dramatic tribute ignored political grudges and hailed Benjamin's science and diplomacy. Marguerite Gérard's allegorical portrait, an etching entitled "To the Genius of Franklin," shows a Zeus-like Benjamin being helped by Minerva, goddess of wisdom, to block lightning and by Mars, god of war, to overthrow autocrats. The Latin motto she included, which came from the French economist and statesman Anne-Robert-Jacques Turgot, translates as: "He snatched lightning from the sky and the scepter from tyrants."[11]

# 17

## A LONG SHADOW

Writing a biography of Benjamin Franklin means contending with the man himself as well as the long shadow he still casts. To take his full measure, we must first separate Benjamin from his personas. Neither Silence Dogood, Poor Richard Saunders, nor Sidi Mehemet Ibrahim spoke entirely for him. He created these characters as mouthpieces for specific causes, and sometimes to sell papers and almanacs. These puppets endure in internet searches and memes.

We also must recognize Franklin wrote even his autobiography with an agenda; from his perspective as an old man, he was trying to burnish his image and instruct his son. To make his arguments more effectual in pamphlets, moreover, he often resorted to sarcasm and downright snark.

Popular images of Franklin abound as a crazed kite-flyer, pithy moralizer, crafty storyteller, and flirty womanizer. The commissioned portraits we have of him are no clearer, depicting him as everything from a wigged gentleman to a frontiersman in a fur cap to a robed divinity.

A fuller take of the man also must process the multiplicities we often ignore in our nation's founders. Franklin owned slaves, but he proposed legislation to abolish the practice. He fathered a son out of wedlock, but he raised and adored that child.[1]

No doubt Franklin has been remembered, if not clearly. He certainly satisfied his own criteria for such historical durability, writing, "If you would not be forgotten, as soon as you are dead and rotten, either write things worth reading, or do things worth writing."[2]

Yet the pendulum has swung back and forth on Franklin's legacy. Biographers carry their own baggage, as do readers of history, who are subject to evolving biases and societal norms. Shifting judgments often expose as much about historians and their times as about Franklin and his.

Since he wrote extensively, the initial lens on Franklin's life was his own.[3] As has been explained, he was not impartial about, willing, or able to tell his entire story. When it came to describing Benjamin's final years negotiating treaties in France and the Constitution in Philadelphia, John Adams took up that task, and this oft-times adversary, according to one historian, explained "how much (Adams) had accomplished in Paris, and how obstructionist, indolent, and dissipated his senior colleague had been."[4]

As years passed, Benjamin's still-living critics mellowed and even Adams in 1811 offered a mostly positive review.

> Franklin had a great genius, original, sagacious, and inventive, capable of discoveries in science no less than of improvement in the fine arts and the mechanical arts. He had a vast imagination.... He had wit at will. He had humor that, when he pleased, was delicate and delightful. He had satire that was good-natured or caustic. Horace or Juvenal, Swift or Rabelais, at his pleasure. He had talents for irony, allegory, and fable that he could adapt with great skill to the promotion of moral and political truth. He was a master of that infantile simplicity which the French call naiveté which never fails to charm.[5]

Sir Humphry Davy, the renowned English chemist who isolated potassium and other elements, exemplified the general praise of Franklin in the early nineteenth century. He called Benjamin's experiments "most ingeniously contrived and happily executed."[6]

It didn't take long, however, before others began using Franklin as a mouthpiece for their messages. Consider Parson Weems, who wrote about him in 1817, nearly thirty years after his death. Much as the minister did for George Washington—conveying the first president's honesty with a fabricated story about a cherry tree—Weems characterized Franklin as a devout Christian, concocting a tale of the dying man gazing blissfully upon a crucifix.

As romanticism displaced reason during the nineteenth century, intellectuals complained that Franklin the rationalist lacked emotion and mysticism. According to poet John Keats, Benjamin was "not (a) sublime man."[7] Henry David Thoreau found Franklin's focus on materialism to be mundane, while Mark Twain, despite continuing Franklin's satiric traditions, mocked Benjamin's maxims for frustrating "boys who might otherwise have been happy."[8] And editor Leigh Hunt wrote that Franklin possessed "few passions and no imagination,"[9] two claims I wholeheartedly reject. In my view, Franklin had more passion than most and, if anything, too much imagination.

After the Civil War and with the advance of industrialism, the pendulum swung back. The historian Frederick Jackson Turner praised Benjamin as "the first great American (whose) greatness lay in his ability to apply to the world a shrewd understanding that disclosed in the ordinary things about him potent forces for helpfulness."[10] Horatio Alger and Andrew Carnegie lauded Franklin's self-help advice to advance virtues, particularly industriousness, as ways to wealth, and the banker Thomas Mellon said reading Franklin's *Autobiography* became "the turning point" of his life.[11]

Into the early twentieth century, William James, John Dewey, and Charles Sanders Peirce all praised Benjamin's practicality and reliance on experience, prompting one historian to claim that Franklin "laid the foundation for the most influential of America's homegrown philosophies, pragmatism."[12]

Benjamin's approval rating fell again as the early twentieth century progressed when Max Weber lambasted Franklin for his "philosophy of avarice" that admired "the earning of more and more money combined with the strict avoidance of all spontaneous engagement of life."[13] Sinclair Lewis, particularly in his novel *Babbitt*, poured on the scorn against Benjamin's bourgeois beliefs. English author D. H. Lawrence dished out more disdain, calling Franklin a "snuff-colored little man," as well as a "dry, moral, utilitarian little democrat" who tried to turn everyone into "virtuous little automaton(s)."[14]

With the passing of another generation, utilitarianism became honorable and Franklin its spokesperson. The Great Depression of the 1930s, according to biographer Walter Isaacson, "reminded people that the virtues of industry and frugality, of helping others and making sure that the community held together, did not deserve to be dismissed as trivial and mundane."[15] With technological and scientific advances in the 1940s, historian I. Bernard Cohen commended Franklin's natural-philosophy achievements, compared them to Isaac Newton's, and wrote that Benjamin "afforded a basis for the explanation of all the known phenomena of electricity."[16]

Yet historians of the early twenty-first century, apart from Joyce Chaplin in 2006,[17] responded to growing partisan polarization and international strife by highlighting Benjamin's diplomatic and political acumen and overlooking his science. Edmund Morgan in 2002 found Benjamin's natural philosophy to be less worthy than his public service, and Isaacson the following year dismissed his scientific work as being that of "a practical experimenter more than a systemic theorist."[18]

Although still considered with George Washington to be among the most popular founding brothers, Benjamin in recent years has faced a bit of scorn.[19] PBS in 2022 questioned whether the kite story "can hold up to modern scrutiny" and suggested the experiment may have been nothing more than "a foolhardy, death-defying stunt."[20] The television show *MythBusters* mockingly imitated that experiment by having lighting strike a kite and fry a dummy of Franklin.[21]

Since Benjamin was one of the first to write and distribute advertising, perhaps there is little wonder in our modern marketing age that his image is used to sell crafts, cookies, and mutual funds. Characterizations of Franklin have even drawn crowds to Broadway musicals, including *1776* (which gives most credit for the Declaration of Independence to John Adams) and *Ben Franklin in Paris* (which portrays Benjamin as a womanizer). Such depictions may add to Franklin's name recognition, but they threaten to render him an eccentric and comic character who elicits neither controversy nor adulation.[22]

What insights might our age offer into Franklin's paradoxes and achievements? Perhaps more interesting, what perspectives on contemporary debates can we glean from his life and works?

I have come to appreciate this complex man's continued relevance. As a vocal set of modern-day activists reject science and dismiss facts, Benjamin's life highlights the importance of verifiable analysis. As some jurists impose their (originalist) view of the Constitution, he— literally an originalist of the Constitution—insists that knowledge and laws evolve with changing circumstances. As zealots impose their religious beliefs, he makes the case for tolerance. As partisans increase their stridency, he shows the value of compromise and civility. As censors ban books and limit debate, he defends printers and free speech. As autocrats seek to centralize authority, he demonstrates what local associations can do by themselves.

In our narrow view of America as either red or blue and our arguments as only for or against, Franklin suggests a more nuanced world, one that is ultimately more fascinating and entertaining. We now can see him with prismatic lenses, rather than bifocals that register at most two views.

Yet we must admit Benjamin is difficult to pigeonhole politically, making him hard for today's adherents to exploit. While certainly an advocate for the middle class, he was more practical than partisan, more concerned about solving community challenges than supporting a party or cause.

The cause he did embrace was science, and the one consistency of his long life was his appreciation for, even idolization of, ingenuity. He sought out the clever and displayed an almost boundless curiosity, utilizing imagination and investigation to understand the natural and political environments around him.

Franklin's scientific approach goes beyond laboratory experiments and integrates his diverse interests. His reliance on reason underscores his support for education and distrust of orthodoxy. Careful observations of natural phenomena permeate his essays as well as discussions at the Junto and American Philosophical Society. His dedication to research reflects the orderliness of his self-improvement maxims. His commitment to cognition underlies his work as essayist, community organizer, and legislator. He showed that scholarship can lead to renown, which he manipulated to obtain critical French support for the American Revolution, settlement of England's surrender, and acceptance of constitutional compromises.

No doubt other founders appreciated science and advanced technology. Thomas Jefferson is credited with numerous inventions and stunning architecture; he was a lover of botany, who collected and experimented with plantings in Virginia; and he studied fossils, turning a section of the White House into his "bone room." George Washington in his Farewell Address supported "the diffusion of knowledge," and John Adams helped establish the American Academy of Arts and Sciences in Boston. Yet Franklin alone considered examination and experimentation his core instincts.

Benjamin moved science from a pastime for gentlemen to a profession for experts and a fascination for the growing middling class.[23] He expanded it beyond the study of natural forces to include the examination of human trends and even politics.

Yet for all my focusing on Benjamin's science, I recognize that his then-revolutionary observations and investigations have been eclipsed, a fact he anticipated when writing that "knowledge" advances with new information and more sophisticated testing equipment. "Invention and improvement are prolific," he added, "and beget more of their kind."[24] Although Benjamin utilized telescopes and microscopes, he would marvel at the complex and exacting tools in modern laboratories. As an independent polymath, he would be surprised by today's specialists as well as the significant research roles now played by governments, universities, and corporations. While he advanced dialogue among European and American technologists, he would be startled by the size and international composition of modern investigative teams.

A time-traveling Franklin, as columnist David Brooks suggested, might not initially understand today's internet or biotech breakthroughs, but he would appreciate their potential to transform our lives. He would share, as well as advance, the techno-enthusiasts' "passion for progress."[25]

Benjamin Franklin's image adorns the $100 bill, the Oval Office, and the shelves of biographies and textbooks. In recognition of his role as postmaster, Franklin's face also appears on perhaps the rarest and most sought-after postage stamp, known as the 1-cent "Z grill," printed in 1868. He stands out even among the nation's founders, in part, for his diverse careers—printer, scientist, inventor, writer, publisher, essayist, businessman, soldier, diplomat, and statesman. Trained as a tradesman rather than a lawyer, this one-time runaway reached the heights of influence through what we want to consider a characteristically American blend of skill, wit, discipline, and ingenuity.

And he was a reliable enemy to the despotic, the dogmatic, and the deluded. Franklin rejected reliance on salvation, preferring to be judged by his works. As for his personal beliefs, he rebuffed religious doctrine, trusting instead reason, common sense, tolerance, and even cheerfulness. He dismissed faith in favor of observation. Most strikingly, in both science and statecraft, he spurned conventional wisdom and arbitrary power.

Let's update the sketches of a wild-haired kite flyer, simple tinkerer, or godlike Prometheus. Fitting for one who viewed life as an experiment, he changed his opinions as new evidence mounted and his observations became clearer. Happiest when in nature or a laboratory, he could be comfortable around a negotiating table or a printing press. Naturally curious and ingenious, his inquiries ranged widely—he explained many of nature's secrets, and he advanced scientific associations and colleges, fire brigades and libraries, and the ideals of our republic.

# NOTES

I would like to acknowledge the extraordinary collection of Franklin's writings and papers by "The Papers of Benjamin Franklin," an online resource made available by a team of scholars at Yale University. The project was established in 1954 under the auspices of Yale and the American Philosophical Society. The entire edition is projected to reach forty-seven volumes and provide access to Franklin's approximately 30,000 extant papers.

## CHAPTER 1: THE KITE

1. *Extract of a Memoir of Mr. Dalibard* (Sparks, 1837), 5:288–93. Read at the Académie des sciences, May 13, 1752.
2. *The Pennsylvania Gazette*, October 19, 1752.
3. Joseph Priestley, *The History and Present State of Electricity* (London, 1767), 179–81. Includes a chapter titled "The Kite Experiment."
4. Priestley, 179–81.
5. *The Pennsylvania Gazette*, October 19, 1752.
6. Priestley, *History and Present State of Electricity*.
7. Benjamin Franklin (Richard Saunders), *Poor Richard Improved* (Philadelphia: Printed and sold by B. Franklin and D. Hall, 1758).
8. Carl Van Doren's extensive biography (*Benjamin Franklin* (New York: Viking Press, 1938) addresses Franklin's science for 27 of its 782 pages; Ronald W. Clark's *Benjamin Franklin: A Biography* (New York: Random House, 1983) offers thirty of its five hundred pages; Esmond Wright's *Franklin of Philadelphia* (Cambridge, MA: Belknap Press, 1986) devotes just eleven of four hundred pages.
9. J. A. Leo Lemay, *The Life of Benjamin Franklin* (Philadelphia: University of Pennsylvania Press, 2006).
10. Gordon S. Wood, "Public Service of Benjamin Franklin," *Encyclopædia Britannica*, accessed January 22, 2024, https://www.britannica.com/biography/Benjamin-Franklin/Public-Service.

11. Edmund Morgan, *Benjamin Franklin* (New Haven: Yale University Press, 2002).
12. Benjamin Franklin to Joseph Banks, September 9, 1782.
13. Walter Isaacson, *Benjamin Franklin* (New York: Simon & Schuster, 2003), 487.
14. I. Bernard Cohen, ed., *Benjamin Franklin's Experiments* (Cambridge, MA: Harvard University Press, 1941).
15. I. Bernard Cohen, *Benjamin Franklin: His Contribution to the American Tradition* (Indianapolis: Bobbs-Merrill, 1953).
16. Louis Untermeyer, *Lives of the Poets: The Story of One Thousand Years of English and American Poetry* (New York: Simon & Shuster, 1959). See also https://quotefancy.com/robert-frost-quotes, accessed January 22, 2024.
17. *Benjamin Franklin: A Film by Ken Burns*, four-hour, two-episode documentary on PBS, April 4–5, 2022. In April 2024, *Franklin*, an Apple TV+ eight-part series starring Michael Douglas, also featured Benjamin's diplomacy in Paris, being based on Stacy Schiff's excellent book, *A Great Improvisation: Franklin, France, and the Birth of America* (New York: Henry Holt, 2005).
18. Aaron Goldman, "Our Founding Flirt," *Washington Post*, April 15, 1990.
19. Alan Taylor, "For the Benefit of Mr. Kite," *The New Republic*, March 19, 2001.
20. Joseph Priestley, "The Kite Experiment," in *History and Present State of Electricity*.
21. I. Bernard Cohen, *Science and the Founding Fathers* (W. W. Norton, 1995).
22. Catherine Drinker Bowen, *The Most Dangerous Man in America* (Boston: Little, Brown, 1974), 54.
23. John Adams to William Tudor, June 5, 1817, in *American Historical Review* 47: 806–7.

## CHAPTER 2: INGENIOUS ANCESTORS

1. Benjamin Franklin, *Autobiography of Benjamin Franklin*, ed. F. W. Pine (New York: Henry Holt, 1916), 7.
2. Benjamin Franklin, *Autobiography*, 8.
3. Benjamin Franklin the Elder's commonplace book, cited in *Papers of Benjamin Franklin* (New Haven: Yale, 1759–1978), vol. 1.
4. Franklin, *Autobiography*, 9.
5. *Benjamin Franklin Writings* (New York: Library of America, 1987), 3:453.
6. Margaret Wood, "Sumptuary Laws," Library of Congress blogs, accessed February 6, 2014. https://blogs.loc.gov/law/2014/02/sumptuary-laws/.
7. Edmund Morgan, *The Puritan Family* (New York: Harper & Row, 1966).
8. *Autobiography*, 12.
9. Nick Bunker, *Young Benjamin Franklin* (New York: Alfred A. Knopf, 2018).
10. Benjamin Franklin, "Epitaph of Josiah and Abiah Franklin."
11. *Autobiography*, 11.
12. *Autobiography*, 16.
13. *Autobiography*, 24.
14. Peter Kalm, *Peter Kalm's Travels in North America* (New York, 1937), 154.
15. Kenneth B. Murdock, ed., *Selections from Cotton Mather* (New York: Hafner Publishing, 1926), 286.
16. Scholars debate the Enlightenment's time span, with most admitting the dates are fluid but some suggesting it began with the death of France's King Louis XIV in 1715 and ended with the death of Immanuel Kant in 1804.
17. Immanuel Kant, "Answering the Question: What Is Enlightenment?" (1784), trans. Ted Humphrey (Indianapolis: Hackett Publishing, 1992). Kant used the Latin phrase *sapere aude*, which also can be translated as "have courage to use your own reason."

18. Immanuel Kant, "What Is Enlightenment?," trans. Mary C. Smith, May 19, 2015, http://www.columbia.edu/acis/ets/CCREAD/etscc/kant.html.

19. Ritchie Robertson, *The Enlightenment* (New York: HarperCollins, 2021), p. viii.

20. Isaac Newton, *Opticks; or, A Treatise of the Reflexions, Refractions, Inflexions and Colours of Light* (London, 1704), and *Philosophiae Naturalis Principia Mathematica* (often called *Principia*) (London, 1767).

21. That date reflects the Gregorian calendar we now use rather than the Julian calendar employed in England and its colonies until 1752. The Julian, or Old Style, version put Benjamin's birthdate on January 6, 1705.

22. The Old South Church, known as the Third Church, to distinguish it from previous Congregational churches. Its congregation first met in 1670 at the Cedar Meeting House and then in 1729 at the Old South Meeting House at the corner of Washington and Milk Streets. The current church on Copley Square was completed in 1873.

23. The Benjamin Franklin Historical Society notes that Benjamin mistakenly wrote that he was born at the corner of Hanover and Union Streets, but city records show Josiah Franklin was a tenant at 17 Milk Street in 1706, the year of Benjamin's birth. The family in 1712 moved to Hanover and Union Streets. Accessed February 26, 2024, https://www.benjamin-franklin-history.org/birthplace.

24. *Autobiography*, 12.

25. Ezra Stiles, *The Literary Diary of Ezra Stiles* (New York: Scribner's, 1901), 2:376. Stiles was a biblical scholar and president of Yale University.

26. *Autobiography*, 13.

27. *Autobiography*, 9.

28. William Temple Franklin, *Memoirs of the Life and Writings of Benjamin Franklin* (London: Henry Colburn, 1818), 1:447.

29. *Autobiography*, 11.

30. *Autobiography*, 5.

31. Arthur Tourtellot, *Benjamin Franklin: The Shaping of Genius, the Boston Years* (Garden City, NY: Doubleday, 1977), 161.

32. *Autobiography*, 11.

33. *Autobiography*, 11.

34. The colonies at the time lacked the lead mines and factories needed to produce such printing machines and type.

35. *Autobiography*, 13.

36. Bernard Fay, *Franklin, The Apostle of Modern Times* (Boston: Little, Brown, 1929), 29.

37. *Autobiography*, 13.

38. Benjamin Franklin, "Will and Codicil," July 17, 1788.

39. *Autobiography*, 13–14.

40. *Autobiography*, 13.

41. *Autobiography*, 13.

42. *Autobiography*, 15.

43. Eric Burns, *Infamous Scribbler: The Founding Fathers and the Rowdy Beginnings of American Journalism* (New York: Perseus Brooks Group, 2006), 54.

44. *Autobiography*, 17.

45. *Autobiography*, 17.

46. *New England Courant*, April 16, 1722.

47. Ralph Lerner, *Revolutions Revisited* (Chapel Hill: University of North Carolina Press, 1994).

48. Silence Dogood, *New-England Courant*, no. 9, July 23, 1722.

49. *New-England Courant*, May 28, 1722.

50. Dogood, *New-England Courant*, no. 13, 24, September 24, 1722.

51. J. A. Leo Lemay, *The Life of Benjamin Franklin* (Philadelphia: University of Pennsylvania Press, 2006).
52. *Autobiography*, 18.
53. John Blake, "The Inoculation Controversy in Boston, 1721–1722," *New England Quarterly* (1952): 489–506.
54. *Autobiography*, 19.
55. *Autobiography*, 19.
56. *Autobiography*, 19.
57. Bunker, *Young Benjamin* Franklin, 131.

## CHAPTER 3: SEARCHING FOR OPPORTUNITY

1. Benjamin Franklin, *Autobiography of Benjamin Franklin*, ed. F. W. Pine (New York: Henry Holt, 1916), 23.
2. *Autobiography*, 27.
3. *Autobiography*, 25.
4. *Autobiography*, 32.
5. *Autobiography*, 32.
6. *Autobiography*, 34.
7. *Autobiography*, 16.
8. Benjamin Franklin to Hugh Roberts, February 26, 1761.
9. *Autobiography*, 33.
10. Tim Hitchcock, "The Urban Contexts of Crimes Tried at the Old Bailey," *The Proceedings of the Old Bailey, London's Central Criminal Court, London 1715–1760*.
11. Ronald W. Clark, *Benjamin Franklin: A Biography* (New York: Random House, 1983).
12. *Autobiography*, 37.
13. *Autobiography*, 38.
14. Jared Sparks, ed., *The Works of Benjamin Franklin* (Boston, 1840), 1:104–5.
15. Benjamin Franklin, "Plan of Conduct, 1726," in Robert Walsh, *Life of Benjamin Franklin* (Philadelphia, 1815–17), 2:51–52.
16. Benjamin Franklin, "Journal of a Voyage, 1726."
17. Papers of Benjamin Franklin, 1:94; diary entry for September 28, 1726.
18. Benjamin Franklin, "Journal of a Voyage, 1726."

## CHAPTER 4: BUILDING A BUSINESS EMPIRE

1. Benjamin Franklin, *Autobiography of Benjamin Franklin*, ed. F. W. Pine (New York: Henry Holt, 1916), 38.
2. *Autobiography*, 43.
3. Carl Van Doren, *Benjamin Franklin* (New York: Viking Press, 1938), 76.
4. *Autobiography*, 40.
5. Explanation by Jim Green in Jeanette Lerman, "Meet Ben Franklin's tragic pal who made Pa.'s paper money hack-proof," *The Philadelphia Inquirer*, August 25, 2017.
6. *Autobiography*, 41.
7. Van Doren, *Benjamin Franklin* (New York: Viking Press, 1938), 76.
8. *Autobiography*, 47.
9. *Autobiography*, 51.
10. *Autobiography*, 44.
11. *Autobiography*, 45.

12. "The Busy-Body," No. 1, *American Weekly Mercury*, February 4, 1729.
13. "The Busy-Body," No. 5, *American Weekly Mercury*, March 4, 1729.
14. *Autobiography*, 48.
15. Benjamin Franklin, "Apology for Printers," *The Pennsylvania Gazette*, June 10, 1731.
16. Franklin's image is on the Pulitzer Gold Medal for public service by an American news organization.
17. *Autobiography*, 49.
18. *Autobiography*, 29.
19. *Autobiography*, 49.
20. Benjamin Franklin, "I Sing My Plain Country Joan" (American Philosophical Society Song; c. 1742).
21. *Autobiography*, 49.
22. *Autobiography*, 69.
23. Poor Richard, *An Almanack For the Year of Christ 1735* (October 30, 1734).
24. Benjamin Franklin, *Poor Richard Improved* (1758).
25. *Autobiography*, 52.
26. *Autobiography*, 45.
27. *Autobiography*, 54–55.
28. *Autobiography*, 53.
29. *Autobiography*, 59. The phrase "cheerful acceptance of imperfection" from Lorraine Smith Pangle, *The Political Philosophy of Benjamin Franklin* (Baltimore: Johns Hopkins University Press, 2007).
30. *Autobiography*, 60–61.
31. *Autobiography*, 55.
32. *Autobiography*, 60.
33. Ralph Lerner, *The Thinking Revolutionary* (Ithaca: Cornell University Press, 1979), 56.
34. *Autobiography*, 61.
35. *Autobiography*, 62.
36. *Autobiography*, 67.
37. Jill Lepore, *Book of Ages: The Life and Opinions of Jane Franklin* (New York: Vintage Books, 2014), 69.
38. *Autobiography*, 66.
39. *The Pennsylvania Gazette*, October 24, 1734.
40. *Autobiography*, 67.
41. *Autobiography*, 79.
42. Benjamin Franklin to Peter Collinson, printed in Franklin, *Experiments and Observations on Electricity Made at Philadelphia in America* (London, 1769), 350.
43. *Autobiography*, 71.
44. "Benjamin Franklin (1706–1790)," Harvard University Portrait Collection, Bequest of Dr. John Collins Warren, 1856.
45. Van Doren, *Benjamin Franklin* (New York: Viking Press, 1938), 123.
46. Benjamin Franklin to Cadwallader Colden, September 29, 1748.
47. Van Doren, *Benjamin Franklin*, 188–89.

## CHAPTER 5: ELECTRICITY AND HEAT

1. Isaac Newton, "General Scholium" (*Scholium Generale*), 1713.
2. Mme. Du Chatelet, *Dissertation sur la nature et la propagation du feu* (Paris, 1744), 118.
3. Isaac Greenwood, "An Experimental Course of Mechanical Philosophy, Lecture III," Evans Early American Imprint Collection, University of Michigan.

4. Franklin's memoirs mistakenly claimed the demonstrations were performed by a Dr. Spence in Philadelphia in 1746. A good review of Franklin's interactions with Archibald Spencer (the gentleman's name was Spencer but Franklin mistakenly wrote "Spence") is I. Bernard Cohen, *Benjamin Franklin's Science* (Cambridge, MA: Harvard University Press, 1990).
5. *Autobiography*, 101.
6. Benjamin Franklin to Peter Collinson, April 29, 1749. Most credit for an electric battery goes to Alessandro Volta, who in 1800 invented the voltaic pile that stored electricity within a stack of metal discs separated by brine-soaked materials.
7. *Autobiography*, 101.
8. I. Bernard Cohen, *Benjamin Franklin's Science*, 52.
9. Benjamin Franklin to Peter Collinson, March 28, 1747.
10. Benjamin Collinson to Peter Collinson, May 25, 1747.
11. Nick Bunker, *Young Benjamin Franklin* (New York: Alfred A. Knopf, 2018), 374. Fluid theories of electricity were updated when electrons were discovered and the effects of magnetism better understood.
12. Catherine Drinker Bowen, *The Most Dangerous Man in America* (Boston: Little, Brown, 1974), 54.
13. Edward Purcell and David Morin, *Electricity and Magnetism* (Cambridge: Cambridge University Press, 2013), 4.
14. Benjamin Franklin, *Experiments and Observations on Electricity Made at Philadelphia in America* (London, 1769).
15. Benjamin Franklin to Peter Collinson, March 18, 1747.
16. Benjamin Franklin to Peter Collinson, 1748.
17. Benjamin Franklin to Cadwallader Colden, April 23, 1752.
18. Joyce Chaplin, *The First Scientific American: Benjamin Franklin and the Pursuit of Genius* (New York: Basic Books, 2006), 108.
19. Benjamin Franklin, "Opinions and Conjectures," July 29, 1750.
20. Benjamin Franklin to Peter Collinson, January 24, 1752.
21. Benjamin Franklin to Cadwallader Colden, April 23, 1752. Franklin rejected the corpuscular theory that suggested light was composed of small, discrete particles.
22. Benjamin Franklin, "Opinions and Conjectures," July 29, 1750.
23. Benjamin Franklin to Peter Collinson, August 14, 1747.
24. Benjamin Franklin to John Franklin, December 25, 1775.
25. Benjamin Franklin to Peter Collinson, July 29, 1750.
26. B. Hindle, *Early American Science* (New York: Science History Publications, 1976).
27. Benjamin Franklin to Peter Collinson, March 28, 1747.
28. Brooke Hindle, *The Pursuit of Science in Revolutionary America, 1735–1789* (Chapel Hill: University of North Carolina Press, 1956).
29. *Autobiography*, 102.
30. Carl Van Doren, *Benjamin Franklin* (New York: Viking Press, 1938), 162. Watson eventually reconciled with Franklin, acknowledging his original work. Watson became noted in 1746 for sending an electrical charge 1,200 feet across the Thames River and instantaneously back again. He was elected vice president of the Royal Society in 1772 and knighted in 1786.
31. Peter Collinson to Benjamin Franklin, September 27, 1752.
32. Benjamin Franklin to John Mitchell, April 29, 1749.
33. Cotton Mather, "The Voice of God in the Thunder," from *Magnalia Christi Americana* (Cotton Mather, 1702).
34. Benjamin Franklin to John Lining, March 18, 1755.

35. Franklin suggested that "for the most part, in thunderstrokes, it is the earth that strikes into the clouds, and not the clouds that strike into the earth."

36. Benjamin Franklin to John Mitchell, April 29, 1749.

37. Benjamin Franklin, "Comments on Hoadly and Wilson's Electrical Pamphlet," January 28, 1759.

38. Franklin, "Opinions and Conjectures," July 29, 1750.

39. Benjamin Franklin to Peter Collinson, March 2, 1750.

40. Benjamin Franklin to Peter Collinson, February 5, 1750.

41. Franklin, "Opinions and Conjectures," July 29, 1750.

42. Franklin never explained why he did not attach a pole to the Academy of Philadelphia's belfry, which was completed in April 1751 and rose approximately eighty feet. He focused on the Christ Church steeple, to be completed in 1754 and soar 196 feet, which would have made it North America's tallest structure.

43. Franklin, "Opinions and Conjectures," July 29, 1750.

44. Franklin, "The Kite Experiment," *The Pennsylvania Gazette*, October 19, 1752.

45. *The Pennsylvania Gazette*, October 19, 1752.

46. I. Bernard Cohen, *Benjamin Franklin's Science* (Cambridge, MA: Harvard University Press, 1990), 98.

47. *Philadelphia Gazette*, October 19, 1752.

48. Tom Tucker, *Bolt of Fate: Benjamin Franklin and His Electric Kite Hoax* (New York: Public Affairs Books, 2003).

49. Benjamin Franklin to Peter Collinson, October 19, 1752.

50. Benjamin Franklin to Peter Collinson, October 19, 1752.

51. Benjamin Franklin to Peter Collinson, October 19, 1752.

52. Priestley, *History and Present State of Electricity* (London, 1767), 179–81.

53. Priestley, *History and Present State of Electricity* (London, 1767), 179–81.

54. Priestley, *History and Present State of Electricity* (London, 1767), 216–17.

55. "A Letter from a Gentleman at Paris to his friend at Toulon, concerning a very extraordinary experiment in electricity," *The Gentleman's Magazine & Historical Chronicle*, June 1752.

56. Henry Brougham, *Works of Henry Lord Brougham* (Edinburgh: Adam and Charles Black, 1872), 6:253.

57. Sir Humphry Davy, "Agricultural Lectures," in *Collected Works* (London: Smith, Elder, 1840), 8:264.

58. Sir Humphrey Davy, quoted in William Cabell Bruce, *Benjamin Franklin Self-Revealed* (CreateSpace, 2017), 2:362.

59. Earl of Macclesfield, "Speech Awarding the Copley Medal," November 30, 1752.

60. Peter Collinson to Benjamin Franklin, May 27, 1756.

61. Immanuel Kant, "The Modern Prometheus," 1755.

62. Van Doren, *Benjamin Franklin* (New York: Viking Press, 1938), 170.

63. Van Doren, 171. Includes the great line about Franklin: "He found electricity a curiosity and left it a science."

64. Benjamin Franklin to Peter Collinson, September 1753.

65. Benjamin Franklin to Peter Collinson, August 14, 1747.

66. Benjamin Franklin to Peter Collinson, April 12, 1748.

67. Benjamin Franklin, "Experiments Supporting the Use of Pointed Lightning Rods," August 18, 1772.

68. Benjamin Franklin to Thomas-François Dalibard, June 29, 1755.

69. Benjamin Franklin to Peter Collinson, September 1753.

70. Benjamin Franklin, "Experiments Supporting the Use of Pointed Lightning Rods," August 18, 1772.

71. Cohen, *Science and the Founding Fathers* (New York: W. W. Norton, 1995), 213–14.
72. *Poor Richard's Almanack* (1753).
73. Cohen, *Science and the Founding Fathers*, 214, 240.
74. Brooke Hindle, *Early American Science* (New York: Science History Publications, 1976).
75. Benjamin Franklin to Lord Kames, October 21, 1761.
76. John Bigelow, ed., *The Works of Benjamin Franklin* (New York: G. P. Putnam's Sons, 1904), vol. 2.
77. Benjamin Franklin, "An Account of the New Invented Pennsylvanian Fire-Places," November 16, 1744.
78. *Autobiography*, 77.
79. *Autobiography*, 82–83.
80. Benjamin Franklin to Cadwallader Colden, February 25, 1763.
81. Franklin's heat experiments became better understood when Joseph Black, a Scottish chemist, introduced the concept of latent heat, defined as the energy absorbed or released by a substance during a change in its physical state.
82. Van Doren, *Benjamin Franklin* (New York: Viking Press, 1938), 157.
83. I. Bernard Cohen, *Science and the Founding Fathers*, 147.
84. Benjamin Franklin to John Franklin, December 8, 1752.
85. Benjamin Franklin to John Franklin, December 8, 1752.
86. "A Proposal for Promoting Useful Knowledge Among the British Plantations in America," May 1743.
87. Cadwallader Colden to Peter Collinson, March 1743.
88. Allen Johnson, ed., *Dictionary of American Biography* (New York: Charles Scribner's Sons, 1929), 26–28.
89. Edwin Wolf II, "James Logan, Bookman Extraordinary," *Proceedings of the Massachusetts Historical Society*, 79:33–46.
90. Benjamin Franklin, "True Merit" (1749).
91. Benjamin Franklin, "Proposals Relating to the Education of Youth in Pennsylvania," October 1749, pp. 14–15, 19.
92. Penn Medicine, "History of the Pennsylvania Hospital," accessed January 24, 2024, https:///www.uphs.upenn.edu/paharc/features/creation/html.
93. *Autobiography*, 80.
94. *Autobiography*, 81.
95. "Plain Truth, or Serious Considerations on the Present State of the City of Philadelphia, and Province of Pennsylvania, by a Tradesman of Philadelphia," November 17, 1747.
96. David Freeman Hawke, *Franklin* (New York: Harper & Row, 1976), 85.
97. "Plain Truth," November 17, 1747.
98. Jonathan Lyons, *The Society for Useful Knowledge* (New York: Bloomsbury Press, 2013).
99. Benjamin Franklin to Governor William Shirley, December 22, 1754.
100. Lyons, *The Society for Useful Knowledge*.
101. Benjamin Franklin to Peter Collinson, June 26, 1755.
102. Benjamin Franklin to Peter Collinson, August 25, 1755.
103. Benjamin Franklin, "Physical and Meteorological Observations, Conjectures, and Suppositions," printed in the Royal Society's *Philosophical Transactions* (1765), 55:182–92.
104. James Cook, *A Voyage toward the South Pole, and Round the World* (1777, repr. The Perfect Library, 2015).

105. Quoted in Benjamin Franklin to Peter Collinson, August 25, 1755.

## CHAPTER 6: FIGHTING THE PENNS

1. Benjamin Franklin, "Observations Concerning the Increase of Mankind, Peopling of Countries, etc., 1751" (S. Kneeland, 1755).
2. Franklin, "Observations Concerning the Increase of Mankind."
3. Conway Zirkle, "Natural Selection before the 'Origin of Species,'" *Proceedings of the American Philosophical Society*, April 25, 1941.
4. Historian Joyce Chaplin emphasized the contrasts between Franklin and Darwin, stating that Benjamin "rejected (Darwin's) idea of annihilation of species" and "believed that material things, created by divine power, could only be destroyed by that power."
5. Jonathan R. Dull, *Franklin the Diplomat* (Philadelphia: American Philosophical Society, 1982), 20.
6. Franklin, "Observations Concerning the Increase of Mankind."
7. Bunker, *Young Benjamin Franklin*, 204.
8. Franklin removed references to the Palatine Boors when he reprinted "Observations" in 1760.
9. Franklin, "Observations Concerning the Increase of Mankind."
10. Franklin's views toward minorities were mixed and sometimes contradictory. Although he sought to protect Native Americans from white mobs, he labeled some Indians "drunken savages who delight in war, take pride in murder," and should be pursued with "large, strong, and fierce dogs." Benjamin also described African Americans as "sullen, malicious, revengeful" and "by nature (thieves)"; yet after visiting a school for Black children, he commented that he left with "a higher opinion of the black race than I had ever before entertained" and concluded that what he thought was enslaved peoples' tendency to thievery might be related more to their situation than nature. Despite these inconsistencies, Franklin, according to historian Emma Lapsansky-Werner, "consistently showed himself to be thoughtful, open, teachable." (Lapsansky-Werner, "Franklin and the Vexing Question of Race in America" [2018], in The Electric Ben Franklin, https://www.ushistory.org/franklin/essays/franklin_race.htm.)
11. William Penn quoted in Horace Mather Lippincott, *Early Philadelphia: Its People, Life, and Progress* (Philadelphia: J. B. Lippincott, 1917).
12. William Penn, *Fruits of Solitude* (Philadelphia: Benjamin Johnson, 1792).
13. Walter Isaacson, *Benjamin Franklin* (New York: Simon & Schuster, 2003), 169.
14. Thomas Penn to Richard Peters, July 5, 1758.
15. *Pennsylvania Gazette*, May 9, 1754.
16. Catherine Drinker Bowen, *The Most Dangerous Man in America*, 140.
17. Benjamin Franklin, "Albany Plan of Union," April 9, 1789.
18. Jill Lepore, *These Truths* (New York: W. W. Norton, 2018), 78.
19. According to historian Ronald Clark, there is no meaningful way to convert these amounts into contemporary values, although it was noted at the time that a common family could live comfortably in Boston on forty pounds a year.
20. Benjamin Franklin, *Autobiography of Benjamin Franklin*, ed. F. W. Pine (New York: Henry Holt, 1916), 109.
21. *Autobiography*, 108.
22. *Autobiography*, 109.
23. Benjamin Franklin to Deborah Franklin, January 1758.

24. Edwin S. Gaustad, *Benjamin Franklin: Inventing America* (Oxford: Oxford University Press, 2004), 68.
25. Thomas Penn to Richard Peters, May 14, 1757.
26. Thomas Penn to Richard Peters, May 14, 1757.
27. Ronald W. Clark, *Benjamin Franklin*, ch. 5.
28. *Autobiography*, 110.
29. Lord Granville was married to the sister of Thomas Penn's wife.
30. *Autobiography*, 111.
31. Van Doren, *Benjamin Franklin* (New York: Viking Press, 1938), 278.
32. William Franklin to Benjamin Franklin, March 2, 1769.
33. Benjamin Franklin to Deborah Franklin, November 22, 1757.
34. *Autobiography*, 111.
35. Benjamin Franklin to Isaac Norris, January 14, 1758.
36. Thomas Penn to Richard Peters, July 5, 1758.
37. Benjamin Franklin to Deborah Franklin, September 6, 1758.
38. Isaacson, *Benjamin Franklin*, 188.
39. Benjamin Franklin to Isaac Norris, June 9, 1759.
40. Van Doren, *Benjamin Franklin* (New York: Viking Press, 1938), 287.
41. David Hume to Benjamin Franklin, May 10, 1762.
42. Benjamin Franklin to Lord Kames, January 3, 1760.
43. Benjamin Franklin to Lord Kames, January 3, 1760.
44. Musschenbroek to Benjamin Franklin, April 15, 1759. In that same letter, however, Musschenbroek encouraged Franklin to repeat his kite experiment and provide particulars such as date and location.
45. Daniel Mark Epstein, *The Loyal Son* (New York, Ballantine Books, 2017).
46. No doubt William twice asked Lord Bute for the position (see R. C. Simmons, "Colonial Patronage: Two Letters from William Franklin to the Earl of Bute, 1762," *William and Mary Quarterly*, 2002, pp. 123–34). H. W. Brands, in *The First American* (New York: Anchor Books, 2002) suggested Bute secretly granted the request in part to reward Benjamin for weakening his political rivals within the Penn faction.
47. James Parton, *Life and Times of Benjamin Franklin* (London: Lume Books, 2017), 1:432.
48. Benjamin Franklin to Giovanni Battista Beccaria, July 13, 1762.
49. Benjamin Franklin to Giovanni Battista Beccaria, July 13, 1762.
50. "The Family Memoirs of the Rev. William Stukeley M.D." Publications of the Surtess Society, 80:iii, 480.
51. Benjamin Franklin to Jane Mecom, November 25, 1762.
52. Walter Isaacson, *Benjamin Franklin* (New York: Simon & Schuster, 2003), 204.
53. Benjamin Franklin to John Pringle, December 1, 1762.
54. John Pringle to Benjamin Franklin, May 1763.

## CHAPTER 7: FRUSTRATION IN THE COLONIES

1. Benjamin Franklin to William Strahan, December 2, 1762.
2. Thomas Penn to James Hamilton, September 1762.
3. At the 1763 peace conference, Britain also received Florida from Spain, while Spain regained Cuba. The Mississippi valley essentially was opened to westward expansion.
4. *Autobiography*, 100.
5. Benjamin Franklin, "*The Interest of Great Britain Considered*," April 17, 1760.

6. "Defense of the Canada Pamphlet, *The London Chronicle*, May 8–15, 1760.

7. Benjamin Franklin, "The Interest of Great Britain Considered," April 17, 1760.

8. Benjamin Franklin, "A Plan for Settling Two Western Colonies," 1779.

9. Daniel Mark Epstein, *The Loyal Son* (New York: Ballantine Books, 2017), 131.

10. Benjamin Franklin, "A narrative of the late massacres, in Lancaster County, of a number of Indians, friends of this province, by persons unknown. With some observations on the same." January 30, 1764.

11. Franklin, "A Narrative of the late massacres."

12. Franklin, "A Narrative of the late massacres."

13. Franklin, "A Narrative of the late massacres."

14. Daniel Mark Epstein, *The Loyal Son* (New York: Ballantine Books, 2017).

15. Benjamin Franklin, "Observations Concerning the Increase of Mankind, 1751."

16. Benjamin Franklin to Lord Kames, June 2, 1765.

17. Benjamin Franklin to Lord Kames, June 2, 1765.

18. John Penn to Thomas Penn, May 5, 1764.

19. Pennsylvania Assembly, "Resolves upon the Present Circumstances," *Votes and Proceedings of the House of Representatives* (Philadelphia, March 24, 1764), 72–74.

20. Benjamin Franklin to William Strahan, December 19, 1763.

21. Benjamin Franklin to Charles Thomson, December 29, 1788.

## CHAPTER 8: FRUSTRATION IN LONDON

1. Joseph J. Ellis, *The Cause* (New York: W. W. Norton, 2021).

2. Benjamin Franklin, "Felons and Rattlesnakes," *The Pennsylvania Gazette*, May 9, 1751.

3. H. W. Brands, *The First American* (New York: Anchor, 2002), 360–63.

4. Benjamin Franklin to John Hughes, August 9, 1765.

5. John Hughes to Benjamin Franklin, September 17, 1765.

6. David Hall to Benjamin Franklin, September 6, 1765.

7. Benjamin Rush to Ebenezer Hazard, November 5, 1765.

8. Edward M. Riley, "The Deborah Franklin Correspondence," *Proceedings of the American Philosophical Society* (June 1951), 95:3.

9. Benjamin Franklin to John Hughes, August 9, 1765.

10. Benjamin Franklin to Jane Franklin Mecom, July 28, 1774.

11. Benjamin Franklin to Charles Thompson, July 11, 1765.

12. *Journal of the First Congress of the American Colonies, in Opposition to the Tyrannical Acts of the British Parliament. Held at New York, October 7, 1765* (New York, 1845), 28.

13. Carl Van Doren, *Benjamin Franklin* (New York: Viking Press, 1938), 329.

14. Jill Lepore, *These Truths* (New York: W. W. Norton, 2018). The historian notes that whites outnumbered Blacks in the colonies by four to one, while Blacks outnumbered whites on the Caribbean islands by eight to one.

15. Benjamin Franklin to Jonathan Williams, April 28, 1766.

16. "The Examination of Doctor Benjamin Franklin before an August Assembly Relating to the Repeal of the Stamp Act," 1766.

17. "The Examination of Doctor Benjamin Franklin."

18. Walter Isaacson, *Benjamin Franklin* (New York: Simon & Schuster, 2003), 229.

19. Isaacson, *Benjamin Franklin*, 229.

20. "Marginalia in Protests of the Lords against Repeal of the Stamp Act," 1766.

21. Charles Thompson to Benjamin Franklin, May 20, 1766.

22. Benjamin Franklin to Charles Thomson, September 27, 1766.

23. Samuel and John Adams were cousins.
24. Benjamin Franklin, "On Railing and Reviling," January 6, 1768.
25. Benjamin Franklin to Lord Le Despencer, July 26, 1779.
26. Benjamin Franklin to William Franklin, July 2, 1768.
27. Van Doren, *Benjamin Franklin* (New York: Viking Press, 1938), 379.
28. Benjamin Franklin to Joseph Galloway, January 9, 1768.
29. Benjamin Franklin, "The Causes of the Present Discontents," *London Chronicle*, January 7, 1768.
30. Marginalia in *The True Constitutional Means for Putting an End to the Disputes between Great-Britain and the American Colonies* (London, 1769), an anonymous pamphlet presumed to be by Benjamin Franklin.
31. Benjamin Franklin, "Dear Sir," *Gentleman's Magazine*, November 28, 1768.
32. Benjamin Franklin to William Franklin, July 2, 1768.
33. Benjamin Franklin to William Franklin, July 2, 1768.
34. Benjamin Franklin to Thomas Cushing, February 5, 1771.
35. Benjamin Franklin to Charles Thomson, March 18, 1770.
36. Benjamin Franklin to Samuel Cooper, June 8, 1770.
37. Benjamin Franklin to Samuel Cooper, June 8, 1770.
38. Benjamin Franklin to Samuel Cooper, February 5, 1771.
39. "Franklin's Account of His Audience with Hillsborough," January 16, 1771.
40. *Benjamin Franklin Writings* (New York: Library of America, 1987), 5:298–304.
41. Benjamin Franklin to Samuel Cooper, February 3, 1771.
42. Benjamin Franklin to Massachusetts Committee of Correspondence, May 15, 1771.

## CHAPTER 9: EVERY KIND OF SCIENCE

1. Benjamin Franklin to William Franklin, August 19, 1772.
2. Colin Schultz, "Why Was Benjamin Franklin's Basement Filled With Skeletons?" *Smithsonian Magazine*, October 3, 2013.
3. Benjamin Franklin to Mary Stevenson, September 14, 1767.
4. James Boswell, *Private Papers*, ed. Geoffrey Scott and Frederick A. Pottle (New York, 1928–1934).
5. Benjamin Franklin to Mary Stevenson, September 14, 1767.
6. Benjamin Franklin to Thomas-François Dalibard, January 31, 1768.
7. Van Doren, *Benjamin Franklin* (New York: Viking Press, 1938), 428.
8. Walter Isaacson, *Benjamin Franklin*, 253.
9. Benjamin Franklin to Duc de la Rochefoucauld, October 22, 1788.
10. Benjamin Franklin to Cadwallader Colden, February 20, 1768.
11. Benjamin Franklin to Cadwallader Colden, September 7, 1769.
12. *Benjamin Franklin Writings* (New York: Library of America, 1987), 5:245.
13. Benjamin Franklin to William Brownrigg, November 7, 1773.
14. Benjamin Franklin to Benjamin Rush, July 14, 1773.
15. Charles Tanford, *Ben Franklin Stilled the Waves* (Oxford: Oxford University Press, 1989), 90.
16. Benjamin Franklin to William Brownrigg, November 7, 1773.
17. Franklin to Brownrigg, November 7, 1773.
18. Franklin to Brownrigg, November 7, 1773.
19. Franklin to Brownrigg, November 7, 1773.
20. Tanford, *Ben Franklin Stilled the Waves*, 84.
21. Tanford, 2.

22. "Pouring oil on choppy water to calm it, does it work and if so how?" Physics Stack Exchange, August 25, 2015.
23. Benjamin Franklin to John Pringle, May 10, 1768.
24. NOAA, "Who First Charted the Gulf Stream?" National Ocean Service website, accessed January 24, 2024, https://oceanservice.noaa.gov/facts/bfranlin.html.
25. Benjamin Franklin to Anthony Todd, October 29, 1768.
26. "Did Ben Franklin Invent Daylight Saving Time?" The Franklin Institute, accessed January 24, 2024, https://www.fi.edu/benjamin-franklin/daylight-savings-time.

**CHAPTER 10: THE CATALYST**

1. Benjamin Franklin to Thomas Cushing, December 2, 1772.
2. Thomas Hutchinson to unknown, January 20, 1769.
3. Benjamin Franklin to Samuel Cooper, July 7, 1773.
4. Diary of John Adams, April 24, 1773.
5. Benjamin Franklin, "To the Massachusetts House of Representatives," July 7, 1773.
6. Benjamin Franklin to Thomas Cushing, December 2, 1772.
7. Benjamin Franklin to William Franklin, September 1, 1773.
8. Lord Dartmouth's comment noted in Benjamin Franklin letter to Thomas Cushing, May 6, 1773.
9. Benjamin Franklin to Thomas Cushing, May 6, 1773.
10. Benjamin Franklin to John Winthrop, July 25, 1773.
11. Benjamin Franklin to Thomas Cushing, March 9, 1773.
12. Benjamin Franklin to Massachusetts House of Representatives, July 7, 1773.
13. Benjamin Franklin to Massachusetts House of Representatives, July 7, 1773.
14. "Rules by Which a Great Empire May Be Reduced to a Small One," *Public Advertiser*, September 11, 1773.
15. "An Edict by the King of Prussia," *The Public Advertiser*, September 22, 1773.
16. Benjamin Franklin to William Franklin, October 6, 1773.
17. Benjamin Franklin to William Franklin, October 6, 1773
18. Benjamin Franklin to Benjamin Rush, July 14, 1773.
19. A fourth ship ran aground off Cape Cod.
20. Benjamin Franklin to the Massachusetts House Committee of Correspondence, February 2, 1774.
21. Benjamin Franklin to Lord Chatham, March 22, 1775.
22. George Washington to Robert Mackenzie, October 9, 1774.
23. Thomas Jefferson to John Randolph, August 25, 1775.
24. George III to Lord North, November 11, 1774.
25. Catherine Drinker Bowen, *The Most Dangerous Man in America* (Boston: Little, Brown, 1974).
26. Jill Lepore, *These Truths* (New York: W. W. Norton, 2018), 91.
27. J. A. Leo Lemay, *The Life of Benjamin Franklin* (Philadelphia: University of Pennsylvania Press, 2006), vol. 3.
28. Benjamin Franklin to the Printer of the *London Chronicle*, December 25, 1773.
29. Van Doren, *Benjamin Franklin* (New York: Viking Press, 1938), 464.
30. "The Preliminary Hearing before the Privy Council Committee for Plantation Affairs on the Petition from the Massachusetts House of Representatives for the Removal of Hutchinson and Oliver," January 11, 1774.
31. Benjamin Franklin to *London Chronicle*, December 25, 1773.
32. Epstein, *The Loyal Son*, 176.

33. Benjamin Vaughn, *Political, Miscellaneous, and Philosophical Pieces Written by Benj. Franklin* (London, 1779), 341.
34. "The Final Hearing before the Privy Council Committee for Plantation Affairs on the Petition from the Massachusetts House of Representatives for the Removal of Hutchinson and Oliver," January 29, 1774.
35. Benjamin Franklin to Thomas Cushing, February 15, 1774.
36. Edward Bancroft, "The Doctor," in *Memoirs*, 358.
37. Van Doren, *Benjamin Franklin* (New York: Viking Press, 1938), 474.
38. Catherine Drinker Bowen, *The Most Dangerous Man in America*, 241.
39. Benjamin Franklin, "A Letter from London," *Boston Gazette*, April 25, 1774.
40. Benjamin Franklin to William Franklin, February 2, 1774.
41. William Franklin to Lord Dartmouth, May 31, 1774.
42. Thomas Percival to Benjamin Franklin, January 10, 1775.
43. Benjamin Franklin to Jane Franklin Mecom, September 26, 1774.
44. Van Doren, *Benjamin Franklin*, 483.
45. *Public Advertiser*, May 21, 1774.
46. Benjamin Franklin to Deborah Franklin, September 1, 1773.
47. Deborah Franklin to Benjamin Franklin, November 20, 1769.
48. Isaacson, *Benjamin Franklin*, 283.
49. Benjamin Franklin, "Journal of the Negotiations in London," March 22, 1775.
50. Franklin Journal, March 22, 1775.
51. William Franklin to Benjamin Franklin, December 24, 1774.
52. William Franklin to Benjamin Franklin, December 24, 1774.
53. Benjamin Franklin to Joseph Galloway, February 25, 1775.
54. Benjamin Franklin to Thomas Walpole, March 16, 1775.

## CHAPTER 11: REVOLUTION

1. Benjamin Franklin to Joseph Priestley, May 16, 1775.
2. Guillaume Thomas Raynal, *Historie Philosophique et Politique* (1774), 8:92.
3. Thomas Jefferson, *Notes on the State of Virginia* (1782), 119–20.
4. Andrea Wulf, "Thomas Jefferson's Quest to Prove America's Natural Superiority," *The Atlantic*, March 7, 2016.
5. Alexander Garden to John Ellis, November 19, 1764, quoted in Lee Alan Dugatkin, *Mr. Jefferson and the Giant Moose: Natural History in Early America* (Chicago: University of Chicago Press, 2009).
6. Benjamin Franklin to Lebeque de Presle, October 4, 1777. See also I. Bernard Cohen, ed., *Benjamin Franklin's Experiments* (Cambridge, MA: Harvard University Press, 1941), 138.
7. John Adams, *Correspondence*, 4:431.
8. William Rachel, ed., *Papers of James Madison* (Chicago: University of Chicago Press, 1962), 1:149.
9. Gordon Wood, *The Americanization of Benjamin Franklin* (New York: Penguin Books, 2005), 158.
10. H. W. Brands, *The First American* (New York: Anchor, 2002), 494.
11. Benjamin Franklin to William Strahan, July 5, 1775.
12. Benjamin Franklin to Joseph Priestley, May 16, 1775.
13. "Proposed Articles of Confederation," July 21, 1775, in *Papers*, 22:120.
14. Benjamin Franklin to Richard Bache, October 19, 1775.
15. "Minutes of Conference with General Washington, October 18–24, 1775, in *Papers*, 22:224.

16. Benjamin Franklin to Joseph Priestley, September 19, 1772.

17. Maya Jasanoff, *Liberty's Exiles: American Loyalists in the Revolutionary World* (New York: Knopf, 2011), 8.

18. Benjamin Franklin to William Franklin, August 1774.

19. William Franklin, "Address to the New Jersey General Assembly," January 13, 1775.

20. Benjamin Franklin to Charles Carroll and Samuel Chase, May 27, 1776.

21. Benjamin Franklin to George Washington, June 21, 1776.

22. Thomas Paine, *Common Sense*, February 14, 1776.

23. Thomas Paine, *Common Sense*, February 14, 1776.

24. Joseph J. Ellis, *The Cause* (New York: W. W. Norton, 2021).

25. *The Declaration of Independence in Congress*, July 4, 1776.

26. "Thomas Jefferson's Anecdotes of Benjamin Franklin," December 4, 1818.

27. Thomas Jefferson to Benjamin Franklin, June 21, 1776.

28. Historian Julian Boyd disagrees, suggesting that the edit looks more like Jefferson's handwriting. Julian P. Boyd, *The Declaration of Independence: The Evolution of the Text as Shown in Facsimile* (Washington, DC: Library of Congress, 1943). Historian Carl Becker, in his *The Declaration of Independence* (New York: Vintage, 1958), argues against crediting anyone with any single edit since substantial uncertainty surrounds those negotiations.

29. *Benjamin Franklin Writings* (New York: Library of America, 1987), 1:408.

30. Howe's comment was not in the minutes but was recalled by John Adams and included within Lyman H. Butterfield, ed., *The Diary and Autobiography of John Adams* (Cambridge, MA: Belknap Press of Harvard University Press, 1966), 422.

31. Lord Howe's secretary, "Lord Howe's Conference with the Committee of Congress," September 11, 1776.

32. Benjamin Franklin to Benjamin Rush, September 27, 1776.

## CHAPTER 12: SCIENCE OPENS THE DOOR

1. The Continental Congress in September 1776 formally changed the new nation's name from the "United Colonies" to the "United States" of America.

2. Benjamin Franklin to Don Gabriel Antonio de Bourbon, December 12, 1775.

3. John Durand, *New Materials for the History of the American Revolution* (New York, 1889), 2–5.

4. The *Reprisal* twice had to evade British warships, whose captains would have imprisoned, and possibly hanged, the American rebel who had recently signed the Declaration of Independence.

5. E. E. Hale and E. E. Hale Jr., *Franklin in France* (Boston: 1887–1888), 1:243.

6. *The Boston Patriot*, May 15, 1811.

7. Stacy Schiff, "Franklin in Paris," *The American Scholar*, March 1, 2009.

8. "American's First Rock Star: Benjamin Franklin in France," *Constitution Daily Blog*, National Constitution Center, December 17, 2015. Accessed February 26, 2024, https://constitutioncenter.org/blog/americas-first-rock-star-benjamin-franklin-in-france.

9. Benjamin Franklin to Jane Mecom, October 25, 1779.

10. Ronald W. Clark, *Benjamin Franklin: A Biography* (New York: Random House, 1983), ch. 11.

11. Joseph J. Ellis, *The Cause* (New York: W. W. Norton, 2021).

12. Van Doren, *Benjamin Franklin* (New York: Viking Press, 1938), 573.

13. Lord Stormont to Lord Weymouth, December 11, 1776.

14. Benjamin Franklin to Polly Stevenson, August 28, 1767.

15. Benjamin Franklin to Emma Thompson, February 8, 1777.
16. Benjamin Franklin to George Whatley, August 21, 1784.
17. Benjamin Franklin to George Whatley, May 23, 1785.
18. Benjamin Franklin to George Whatley, May 23, 1785.
19. Comte de Vergennes to Lord Stormont.
20. *Benjamin Franklin Writings* (New York: Library of America, 1987), 6:477.
21. Vergennes to Conde d'Aranda, December 28, 1776.
22. Bancroft hid his clandestine activities until his death in 1821; only late in the nineteenth century did previously unknown documents reveal his spying.
23. Horace Walpole to William Mason, February 27, 1777.
24. Franklin, *Writings*, 7:11.
25. Benjamin Franklin, "Comparison of Great Britain and America as to Credit, in 1777" (before September 8, 1777).
26. Benjamin Franklin to Richard Bache, May 22, 1777.
27. Benjamin Franklin, "On Recommendations" (date unknown).
28. Benjamin Franklin, "Model of a Letter of Recommendation of a person you are unacquainted with," April 2, 1777.
29. Benjamin Franklin to Margaret Stevenson, January 25, 1779.
30. John Adams, diary entry.
31. Temple Franklin to Sally Franklin (Bache), November 25, 1777.
32. Benjamin Franklin to Jean-Louis Giraud Soulavie, September 22, 1782.
33. Benjamin Franklin to Joseph Priestley, February 8, 1780.
34. Benjamin Franklin to John Paul Jones, April 28, 1779.
35. Van Doren, *Benjamin Franklin* (New York: Viking Press, 1938), 555.
36. Clark, *Benjamin Franklin*, 328.
37. Benjamin Franklin to Thomas Cushing, February 27, 1778.
38. B. F. Stevens, *Facsimiles of Manuscripts in European Archives Relating to America, 1773–1783*, vol. 5, no. 489.
39. "Excerpts from the Papers of Dr. Benjamin Rush," *Pennsylvania Magazine of History and Biography* (1905), 29:28.
40. Clark, *Benjamin Franklin*, 351.
41. Clark, *Benjamin Franklin*, 341.
42. Duc de Croy, *Journals inedit* (Paris, 1906–1907), 4:78.
43. Van Doren, *Benjamin Franklin*, 593.
44. Edmund Morgan, *Benjamin Franklin* (New Haven: Yale University Press, 2002).
45. Arthur Lee to Benjamin Franklin, April 2, 1778.
46. Benjamin Franklin to Arthur Lee (unsent), April 4, 1778.
47. Charles Andrews, *A Note on the Franklin-Deane Mission to France Yale University Library Gazette*, 2:65.
48. Richard Henry Lee also attacked Franklin, asking Samuel Adams, "How long, my dear friend, must the dignity, honor, and interest of these United States be sacrificed to the bad passions of that old man under the idea that his being a philosopher?" (Richard Henry Lee to Samuel Adams, September 10, 1780.)
49. Benjamin Franklin to Robert R. Livingston, March 4, 1782.
50. Benjamin Franklin to Robert R. Livingston, July 22, 1783.
51. Stacy Schiff, *Great Improvisation: Franklin, France, and the Birth of America* (New York: Henry Holt, 2005), 2.
52. Letter to Robert R. Livingston, May 25, 1783, *Papers of John Adams*, 14:492–93.
53. Benjamin Franklin to Robert Livingston, July 22, 1783.
54. Benjamin Franklin "To All Captains and Commanders of American Armed Ships," March 10, 1779.

55. Schiff, *Great Improvisation*, 278.
56. Benjamin Franklin, "The Nature and Necessity of a Paper Currency," April 3, 1779.
57. Karl Marx, *A Contribution to the Critique of Political Economy*, trans. N. I. Stone (1859; repr., Chicago: Charles H. Kerr, 1904), 62.
58. Benjamin Franklin, "To the Royal Academy of Farting," May 19, 1780.
59. Benjamin Franklin to the Committee for Foreign Affairs, May 26, 1779.
60. Benjamin Franklin to John Jay, October 4, 1779.
61. Benjamin Franklin to Sarah Bache, June 3, 1779.
62. Benjamin Franklin to John Jay, October 2, 1780.
63. Extrapolation from the 2009 estimate of $13 billion by Stacy Schiff, "Franklin in Paris," *The American Scholar*, March 1, 2009.
64. Benjamin Franklin to Samuel Huntington, August 9, 1780.
65. Vergennes to John Adams, July 29, 1780.
66. Benjamin Franklin to the Continental Congress, March 12, 1781.
67. Ralph Izard to Richard Lee, October 15, 1780.
68. Benjamin Franklin to Richard Bache, June 2, 1779.
69. Conrad-Alexandre Gérard to Comte de Vergennes, July 18, 1779.
70. Marquis de Lafayette to Comte de Vergennes, August 16, 1779.
71. Also invited were Thomas Jefferson, who could not leave the United States, and Henry Laurens of South Carolina, who was captured by a British warship and held in the Tower of London until the war's end.
72. Vergennes to la Luzerne, December 4, 1780.
73. Arthur Lee to James Warren, August 1789.

## CHAPTER 13: PEACEMAKER

1. Benjamin Franklin to Josiah Quincy Sr., September 11, 1783.
2. Benjamin Franklin to Robert Morris, July 26, 1781.
3. *Journal of Benjamin Franklin*, March 21, 1782, to July 1, 1782. Transcript in the National Archives, Records of the Continental Congresses and Constitutional Convention.
4. Benjamin Franklin, *Journal of Peace Negotiations*, May 9–July 1, 1782.
5. Benjamin Franklin, *Journal of Peace Negotiations*, May 9–July 1, 1782.
6. Richard Morris, *The Peacemakers* (New York: Harper & Row, 1965), 274.
7. L.S. Livingston, *Franklin and His Press at Passy* (New York, 1914), 58–67.
8. Stacy Schiff, *Great Improvisation: Franklin, France, and the Birth of America* (New York: Henry Holt, 2005), 404.
9. Benjamin Franklin to Samuel Cooper, December 26, 1782.
10. John Adams Diaries, 3:37.
11. "Conditional Peace Treaty between Great Britain and the United States," November 29, 1782.
12. Vergennes to Benjamin Franklin, December 15, 1782.
13. Benjamin Franklin to Vergennes, December 17, 1782.
14. Vergennes to la Luzerne, December 19, 1782.
15. Benjamin Franklin to Vergennes, December 17, 1782.
16. Benjamin Franklin to Robert R. Livingston, December 5, 1782.
17. Benjamin Franklin to Robert Morris, December 23, 1782.
18. The Peace Treaty of 1783, which ended the American Revolutionary War, is not to be confused with the Treaty of Paris of 1763 that ended the French and Indian War (also known as the Seven Years' War between Great Britain and France).
19. Van Doren, *Benjamin Franklin* (New York: Viking Press, 1938), 696–97.
20. Walter Isaacson, *Benjamin Franklin* (New York: Simon & Schuster, 2003), 417.

21. Herbert Klinghoffer, "Matthew Ridley's Diary during the Peace Negotiations of 1782," *William and Mary Quarterly* 20, no. 1 (January 1963): 132.
22. Benjamin Franklin to Josiah Quincy Sr., September 11, 1783.
23. Benjamin Franklin to Robert R. Livingston, December 5, 1782.

## CHAPTER 14: MORE TO DISCOVER

1. Benjamin Franklin, "Meteorological Imaginations and Conjectures," May 1784.
2. Benjamin Franklin to American Philosophical Society, June 25, 1784. Part of Benjamin Franklin, "Loose Thoughts on a Universal Fluid," June 25, 1784.
3. Benjamin Franklin to David Rittenhouse, June 25, 1784.
4. Benjamin Franklin to James Bowdoin, May 31, 1788.
5. Benjamin Franklin to Joseph Banks, July 27, 1783.
6. Benjamin Franklin to Benjamin Rush, December 26, 1783.
7. Benjamin Franklin to Joseph Banks, November 7, 1783.
8. Benjamin Franklin to Joseph Banks, August 30, 1783.
9. Benjamin Franklin to Joseph Banks, December 1, 1783.
10. Benjamin Franklin to Jan Ingenhousz, January 16, 1784.
11. Benjamin Franklin to Sir Joseph Banks, November 21, 1783.
12. Claude-Anne Lopez, *Mon Cher Papa* (New Haven: Yale University Press, 1966), 222.
13. Benjamin Franklin to La Sabliére de La Candamine (draft), March 19, 1784.
14. Alfred Binet and Charles Féré, *Animal Magnetism* (New York, 1888), 18–25.
15. Benjamin Franklin to Temple Franklin, August 25, 1784.
16. Thomas Jefferson, Eulogy read at the American Philosophical Society in memory of Benjamin Franklin, March 1, 1791.
17. Thomas Jefferson to Rev. William Smith, February 19, 1791.
18. Thomas Jefferson to Abigail Adams, June 21, 1785, *Papers of Thomas Jefferson*, 8:241.
19. Benjamin Franklin, *Journal* (unpublished), June 27, 1784.
20. Benjamin Franklin to Captain Nathaniel Falconer, July 28, 1783.
21. Benjamin Franklin to David Hartley, July 5, 1785.
22. *Benjamin Franklin Writings* (New York: Library of America, 1987), 9:307.
23. Vergennes to François Barbé de Marbois, May 10, 1785.
24. Fawn Brodie, *Thomas Jefferson* (New York: W. W. Norton, 1974), 425.
25. Benjamin Franklin Bache, diary entry entitled "Dr. Franklin's Return from France in 1785," June 1785.
26. Jefferson Papers, 8:129.
27. Benjamin Franklin, "Description of a new Stove for burning of Pitcoal, and consuming all its Smoke," unpublished; written at sea, 1785.
28. Franklin, "Description of a new Stove for burning of Pitcoal."
29. Benjamin Franklin journal, September 14, 1785.

## CHAPTER 15: THE CONSTITUTIONAL EXPERIMENT

1. I. H. Butterfield, *Letters of Benjamin Rush* (Princeton, 1951), 1:389–90.
2. Benjamin Franklin to Thomas Paine, September 27, 1785.
3. Benjamin Franklin to Jane Franklin Mecom, November 4, 1787.
4. Benjamin Franklin to Jonathan Williams, February 16, 1786.
5. Benjamin Franklin to Jonathan Shipley, February 24, 1786.
6. Benjamin Franklin to Marsilio Landriani, October 14, 1787.

7. *Pennsylvania Gazette*, October 5, 1785.
8. *Pennsylvania Packet*, December 5, 1785.
9. Benjamin Franklin to la Rochefoucauld, October 22, 1788.
10. *Rules and Regulations of the Society for Political Enquiries, Established at Philadelphia, 9th February 1787* (Philadelphia: Robert Aitken, 1787), 1–2.
11. Alan Houston, *Benjamin Franklin & the Politics of Improvement* (New Haven: Yale University Press, 2008), 218.
12. Benjamin Franklin to John Jay, January 6, 1784.
13. Benjamin Franklin to Louis-Guillaume Le Veillard, April 15, 1787.
14. Benjamin Franklin to John Hunter, November 24, 1786.
15. Benjamin Franklin to Mary Hewson, May 6, 1786.
16. Benjamin Franklin to Jonathan Shipley, February 24, 1786.
17. Catherine Drinker Bowen, *Miracle at Philadelphia* (Boston: Back Bay Books, 1986).
18. Max Ferrand, *Benjamin Franklin's Memoirs, Huntington Library Bulletin* (1936), 3:91.
19. Benjamin Franklin (Medius), "On the Labouring Poor," *The Gentleman's Magazine*, April 1768.
20. Benjamin Franklin, "Convention Speech on Salaries," June 2, 1787.
21. *Madison Journal*, June 2, 1787.
22. Max Ferrand, ed., *The records of the Federal convention of 1787*, 2:65.
23. Ferrand, Records of Convention, 2:236–37.
24. Isaacson, *Benjamin Franklin*, 447.
25. The Pennsylvania Abolition Society to the United States Congress, February 3, 1790. See also Emma Lapsansky Werner, "Franklin and the Vexing Question of Race in America" (2018). The Electric Ben Franklin, https://www.ushistory.org/franklin/essays/franklin_race.htm.
26. Benjamin Franklin, "Sidi Mehemet Ibrahim on the Slave Trade," *Federal Gazette*, March 23, 1790.
27. Ferrand, Records of Convention, 1:488.
28. W. P. Cutler and Julia P. Cutler, *Life, Journals, and Correspondence of Rev. Manasseh Cutler* (Cincinnati, 1888), 1:267–70.
29. Ferrand, Records of Convention, 2:641–43.
30. *Federalist No. 9*, "The Union as a Safeguard against Domestic Faction and Insurrection," November 21, 1787.
31. Ferrand, Records of Convention, 2:648.
32. Gillian Brockell, "'A republic, if you can keep it': Did Ben Franklin really say Impeachment Day's favorite quote?" *Washington Post*, December 18, 2019.

## CHAPTER 16: CLOSING THE BOOKS

1. Benjamin Franklin to Duc de La Rochefoucauld, October 24, 1788.
2. John Bigelow, ed., *The Life of Benjamin Franklin, Written by Himself* (Philadelphia: J. B. Lippincott, 1875), 416–17.
3. Benjamin Franklin to Alexander Small, February 17, 1789.
4. Benjamin Franklin to Pierre-Samuel du Pont de Nemours, June 9, 1788.
5. Benjamin Franklin to Jean-Baptiste Leroy, 1789.
6. Benjamin Franklin to Louis-Guillaume Le Veillard, September 5, 1789.
7. Benjamin Rush to Richard Price, referenced in John Bigelow, *The Works of Benjamin Franklin* (New York: G.P. Putnam, 1904), 1:531.
8. Dr. John James, quoted in F. A. Willius and T. F. Keys, "The Medical History of Benjamin Franklin," *Proceedings of the Mayo Clinic*, June 1942, 17:416.

9. Count Mirabeau, "Announcement to the General Assembly," June 1790.
10. Robert Middlekauff, *Benjamin Franklin and His Enemies* (Berkeley: University of California Press, 1996), 103.
11. Marguerite Gerard, "To the Genius of Franklin," 1778. Philadelphia Museum of Art.

## CHAPTER 17: A LONG SHADOW

1. Benjamin remained a dutiful father until William became an English loyalist.
2. Poor Richard, *An Almanac For the Year of Christ 1738*, preface by Mistress Saunders, 1738.
3. When finally compiled by Yale University's thorough researchers, Franklin's papers, some 30,000 total documents, will fill forty-seven volumes.
4. Stacy Schiff, *A Great Improvisation: Franklin in France* (New York: Henry Holt, 2005).
5. John Adams, *Boston Patriot*, May 15, 1811.
6. Carl Becker, *The Declaration of Independence* (New York: Vintage, 1958), 16.
7. John Keats to George and Georgian Keats, October 31, 1818.
8. Mark Twain, "The Late Benjamin Franklin," ca. 1870.
9. Leigh Hunt, *Autobiography* (New York: Harper, 1850), 1:130–32.
10. Frederick Jackson Turner, review of "Franklin in France," *The Dial*, May 1887, 8:85.
11. Irvin G. Wyllie, *The Self-Made Man in America: The Myth of Rags to Riches* (New Brunswick: Rutgers University Press, 1954), 15–16.
12. Walter Isaacson, *Benjamin Franklin* (New York: Simon & Schuster, 2003), 491.
13. Max Weber, *The Protestant Ethic and the Spirit of Capitalism* (New York: HarperCollins, 1930), 52–53.
14. D. H. Lawrence, "Benjamin Franklin," *Studies in Classic American Literature* (New York: Viking, 1923), 10–16.
15. Isaacson, *Benjamin Franklin*, 484.
16. I. Bernard Cohen, *Benjamin Franklin's Experiments* (Cambridge, MA: Harvard University Press, 1941), 73.
17. Joyce E. Chaplin, *The First Scientific American: Benjamin Franklin and the Pursuit of Genius* (New York: Basic Books, 2006).
18. Isaacson, *Benjamin Franklin*, 493.
19. Fred Backus, "George Washington Is America's Favorite Founding Father—CBS News Poll," CBS News, July 2, 2021.
20. "Ben Franklin's kite story charged with confusion," WHYY (a public radio station in Philadelphia), November 12, 2012.
21. MythBusters Episode 48, "Franklin's Kite," March 8, 2006.
22. Alan Taylor, "For the Benefit of Mr. Kite," *The New Republic*, March 19, 2001.
23. Paraphrasing Carl Van Doren, *Benjamin Franklin* (New York: Viking Press, 1938).
24. Benjamin Franklin to John Lothrop, May 31, 1788.
25. David Brooks, "Our Founding Yuppie," *The Weekly Standard*, October 23, 2000.

# INDEX

lightning rod and, 64–66, 125, 142, 190
London missions and, 89, 92, 220n44
single-fluid thesis, 54
theories of lightning, 59–60, 217nn35,42
BF's French mission, 151–69
John Adams and, 164–65, 168
appearance and, 155–56, 163
assistance negotiations, 161–62, 166–67, 168
BF as scientist and, 153, 155, 159–60, 165–66
British espionage and, 157–58, 226n22
British responses, 155, 162–63
celebrity and, 153–54, 155
delegation disagreements, 152, 157, 163–64, 168–69, 226n48
departure from France, 186–87
minister plenipotentiary position, 165, 166–67
negotiation approaches, 151–52
peace treaty negotiations, 169, 171–72, 173–77
planning for, 149–50
return from, 186–87, 189
Treaty of Paris and, 98, 149, 151, 154, 156
Vergennes and, 156–57
voyage to France, 152–53, 225n4
war news and, 158–59, 160, 161, 166, 167–68
writings and, 153, 158
BF's inventions
bifocals, 156
catheter, 71
flippers, 19
glass armonica, 93–94
lightning rod, 64–66, 125, 142, 190
matching grant, 75
phonetic alphabet, 118
stoves, 68–69, 89, 188
street lamps, 69
BF's late life
family, 191
health issues, 191, 192, 200–201
political involvement, 189–90
scientific interests, 190, 196, 199–200
Society for Political Enquiries founding, 190–91

BF's London mission (1757–62), 85–95
end of, 94
glass armonica invention, 93–94
illness, 89–90
land speculation and, 100
negotiation failure, 90, 91–92, 94
payment for, 85, 219n19
science and, 86, 87, 89, 90–91, 95
Scotland visit, 92
voyage, 85–86
writing and, 87–88
BF's London mission (1764–74), 107–16
Boston Massacre and, 114–15
departure from Philadelphia, 104–5
end of, 139–40, 143
flirtations and, 138
Hutchinson letters affair, 127–30, 134–36
increasing conflict, 115–16
Paris sojourn, 118–19
Privy Council rebuke, 135–37, 162
reconciliation proposals, 138–39
science and, 117, 118–25, 137
Stamp Act and, 108–12
Townshend Acts and, 113, 114
writing and, 120, 130–31
BF's networking
French mission and, 153, 155, 159–60, 165–66
London missions and, 87–88, 117–18, 120–21
London sojourn and, 30–31
political positions and, 47
postmaster position and, 48, 76, 101
printing business and, 37
Revolutionary War treaty negotiations and, 171–72
BF's political involvement
Constitutional Convention, 191–97, 207
Pennsylvania Assembly and, 47, 76, 85, 90, 91, 97, 103–4
Pennsylvania presidency, 189–90
See also BF's role in American Revolution; BF's role in British-colonial relations
BF's role in American Revolution
Canada mission, 146
Declaration of Independence and, 147, 148, 152, 225nn4,28
demographic studies and, 80